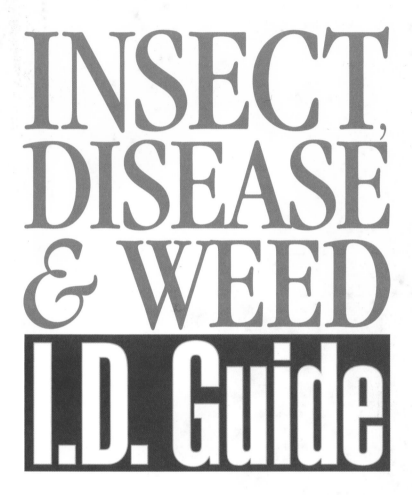

INSECT, DISEASE & WEED
I.D. Guide

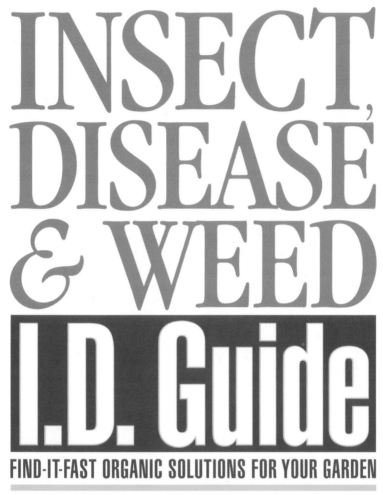

INSECT, DISEASE & WEED
I.D. Guide

FIND-IT-FAST ORGANIC SOLUTIONS FOR YOUR GARDEN

Jill Jesiolowski Cebenko & Deborah L. Martin, editors

Anna Carr, Linda Gilkeson, and Miranda Smith, writers

RODALE

RODALE

**WE INSPIRE AND ENABLE PEOPLE TO IMPROVE
THEIR LIVES AND THE WORLD AROUND THEM**

Rodale Organic Living Books

Editorial Director: Christopher Hirsheimer

Executive Creative Director: Christin Gangi

Executive Editor: Kathleen DeVanna Fish

Art Director: Patricia Field

Content Assembly Manager:
Robert V. Anderson Jr.

Studio Manager: Leslie M. Keefe

Copy Manager: Nancy N. Bailey

Project Coordinator: Kerrie A. Cadden

Editors: Jill Jesiolowski Cebenko and
Deborah L. Martin

Writers: Anna Carr, Linda Gilkeson, and
Miranda Smith

Cover and Interior Book Designer:
Nancy Smola Biltcliff

Interior Illustrators: Robin Brickman and
Thomas Quirk

Cover Illustrator: Robin Brickman

Photography Editor: Lyn Horst

Photography Assistant: Jackie L. Ney

Layout Designer: Keith Biery

Researchers: Diana Erney and
Sarah Wolfgang Heffner

Copy Editors: Stacey Ann Follin,
Linda Brunner, and Barbara Webb

Product Specialist: Jodi Schaffer

Indexer: Lina Burton

Editorial Assistance: Judy Anderson
and Susan L. Nickol

**Library of Congress
Cataloging-in-Publication Data**

    Insect, disease & weed I.D. guide : find-it-fast organic solutions for your garden / Jill Jesiolowski Cebenko and Deborah L. Martin, editors.

        p.   cm.

    Includes bibliographical references (p.).

    ISBN 0–87596–867–8 (hardcover : alk. paper)

    1. Garden pests. 2. Plant diseases. 3. Weeds. 4. Organic gardening. I. Title: Insect, disease and weed I.D. guide. II. Cebenko, Jill Jesiolowski. III. Martin, Deborah L.

SB603.5 .I575 2001

632'.96—dc21   2001002548

ISBN 0–87596–882–1 (paperback)

Distributed in the book trade by St. Martin's Press

2 4 6 8 10 9 7 5 3 1 hardcover
2 4 6 8 10 9 7 5 3 1 paperback

We're always happy to hear from you. For questions or comments concerning the editorial content of this book, please write to:

Rodale Book Readers' Service
33 East Minor Street
Emmaus, PA 18098

Look for other Rodale books wherever books are sold. Or call us at (800) 848-4735.

For more information about Rodale Organic Living magazines and books, visit us at

www.organicgardening.com

RODALE
Organic Gardening Starts Here!

Here at Rodale, we've been gardening organically for more than 50 years—ever since my grandfather J. I. Rodale learned about composting and decided that healthy living starts with healthy soil. In 1940 J. I. started the Rodale Organic Farm to test his theories, and today the nonprofit Rodale Institute Experimental Farm is still at the forefront of organic gardening and farming research. In 1942 J. I. founded Organic Gardening magazine to share his discoveries with gardeners everywhere. His son, my father, Robert Rodale, headed Organic Gardening until 1990, and today a fourth generation of Rodales is growing up with the magazine. Over the years we've shown millions of readers how to grow bountiful crops and beautiful flowers using nature's own techniques.

In this book, you'll find the latest organic methods and the best gardening advice. We know—because all our authors and editors are passionate about gardening! We feel strongly that our gardens should be safe for our children, pets, and the birds and butterflies that add beauty and delight to our lives and landscapes. Our gardens should provide us with fresh, flavorful vegetables, delightful herbs, and gorgeous flowers. And they should be a pleasure to work in as well as to view.

Sharing the secrets of safe, successful gardening is why we publish books. So come visit us at the Rodale Institute Experimental Farm, where you can tour the gardens every day—we're open year-round. And use this book to create your best garden ever.

Happy gardening!

Maria Rodale

Maria Rodale
Rodale Organic Living Books

Contents

How to Use This Book

There's a lot going on in your garden. Seeds sprouting, roots stretching, buds opening, fruits forming. Insects are buzzing, flying, and crawling around, while other tiny critters creep and sleep within the soil. Even the breeze carries pollen, petite flies, microscopic spores, and fluffy, floating seeds. If you stand quietly in your garden, just for a minute or two, you'll begin to notice the remarkable amount of activity that's taking place all around you.

The good news is that nearly all of that traffic in your garden is good for it. Soil-dwelling insects and earthworms "till" the soil, making spaces where water can flow and roots can grow. Bacteria and fungi help to break down fallen leaves and old plant matter into nutrients for new seedlings. Even weeds can serve good purposes, providing food and shelter for beneficial insects and protecting the soil from erosion by wind and rain.

Of course, along with the many benefits your garden gains from its healthy population of flying, crawling, climbing, and growing organisms, it will also suffer a few injuries. Pests will come and bite holes in your plants. Spores will spread and cause leaves to darken and wither. Weeds with pretty flowers will turn out to have aggressively spreading roots that hog all the water and nutrients intended for your vegetables.

The key for you, the gardener, is knowing which things are which. Being able to tell the good guys from the villains. And knowing what—if anything—to do when something's chewing on, growing on, or crowding out your favorite plants. That's where this book can help.

Start with the keys, tables, and other helpful tools that begin each of the three sections: Insects, Diseases, and Weeds. Follow the descriptions to the most likely match for the insect, disease, or weed you're trying to identify. Turn to the page that's indicated in the key or table and use the illustration and description there to learn what's bugging your garden. You may be surprised to find out that the menacing-looking beetle you spotted is a slug-gobbling beneficial. Or that the dark spots on your tomato plants won't harm the ripening fruits. In each entry you'll find clear information about the featured insect, disease, or weed, including important details about its life cycle and how, when, and if you should try to control it, using safe, natural, organic methods.

Let this book be your guide to your garden. Let it introduce you to the many seasonal visitors and year-round residents that live there—mostly in harmony—with the flowers, fruits, vegetables, and other plants that you've chosen to grow. You'll probably be pleas-

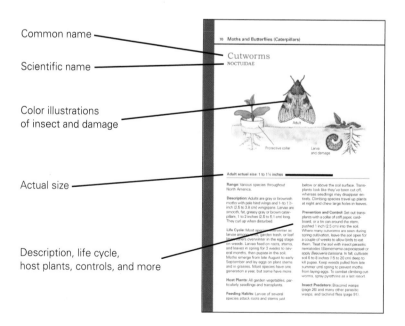

Common name

Scientific name

Color illustrations of insect and damage

Actual size

Description, life cycle, host plants, controls, and more

antly surprised by how few of the things that you encounter are actual problems that require you to intervene on your plants' behalf. But when intervention is needed, you'll be prepared and informed, and you'll know just what to do.

Common name

Scientific name

Color photo(s) of symptoms

Description, life cycle, host plants, controls, and more

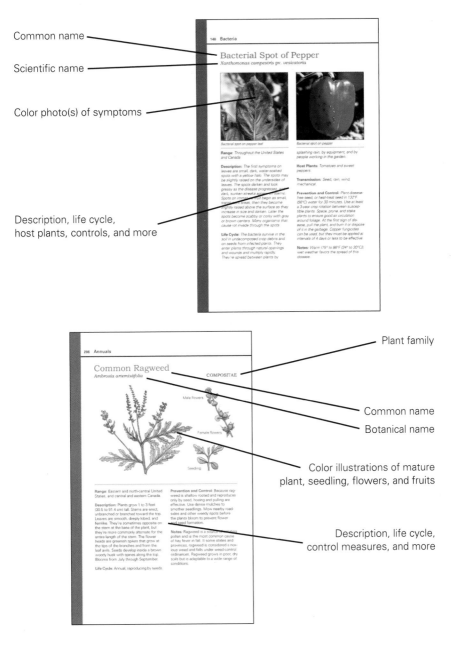

Plant family

Common name

Botanical name

Color illustrations of mature plant, seedling, flowers, and fruits

Description, life cycle, control measures, and more

Insects

An Overview

With an estimated 30 million species of insects on the planet, it's surprising that few of us actually know much about them. Centipedes, spiders, ticks, and other creeping creatures are commonly mistaken for insects, but they're only distant relatives. What then *is* an insect?

Insects are animals in the class Insecta, which is part of the greater group of animals known as Arthropods, meaning creatures with jointed legs. Arthropods have a hard, jointed skeleton on the outside of their body, called an *exoskeleton*. Crabs, lobsters, millipedes, mites, and spiders are also arthropods, but insects are a unique group. They have only six legs, and many have wings in the adult stage. Mites and spiders also have jointed legs, but they have eight legs and no wings, so they belong to a different class within Arthropoda.

The class Insecta is further divided into *orders*. Orders are large groupings of insects with similar

1

overall characteristics. Members of the order Coleoptera (beetles), for example, can usually be recognized by the hard or leathery top wings that meet in a straight line down the center of the back. Each order contains one or more *families,* whose members share more specific characteristics within the larger order. The family name always ends in "idae." The most basic levels of classification used to identify insects are *genus* and *species.* The genus name, which is always capitalized, refers to a small group of closely related members of a family. The species name, which isn't capitalized, describes insects that are so alike that they can mate and have fertile offspring. Thus, both the asparagus beetle and the spotted asparagus beetle belong to the genus *Crioceris* because they're very similar in shape, behavior, life cycle, and what they eat. They aren't exactly alike, however, and can't crossbreed, so they're considered separate species: *asparagi* and *duodecimpunctata,* respectively.

Where entries in this guide refer to a group of similar insects from one family, you'll see the family name listed (for example, the ground beetles, Carabidae). Where similar species in a genus are described, you may see the genus name followed by the abbreviation "spp."—this means more than one species is being described. Because the scientific names of insects may be changed as researchers learn more about them, you'll find that some of the names in this book are different from names found in older texts.

Using This Guide

The type of insect appears in the upper corner of each entry in this section. To find an insect you want to identify, check the descriptions in the chart, "Key to Common Garden Insects" (larval stage, and nymph and adult stages), on pages 20–23. This chart will tell you what group the insect is likely to belong to so that you can look up the right entry.

Insect Biology

The bodies of insects are divided into three sections: *head, thorax,* and *abdomen.* On their heads, insects have a pair of antennae, or feelers, and a pair of larger, compound eyes. Many have other simple eyes (called *ocelli*) as well. The thorax, or middle section, is where legs and wings, if they have them, are attached. The abdomen has most of the digestive and reproductive organs as well as breathing holes. Insects breathe through a system of small round openings, or *spiracles,* along the sides of their bodies. These open into small, branching tubes, known as *trachea,* that carry oxygen throughout their internal tissues.

Insects breathe through a system of small, round openings, or spiracles, along the sides of their bodies.

Exoskeleton. Insect external skeletons are thickened and ridged at various points, both for strength and to support the muscles that are attached inside. The surface is covered with a waterproof layer of waxes and oils that keep the insect from drying up. Insects also have thousands of sensory hairs scattered over the surface of their bodies. These are connected to nerve endings so the insect can detect changes in the environment (colder, hotter, more or less humid, and so on) and in the positions of its own body.

Because their bodies are encased in rigid shells, immature insects have to keep shedding their exoskelton in order to grow bigger. They feed until they're a tight fit inside their exoskeleton, then grow a soft new shell underneath. They split the old exoskeleton to crawl out, then the new one expands and quickly hardens in the air. This process is called *molting.* With each molt the young insect gets bigger, until it reaches its full size. The stage between each molt is called an *instar.* Most insects pass through three to six instars, but some have many more. Once the insects become adults, they no longer need to molt because they no longer need to grow.

STRUCTURE OF A TYPICAL INSECT

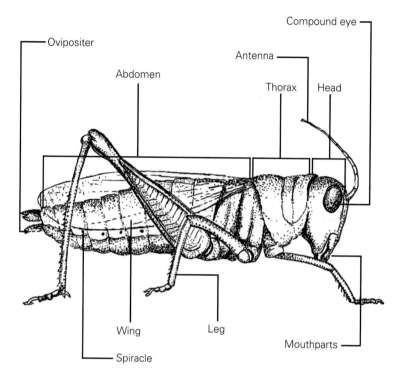

Eyes. Most adult insects have compound eyes made up of many separate hexagonal lenses fitted together. Some, such as flies and dragonflies, have enormous eyes with very high resolution, so they detect the slightest motion. Most insects, however, have eyes adapted to see only certain colors and shapes. Insects see a range of colors, including yellow, green, blue, violet, and even ultraviolet. A very few species, such as apple maggot flies, are known to see red.

Besides compound eyes, most insects also have simple, single-lens eyes called *ocelli*. These simple eyes generally just detect light and dark shapes. Insect larvae don't have compound eyes, so they must rely on these simple eyes to find their way around. The ocelli of some caterpillars that feed on leaves can detect vertical dark shapes, which is enough to allow them to detect a stem or trunk to climb.

Legs. In adult insects, one or more pairs of legs can be highly modified so that they serve different purposes—jumping hind legs in grasshoppers and grasping front legs in mantids are examples. Besides the six legs, some immature insects, such as caterpillars, have up to five pairs of fleshy false legs, called *prolegs*. These have sucker feet to help the caterpillar hang onto plants.

Wings. Although all insects are wingless when they're immature, most adults have two pairs of wings. Flies are an exception in that they have one pair of wings. A few species never have wings, and in some species only males have wings. Others, such as aphids, may or may not have wings, depending on the conditions. A framework of rigid veins supports the wings. They're controlled by a set of strong muscles inside the thorax. Some insects can move each pair of wings separately, whereas others move them together. They can even twist the wing surfaces to provide lift and thrust during flight. Some flies can beat their wings up to 1,000 times per second. Some insects are strong, agile fliers, darting and hovering at will. Others are poor fliers, tumbling to the ground to make a landing or unable to fly against a breeze.

Insect Life Cycles and Behavior

All insects come from an egg that hatches into an immature insect or *larva* (plural *larvae*). As larvae grow, they eventually change to adults through a process called *metamorphosis.* There are two basic types of life cycles: "incomplete" metamorphosis and "complete" metamorphosis.

True bugs, aphids, crickets, earwigs, grasshoppers, mantids, scales, thrips, and whiteflies pass through three basic forms—*egg, larva,* and *adult.* This is called *simple* or *incomplete metamorphosis* (see the

INCOMPLETE METAMORPHOSIS

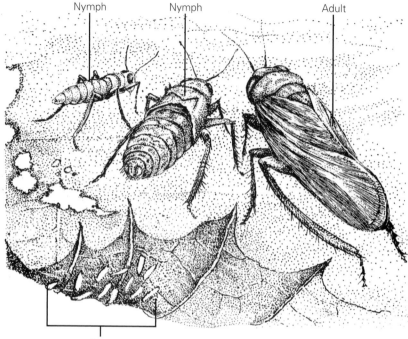

Nymph　　　　Nymph　　　　　　　Adult

Eggs

illustration above). This is because the larvae, also called *nymphs*, more or less resemble the adults, but they don't have fully developed wings or reproductive organs. After they've reached full size, the nymphs pass through one last molt to become adults. In these insects, the adults and nymphs usually eat similar food and are commonly found together on the same plants.

Most other insects—including bees, beetles, butterflies, flies, lacewings, moths, and wasps—go through *complete metamorphosis* (see the illustration on page 8), in which they pass through four distinctly different life stages—*egg, larva, pupa,* and *adult.* The larvae of these insects don't look anything like the adults. Many are soft grubs, maggots, or caterpillars. Some have tiny legs, and others are legless; some are covered with spines or tufts of hair, and others are naked. The larvae molt several times as they grow, but each stage (instar) usually looks much like the previous one, only larger.

When the larva reaches its last instar, it stops feeding and molts into an immobile form called a *pupa.* Some insects spin a cocoon or web, or roll a leaf around their bodies to protect themselves during this period of development. Inside the pupa, the whole insect completely changes. The larval structures and tissues dissolve and new adult features—such as legs, wings, and reproductive organs—develop. When the adult is completely formed, the insect splits open the pupa and emerges. It's soft and pale at first, with crumpled, wet wings; but in a short time, the exoskeleton hardens and the wings expand and become rigid. The adults usually have a different diet than their larvae—typically the adults sip nectar, whereas the larvae eat leaves or prey on other insects.

Feeding. As a group, insects feed on all kinds of things: plants, animals and other insects, pollen, nectar, decaying organic matter, blood, and other materials. What each species eats, however, is usually limited to only one type of plant or group of related plants, or one type of prey. Cabbage root maggots, for example, feed only on cabbage-family plants and would starve on carrots. Aphid midge larvae feed only on aphids and couldn't survive on other types of insects.

Insects generally consume food in one of two ways: by chewing or sucking. Insects that chew have sturdy jaws. The jaws are toothed and can be used to tear food as well as to mash and chew it. Insects that suck their food have long, styluslike mouthparts. Aphids, stinkbugs, and others with sucking mouthparts pierce the leaves or stems of a plant with a beak that has a fine tube inside for sucking plant sap. Butterflies and moths lack the piercing organs; instead, they have a long retractable tube, or *proboscis,* through which they sip nectar from flowers.

Most insects have taste organs in the areas around their mouthparts. Some insects use their antennae to taste things, and certain butterflies even have taste buds on their feet. This sense of taste is usually very selective, so subtle changes in the quality of host plants may make the plants unattractive to an insect.

COMPLETE METAMORPHOSIS

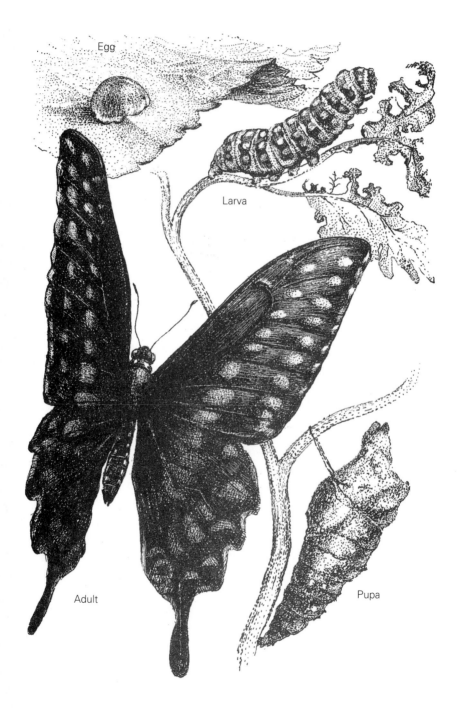

Although insects don't have a sense of smell as we know it, they do have a similar sense that is very acute. They can detect very subtle changes in odors of plants and find mates by detecting the odors that females give off. The senses of smell, taste, and sight come into play when insects are deciding which plant to eat—and some methods of protecting plants from pests depend on fooling these senses. For example, spraying a fine white coating of kaolin clay on apples changes the color and smell so that the codling moth doesn't recognize the apple tree as a host plant.

Managing Garden Insects

Using this guide, you can identify both pests and beneficial insects and learn about their life cycles. Correctly identifying insects is the all-important first step because many species we see in our gardens are beneficial. They may be there to eat pests or to pollinate flowers so that fruit will form. We now know a lot more about how important beneficial insects are in controlling pests and why they're a gardener's best friend. Organic growers have always reported fewer pest problems than growers using pesticides—and those natural enemies are a big part of the reason (plant health comes into it too, of course!).

Once you have identified problem insects, keep an eye on the situation for a while before you take action. It's a good idea to check problem plants every few days. Use a hand lens or magnifying glass to look closely. Keep a garden notebook to jot down notes and make sketches. Check to see whether there are more or fewer pest insects than the last time you looked, and watch for the appearance of their natural enemies.

The next step is to decide whether or not controls are necessary. Because many garden plants tolerate quite a lot of damage, you don't necessarily need to leap to the rescue because a plant has a few holes chewed in the leaves. By tolerating the presence of some plant-eating species, you can ensure that their natural enemies are always around to feed on the pests. On the other hand, in some years and some regions, certain pests can seriously damage crops. By knowing as much as you can about what the pest looks like and what its life cycle is, you'll know the best time to apply a treatment, if it's needed. You'll also be able to plan ways to prevent that species from becoming a problem next year.

It helps to think of pest management as a process of making changes in the garden that add up to an environment that's less favorable for the pests. For example, planting flowers that are rich in pollen and nectar between the vegetables helps attract beneficial insects. After this you may notice aphids seem to be less of a problem—and you may find that you can stop spraying soap to control the problem. Once you stop using the pesticide (that's right, soap *is* a pesticide, and it kills both pests and beneficial insects), you may notice that aphids hardly ever reach noticeable numbers. Your garden has become a safe haven for the many insects that eat aphids, and now they're doing the work.

Even though botanical pesticides—such as rotenone, ryania, and sabadilla—come from plants, they're very toxic. They kill pests and beneficials alike and are poisonous for you too—so we won't be recommending them in this guide. Two other botanicals, pyrethrins (from pyrethrum daisies) and neem (from a subtropical tree) are less toxic and can be useful in some cases where there are few other options. Nowadays, however, organic gardeners have so many other methods and low-toxicity products available that using even these two pesticides is rarely necessary.

The following is a review of methods that organic gardeners use to manage pests. Although you'll see many different methods listed under the pest entries, one or two may be all you need to get a satisfactory level of control. However, for pests that are hard to control, use a variety of methods that target the different life stages of the pests. Each method alone might not seem to have much of an impact, but when combined these methods can be very effective. For example, to manage a troublesome caterpillar population, you might use an oil spray to kill the eggs and plant flowers to attract caterpillar predators. You could also hand-pick the caterpillars and plow under crop residues to kill the pupae. Putting all these measures together can provide satisfactory control, not to mention a much smaller pest population next year.

Prevention

Healthy plants. Healthy, robust plants have some amazing ways to defend themselves against pests, ranging from obvious physical defenses, such as spiny or hairy leaves or tough bark, to chemical defenses that they can mobilize in response to attack. When a leaf-eating caterpillar attacks, some plants can increase the levels of various compounds in their tissues to make their leaves less desirable. They can even inhibit the growth of the caterpillars. The odors of the plant compounds also literally "call" beneficial insects that respond to the characteristic odor of these plant chemicals as a cue to come looking for caterpillars to attack.

Fertilizing and watering for healthy plants doesn't necessarily mean encouraging rapid or overly vigorous growth. Although drought or nutrient stress can make plants more susceptible to borers and other pests, studies have consistently found that too much water and fertilizer can also make plants more susceptible to some kinds of pests. This may be partly because when plants are growing rapidly, they have less of their own defense compounds in their tissues. They also may have softer tissues that are easier for sucking insects to pierce.

Attract natural enemies. A garden with a rich variety of predatory and parasitic insects, spiders, and birds and other animals typically has fewer pest problems because the predators keep the pests in check. To lure beneficial insects into your garden, provide them with an attractive supply of food. Because the adults of many beneficial insects feed only on pollen and nectar, you can attract them by including flowers in the garden. Once they have eaten, the adult females then search through the garden for a good place to lay their eggs, which later hatch into predatory larvae. Small-flowered plants in the carrot family (such as coriander, dill, and fennel) and the mustard family (such as broccoli, kale, and radishes) are excellent, as are many herbs in the mint family. Many pretty ornamentals and many weeds (such as corn spurry, Queen-Anne's-lace, and wild mustard) are excellent insect plants. There are annuals, biennials, and perennials to suit any garden, either planted among the vegetables or in borders and beds on the edges. And don't neglect the beetles and other predators that live in the soil. You can provide safe refuges for them by having permanent walkways and perennial beds among the garden annuals. Using mulches and growing cover crops, such as white clover, also make your garden more hospitable to them.

Resistant varieties. Some plant varieties can tolerate more insect damage than others, and some varieties actually resist attack. This might be because they have hairy leaves or tougher stems or thicker husks. Some varieties are also less attractive to insects because they have different amounts of certain compounds in their leaves. Check descriptions in seed catalogs for varieties with insect resistance.

Diverse planting. You can help prevent an over-population of particular plant-eating insects by mixing up plantings. Most insects feed on only certain kinds of related plants. By interplanting favored host plants with other vegetables and flowers, you can help keep the pest populations from increasing as quickly. Sometimes the diverse heights and growth habits of mixed plantings slows down the pests as they look for host plants.

Cultural Controls

Remove alternate hosts. Keeping down particular weeds around the garden is a good strategy if it removes alternate host plants that would harbor crop pests. As mentioned above, however, many weeds have flowers that attract and feed beneficial insects. If pests that are feeding on nearby weeds are also attacking plants in your garden, then removing those weeds could help reduce the pest numbers. If you don't have that pest problem, however, then there's no need to worry about those weeds.

Crop rotation. For insects that feed on plant roots and overwinter in the soil, it's important to rotate crops so that large numbers of pests don't build up in one place. Crop rotation is an essential part of using some types of barriers successfully (see "Barriers" on page 14). For insect management, try to rotate crops so that the same family of plants isn't grown in the same place 2 years in a row (see the disease section on page 125 for recommendations on longer rotations that might be needed to prevent buildup of plant pathogens in the soil). Rotations work best in a garden that uses permanent raised beds, rather than a garden that's completely tilled at one time.

Shift planting times. By planting early or late, you can avoid the time of year when some crops are most likely to be injured by certain insects. For some pests, this can give very good results in most years. For species that lay eggs on leaves, you can get an accurate idea of when to expect damage by watching for the eggs and observing when they hatch out.

Physical Controls

Cultivation. Many insects overwinter on or under crop debris left on the soil. One way to keep their numbers down is to shred, compost, or till under the crop residues as soon as harvest is over. If done without delay, there's a better chance of killing the pests and less chance of killing beneficial insects that also crawl under crop debris to spend the winter. Plowing the soil 6 inches (15.2 cm) deep or more in fall or early spring is recommended for some pests because it kills larvae and pupae and exposes them to attack by birds, but it can also kill beneficial insects.

So how do you decide what to do? First, keep in mind that no one rule fits every case. If you don't have a problem with the species that cultivation controls, then it's usually better not to cultivate, which could kill overwintering lady beetles and other beneficial insects. Instead, apply clean mulch, such as shredded leaves or clean straw, to provide the beneficials with a safe place to overwinter, while at the same time protecting and enriching the soil.

Barriers. You can keep insects from laying eggs or feeding on certain plants by setting up barriers between them and your plants. Floating row covers or other fine-mesh screens are particularly valuable because they can be used to completely cover plants, yet they let in rain and sun. They're most useful on seedlings and small- to medium-height plants. Always rotate crops when using such barriers to make sure that no overwintering pests are emerging from the soil under the covers. Paper, cardboard, or small tin cans can be used as collars around the stems of transplants to prevent cutworm damage. Place squares of tar paper on the soil around the stems of cabbage plants to keep the adult root maggot fly from laying eggs beside the stem.

Sticky traps. In some cases, sticky traps can be used to capture insects and prevent their populations from getting too high. Unfortunately traps used outdoors can also capture beneficial insects, so they aren't recommended except in particular cases. For example, red sticky traps are effective at catching apple maggot flies and are especially useful because most other species aren't attracted to red. In contrast, although yellow sticky traps are great for catching whiteflies and fungus gnats on indoor plants, they should be used with great caution outdoors because they also attract the tiny parasitic wasps that attack aphids. White sticky traps catch tarnished plant bugs but also trap beneficial aphid midge adults.

Trap plants. Some insect species can be lured away from crop plants onto trap plants that are more attractive. These can be grown between the rows of crops to attract pests for the growing season. The most usual method, however, involves watching the trap crop and destroying it along with the pests when they start to build up.

Hand-picking. In the home garden, it may be practical to simply pick off large, slow-moving insects and egg masses by hand and squash them or drop them into a pail of soapy water. Just be really sure you've identified the problem so that you don't mistakenly control the good guys! Sadly, many people kill lady beetle larvae and pupae (page 49) because they look nothing like the familiar adult beetles.

Biological Controls

Some species of beneficial insects, mites, and nematodes (a type of worm) are reared commercially for sale to growers. Most species are sold for use in commercial greenhouse crops, but a few can be successfully used by gardeners. The main drawback is that they're relatively expensive. Before purchasing them, make sure that they're going to work on your pest species and in your location. For the best chance of success, learn as much as you can about the biological controls and always follow instructions from the supplier on how to handle and release them.

Insects and mites. Some of the more useful predators for outdoor gardens include aphid midges (page 83), which are used to control various aphids in fruit trees, shrubs, and cabbage-family plants; and some species of predatory mites (*Amblyseius fallacis, Metaseiulus occidentalis,* and others), which are used to control spider mites in orchard trees. Lacewings (page 92) may be useful in some situations to control various soft-bodied insects. Although you'll see both convergent lady beetles (page 49) and praying mantids (page 117) offered for sale, they aren't necessarily good buys. This species of lady beetle usually flies away when released, and the praying mantids eat anything, including beneficial insects and butterflies, so they wouldn't be useful additions to your garden. It's usually best to stick to making your local lady beetles happy!

Insect parasitic nematodes. Nematodes are a large group of worms. Some cause plant diseases (page 128), others break down organic matter (they're found throughout compost), and others attack insects.

Several species of insect parasitic nematodes are sold by garden suppliers. These might include the following: *Steinernema carpocapsae,* which is useful for cutworms and other insects; *Heterorhabditis megidus*, which is most useful for larvae of root weevils; and *Heterorhabditis bacteriophora* and *Steinernema glaseri*, which attack Japanese beetle and June beetle larvae. Nematodes are sold in a dormant stage, which is mixed with water and applied to the soil. Use plenty of water to soak the nematodes into the soil so that they reach the root zone where the targets pests are feeding.

Microbial insecticides. Certain species of bacteria and fungi are available as biological controls for pests. These are called microbial pesticides because they contain living organisms. A great advantage of microbial insecticides is that they're more specific than insecticides that kill by poisoning. One example is milky spore disease (*Bacillus popilliae*), an old product that has been used for years on Japanese beetle grubs.

BT (Bacillus thuringiensis). The BT bacteria are a group of bacteria that infect insects. *BT* var. *kurstaki* has been used for more than 30 years to control certain caterpillars. It causes the caterpillars to stop feeding immediately and eventually die of the bacterial disease. For best results it's usually sprayed while the caterpillars are still small. The bacteria last only a few days in the environment, so repeat sprays may be needed. *BT* var. *tenebrionis* controls beetle larvae, such as Colorado potato beetles. *BT* var. *israelensis* controls fungus gnats and mosquitoes.

Beauveria bassiana. This fungus disease infects a wide variety of insects. The affected insects eventually become covered with white mold. *Beauveria* is less selective than the BTs, so it should be used with caution to protect nontarget insects. Like BT, however, it has no effect on earthworms, birds, and other animals.

Sprays and Other Controls

If after you've tried preventive, cultural, and biological controls the insects still get out of hand temporarily, you should ask whether it's *really* necessary to take action? If it is, then it's a good idea to start with the least toxic methods first. You can work up to stronger stuff as a last resort if it becomes necessary. Once you've achieved control, think about what you can do to prevent the problem from happening next year. For example, if you felt compelled to spray pyrethrins to save your seedlings from flea beetles this year, then next year prevent the problem entirely by covering the beds with floating rows covers before the seedlings come up.

Even the most "natural" or apparently harmless (to people!) homemade sprays can seriously upset the natural balance in your garden if they're widely applied. Most sprays can harm beneficial insects, so spray only when absolutely necessary, and treat only plants that have the problem. The following list starts with the least toxic sprays first, followed by increasingly more toxic products.

Water. Sprayed forcefully on foliage, water sprays control aphids, mites, and many other small, leaf-eating insects that feed in out-of-the-way places. The predators that the water knocks off the plants can climb back onto the plants. Aphids can climb back up too, but most of them will have their mouthparts damaged by being torn away from the leaf, so they can't start feeding again. One or two water sprays per week is usually all that's needed.

Kaolin. Products containing this naturally occurring fine clay (china clay), which is mixed with water and sprayed on plants, are available for organic gardeners (one such product is called Surround). Kaolin works by coating the plants with a thin white film, which seems to stop insects from laying eggs or eating leaves, partly because the insects no longer recognize the plant as food and partly because they don't like the clay particles on their feet. Although the plants may look strange in white, the clay coating seems to benefit them because they grow well and are protected from sunburn. To be effective, kaolin sprays must thoroughly cover the plant. Kaolin is usually applied at 7- to 21-day intervals during the time pests are present, to maintain the clay barrier as the plants grow.

Soap. Soaps can be used to control aphids, small caterpillars, mites, and other soft-bodied insects. Soap kills only on contact, so it doesn't affect insects crawling on leaves after it has dried. Commercial soap products are available. If you make a homemade soap spray, use pure liquid soap (not detergent), and don't add more than 1 to 2 tablespoons (15 to 30 ml) per gallon (3.8 liters) of water—higher concentrations may burn plant leaves.

Oils. In the past, oils were used as sprays only when trees were dormant because the oils injured the leaves. Now, the petroleum-based, "narrow-range oils" can also be used on many growing plants because the oils are so precisely refined that they don't harm the leaves. Oil sprays on dormant trees smother eggs and pupae of overwintering insects, whereas summer sprays (these are more diluted than dormant sprays) are useful for difficult-to-control pests such as mealybugs, scales, and others. As with soaps, only insects or eggs that come in direct contact with the spray are affected.

Vegetable oils, such as canola oil and jojoba oil, can be used in sprays instead of the petroleum-based, narrow-range oils. Both have the same type of effect on insects and their eggs as narrow-range oils. Canola oil can be used for many different pests on various crops. Jojoba oil seems to be most effective on whiteflies (as well as some plant disease fungi).

Homemade oil sprays can be made by mixing 1 cup (237 ml) of vegetable oil with 1 tablespoon (15 ml) of liquid soap. Mix these together well, then measure out 1 tablespoon (15ml) of this mixture per quart (0.95 l) of water to make a spray.

Diatomaceous earth (DE, or silicon dioxide). DE is made from ground-up skeletons of fossilized, single-celled animals. It works by causing insects to dry up when they come in contact with the sharp particles. Even though it's nontoxic, it does kill beneficial insects. Unlike soaps or oils, which are harmless after they're applied, DE continues to affect insects as long as it's present. That means it should be used only on very small areas in the garden, such as at the base of plant stems to prevent root maggot flies from laying eggs. It should be used rarely (if ever) on leaves. Always buy DE sold for use as an insecticide and not the DE sold for use in pool filters. The latter product is cheap, but it's heated and cracked to a particle size that can harm your lungs if you breathe in the dust. Because the DE sold to be used as an insecticide is also a dust, it's always a good idea to wear a dust mask when using it to avoid inhaling it.

Botanical Insecticides

Essential oils. Homemade sprays from garlic and strong-smelling herbs, such as thyme and mint, have long been known to repel pests. Several commercial products are becoming available, including garlic oil and the distilled oils of various herbs, such as mint, thyme, and cinnamon. As with any pesticide, however, these oils should be used with caution. Note that mint oil isn't the same as pennyroyal oil, which is toxic and should never be used on food plants.

Neem. The subtropical neem tree (*Azadiracta indica*) contains compounds called "azadiractins," which have been used for many years in India and other countries as a low-toxicity insecticide. Azadiractins repel insects and affect their development. Neem is one of the few natural insecticides that can be used to control leafminers. Although it's so harmless to people that it's also used in toothpaste and other products, it can affect the predators that eat pests sprayed by neem. As with other insecticides, neem should be used with caution and only as a last resort.

Pyrethrins. These active compounds are extracted from the flowers of pyrethrum daisies. They're as quick-acting as a contact insecticide. Pyrethrins are moderately toxic to people and animals, so they should be used only as a last resort. They're effective against many different insects—including aphids, beetles, caterpillars, and leafhoppers—and also kill beneficial insects as well. They break down in the environment in a few days, so their effect isn't long-lasting. If you're choosing a pyrethin product, look for one that doesn't contain piperonyl butoxide, which is a synthetic additive.

Key to Common Garden Insects

Larvae

WORMLIKE

NOTES
Prolegs are plump, fleshy false legs that enable the larva to move more easily. Caterpillars have hooked prolegs, enabling them to hang effortlessly from the host plant.

Physical characteristics in black

Behavioral characteristics in green

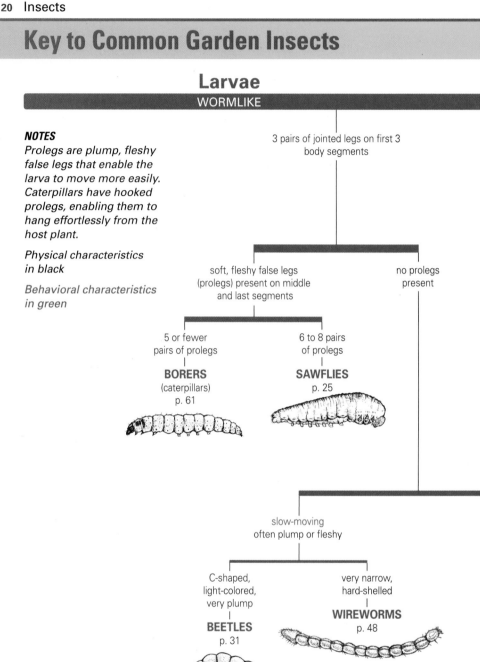

3 pairs of jointed legs on first 3 body segments

soft, fleshy false legs (prolegs) present on middle and last segments

no prolegs present

5 or fewer pairs of prolegs

BORERS
(caterpillars)
p. 61

6 to 8 pairs of prolegs

SAWFLIES
p. 25

slow-moving
often plump or fleshy

C-shaped, light-colored, very plump

BEETLES
p. 31

very narrow, hard-shelled

WIREWORMS
p. 48

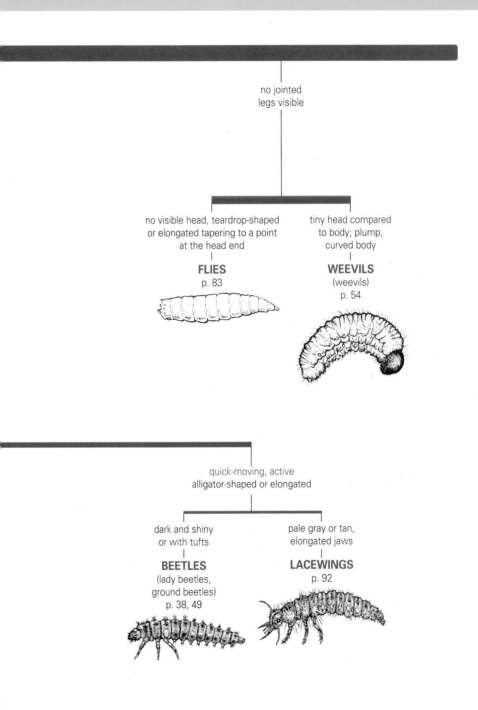

no jointed
legs visible

no visible head, teardrop-shaped
or elongated tapering to a point
at the head end

FLIES
p. 83

tiny head compared
to body; plump,
curved body

WEEVILS
(weevils)
p. 54

quick-moving, active
alligator-shaped or elongated

dark and shiny
or with tufts

BEETLES
(lady beetles,
ground beetles)
p. 38, 49

pale gray or tan,
elongated jaws

LACEWINGS
p. 92

Key to Common Garden Insects

Adults and Nymphs

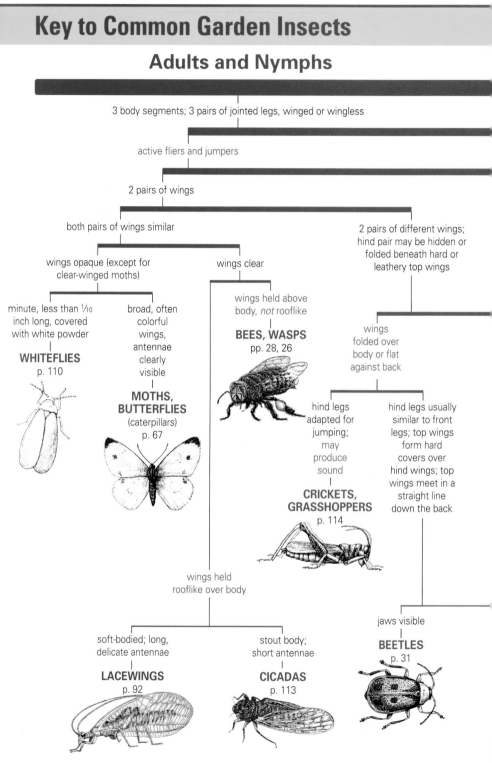

3 body segments; 3 pairs of jointed legs, winged or wingless

active fliers and jumpers

2 pairs of wings

both pairs of wings similar

2 pairs of different wings; hind pair may be hidden or folded beneath hard or leathery top wings

wings opaque (except for clear-winged moths)

wings clear

minute, less than 1/10 inch long, covered with white powder

WHITEFLIES
p. 110

broad, often colorful wings, antennae clearly visible

MOTHS, BUTTERFLIES
(caterpillars)
p. 67

wings held above body, *not* rooflike

BEES, WASPS
pp. 28, 26

wings folded over body or flat against back

hind legs adapted for jumping; may produce sound

CRICKETS, GRASSHOPPERS
p. 114

hind legs usually similar to front legs; top wings form hard covers over hind wings; top wings meet in a straight line down the back

wings held rooflike over body

soft-bodied; long, delicate antennae

LACEWINGS
p. 92

stout body; short antennae

CICADAS
p. 113

jaws visible

BEETLES
p. 31

NOTES: *Physical characteristics are in black;* *behavioral characteristics are in green.*

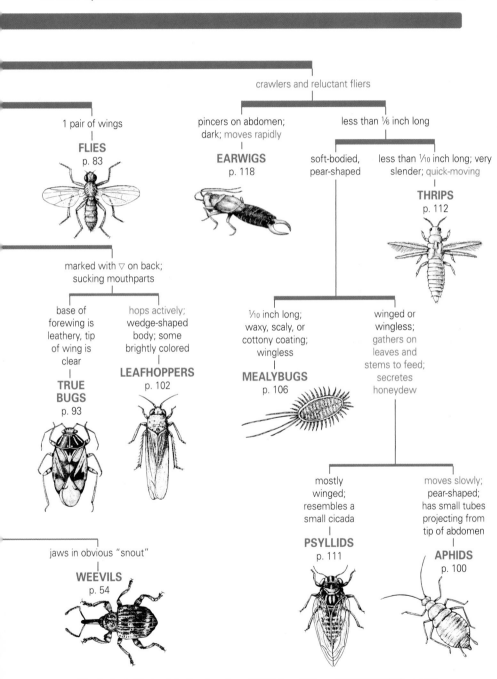

crawlers and reluctant fliers

1 pair of wings

FLIES
p. 83

pincers on abdomen;
dark; moves rapidly

EARWIGS
p. 118

less than ⅛ inch long

soft-bodied,
pear-shaped

less than ⅒ inch long; very
slender; quick-moving

THRIPS
p. 112

marked with ▽ on back;
sucking mouthparts

base of
forewing is
leathery, tip
of wing is
clear

**TRUE
BUGS**
p. 93

hops actively;
wedge-shaped
body; some
brightly colored

LEAFHOPPERS
p. 102

⅒ inch long;
waxy, scaly, or
cottony coating;
wingless

MEALYBUGS
p. 106

winged or
wingless;
gathers on
leaves and
stems to feed;
secretes
honeydew

jaws in obvious "snout"

WEEVILS
p. 54

mostly
winged;
resembles a
small cicada

PSYLLIDS
p. 111

moves slowly;
pear-shaped;
has small tubes
projecting from
tip of abdomen

APHIDS
p. 100

Also included in book but not on key: SCALES, p. 107, and NONINSECTS, p. 119

Ants
FORMICIDAE

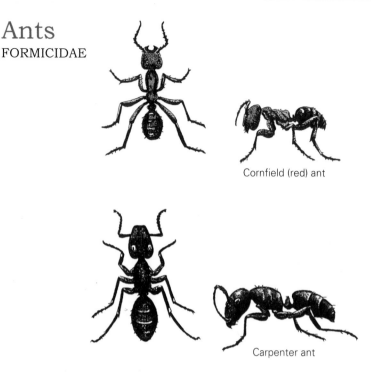

Cornfield (red) ant

Carpenter ant

Adult actual size: ⅙ to ¾ inch

Range: Many species throughout North America.

Description: Adults of most species are tan, reddish brown, or black, ⅙ to ¾ inch (4.2 to 19.1 mm) long, with a narrow "waist." Wingless workers are most commonly seen; winged ants appear in mating swarms. Ants are highly social, with many workers living together in large colonies, each with one or more queens.

Life Cycle: The queen lays eggs in a nest. The nest can be above or below ground and in large chambers, mounds, or small natural crevices. Workers care for the eggs and larvae, feed the queen, and defend the nest. Colonies hibernate for the winter, and the queen resumes laying eggs in spring.

Feeding Habits: Many ants are important predators of insect eggs and larvae. Some species are scavengers of plant or animal matter, whereas others feed on nectar and the honeydew that aphids and other sucking insects produce. These ants can become a problem when they protect the sucking insects from predators.

Prevention and Control: Where ants are causing serious problems by protecting plant pests, set out commercial or homemade bait containing boric acid and sugar (mix 3 tablespoons [45 ml] sugar, 2 cups [473 ml] water, and 1 teaspoon [5 ml] boric acid) along ant trails. Control fire ants, which sting, by pouring boiling water into nest mounds. Nests of other species found in garden soil can also be eliminated with boiling water, digging, or deep cultivation.

European Apple Sawfly
Hoplocampa testudinea

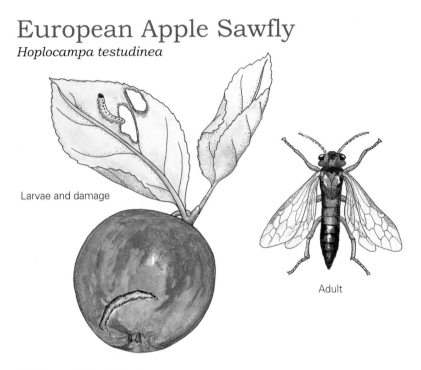

Larvae and damage

Adult

Adult actual size: ⅕ inch ▬

Range: Northeastern United States and into Canada.

Description: Adults are brown, ⅕ inch (5.1 mm) long, with a yellow head and yellow antennae and eyes; wings are clear with tiny black hairs. Larvae are white to tan with seven pairs of legs; their heads and tails are brown to black. The eggs, which are colorless and shiny, are laid at the base of apple blossoms.

Life Cycle: The pupae overwinter in cocoons just below the surface of the soil. Adults emerge and lay eggs about the time apple trees bloom. The larvae feed on fruit until late June, and then drop to the soil to spin cocoons. There's one generation per year.

Host Plants: Apple and crabapple.

Feeding Habits: Larvae first mine under the skin of developing fruit, leaving a spiral scar; later they tunnel into the core, leaving behind wet, reddish brown sawdust.

Prevention and Control: Prompt, early removal of infested fruit prevents larvae from moving onto new fruit. For serious problems, one well-timed spray of canola oil, after flower petals fall, controls newly hatched larvae. Spraying is risky to bees and rarely necessary, except in commercial apple-growing areas where sawfly populations may be high.

Similar Insects: Codling moth larvae (page 69).

Braconid Wasps
BRACONIDAE

Female parasitizing an aphid

Parasitized caterpillar

Adult

Adult actual size: ¹⁄₁₀ to ½ inch ▬▬▬▬

Range: Many species throughout North America.

Description: Adults are black, brown, or reddish brown, ¹⁄₁₀ to ½ inch (2.5 to 12.7 mm) long, with a narrow waist. Larvae are tiny white grubs that parasitize other insects.

Life Cycle: Female wasps inject their eggs into the bodies of host insects; some species sting the host to paralyze it, then lay eggs on it. Larvae feed on, or inside, the host, emerging to spin cocoons on the host body or nearby. Most species overwinter as larvae or pupae inside their hosts. There are several generations per year.

Feeding Habits: Adults lay eggs in the larvae of caterpillars, beetles, aphids, flies, and other insects. The white or tan cocoons are commonly seen on the backs of hornworms and other caterpillars.

Attract and Protect: Attract female wasps by growing small-flowered plants rich in nectar, which they need for food. Plant caraway, coriander, dill, sweet fennel, spearmint, tansy, and other herbs; flowering buckwheat, white sweet clover, golden marguerite, potentilla, and statice are also attractive. Allow some wild areas to grow with weeds such as corn spurry, common knotweed, mustard, stinging nettle, Queen-Anne's-lace, and yarrow.

Yellow Jackets
Vespula spp.

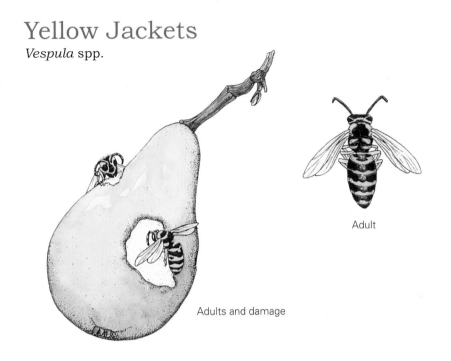

Adult

Adults and damage

Adult actual size: ½ to ¾ inch ▬▬▬▬

Range: Various species throughout North America.

Description: Adults are shiny, black-and-yellow striped, and ½ to ¾ inch (12.7 to 19.1 mm) long; they have two pairs of transparent wings. They're social insects that live in large colonies of workers with a queen, in paper nests they construct of wood fiber. Some species build their nests underground, whereas others hang them from tree branches or other high supports. The larvae are pearly white grubs, reared in cells in the nests.

Life Cycle: The queen wasp overwinters under loose bark or in other protected sites. In spring, she builds a small cluster of paper cells and lays eggs to establish a new colony. As the number of wasps in the colony increases, workers add more layers to the nest. All except the queen wasp die off in the fall, and the old nest isn't reused the following year.

Feeding Habits: Adult wasps capture caterpillars, flies, and other insects to feed the developing young. In late summer, when they're no longer raising young, the wasps are more attracted to fruit, honeydew from aphids, and other sweet foods.

Prevention and Control: Nests that pose a danger can be physically removed if necessary or sprayed with wasp-control products containing pyrethrins or mint oil. To temporarily reduce numbers of yellow jackets at a picnic, place wasp traps around the area. Bait traps with meat or fish early in the season, and use sugary foods later. Nests in the ground can be vacuumed out by a professional pest control service or suffocated by covering the entrance at night with plastic or old carpeting held down by a thick layer of soil.

Similar Insects: Flower flies (page 88).

Bumblebees
Bombus spp.

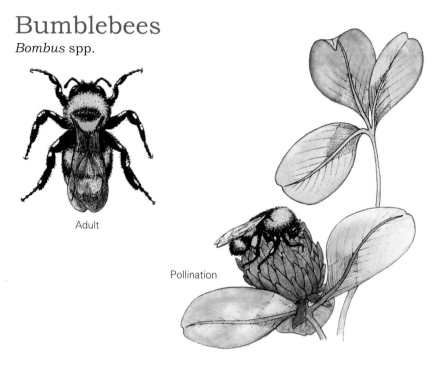

Adult

Pollination

Adult actual size: ½ to 1 inch ▬▬▬▬▬▬

Range: Many species throughout North America.

Description: Adults are large, stout, very fuzzy bees, ½ to 1 inch (12.7 to 25.4 mm) long, with transparent wings. Most are brownish orange to black with bands of yellow or orange hair on their bodies. They're social insects that live in small colonies with a single queen.

Life Cycle: Only young queen bumblebees overwinter in protected sites. In spring, the queen finds an old mouse burrow or other natural chamber to make a nest in. She feeds and cares for the first brood of larvae, which become workers when mature. They collect food and care for the larvae while the queen continues to lays eggs. Most of the bees die in fall.

Feeding Habits: Bumblebees are extremely valuable native pollinators. They fly in cool weather and are the only bees big enough to "buzz pollinate" blueberry, cranberry, and tomato plants or to pollinate plants with deep flowers. Bumblebee colonies store little honey, so they need a steady supply of nectar, or they die out. Native bumblebees are disappearing where native flowers have been replaced by cultivated crops or flowers with little nectar.

Attract and Protect: Preserve natural areas with perennial wildflowers and weeds such as goldenrod, tall ironweed, and Joe-Pye weed. Plant ornamental *Alliums*, meadow clary (*Salvia pratensis*), anchusas, catmint, red clover, heirloom varieties of foxglove, hollyhocks, single-flowered larkspur, nasturtiums, and snapdragons.

Similar Insects: Flower flies (page 88).

Honeybee
Apis mellifera

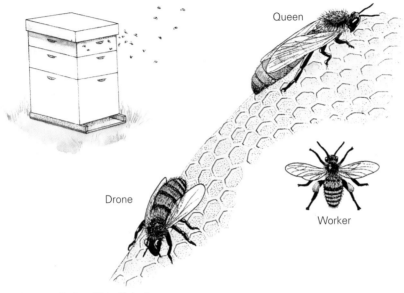

Queen

Drone

Worker

Adult actual size: ¼ to ¾ inch

Range: Throughout North America.

Description: Adults are ½ to ¾ inch (12.7 to 19.1 mm) long and golden yellow, with darker stripes on the abdomen and darker thoraxes covered with short hairs. Honeybees are highly social and live in large colonies of workers, each with a queen.

Life Cycle: The queen lays eggs continually, except during extremely cold periods. Worker bees collect pollen and nectar to feed the developing larvae, keep the hive clean, and defend it. A few larvae are reared to become queens; after a mating flight with males, the young queens leave with swarms of workers to start new colonies. Colonies spend the winter in their hives, feeding on honey.

Feeding Habits: Worker bees feed on nectar from many different plants and, in the process, transfer pollen from one flower to another, or from the male to the female part of a single flower. They're important pollinators of many fruits, vegetables, and other crops.

Attract and Protect: Parasitic mites have decimated honeybee colonies in recent years; in some areas, nearly all wild colonies have died out. Avoid using sprays to control insects, particularly on orchard trees when flowers are blooming; if it's necessary to spray, choose organic options, and apply them in the evening, after bees have returned to the hive. To make up for the loss of these pollinators, attract native pollinators such as bumblebees (opposite page) and orchard mason bees (page 30), which are immune to parasitic mites.

Similar Insects: Flower flies (page 88).

Orchard Mason Bee, Blue Orchard Bee

Osmia lignaria

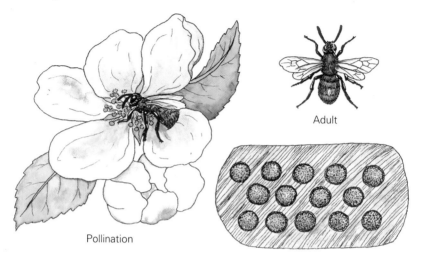

Adult

Pollination

Nesting block with filled cells

Adult actual size: ⅓ inch ▬

Range: Western North America; related species in the East.

Description: Adults are small bluish black bees, ⅓ inch (8.5 mm) long. They carry pollen on hairs on the underside of their abdomen. The larvae are small white grubs.

Life Cycle: Adult orchard mason bees emerge very early in spring. After mating, the females nest in tree holes that insects or birds have made, in hollow plant stems, or in cracks under building siding. They collect a ball of pollen and nectar, lay an egg on it, then use mud to seal off the cell. They continue laying eggs until the hole is full, and then they move on to another hole. The larvae develop into adults by fall but stay inside the cell until they chew their way out the following spring. Orchard mason bees are active only about 3 months of the year; there's one generation per year.

Feeding Habits: Orchard mason bees are important pollinators of fruit and nut crops. They pollinate more blossoms each day and work in weather too cool or damp for honeybees. They prefer orchard fruit flowers, but they also visit dandelion, mustard, pussy willow, and other early-spring flowers.

Attract and Protect: To compensate for limited orchard mason bee numbers from lack of nest sites, provide nesting blocks of wood drilled with holes 5/16 inch (8 mm) in diameter and 4 to 6 inches (10.2 to 15.2 cm) deep, or use a bundle of specially designed heavy cardboard straws (which are sold for this purpose) in a waterproof shelter. Nests must be attached to a wall or post, preferably on the east or south side of a building with protection from rain.

Asparagus Beetle
Crioceris asparagi
Spotted Asparagus Beetle
Crioceris duodecimpunctata

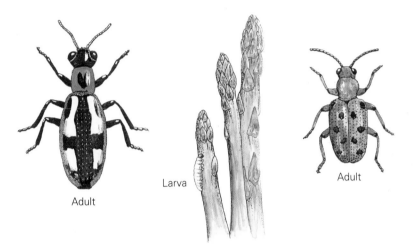

Adult

Larva

Adult

Adult actual size: ¼ to ⅓ inch ▬▬

Range: Widespread throughout North America.

Description: *C. asparagi* adults are metallic blue to black, with 4 white spots and reddish edges on their backs; *C. duodecimpunctata* adults are orange with 12 black spots on their backs. Both are shiny and ¼ to ⅓ inch (6.4 to 8.5 mm) long. Larvae are plump, gray or greenish, less than ⅓ inch (8.5 mm) long, with black heads and legs. Eggs are black and shiny and are laid on young spears or stems.

Life Cycle: Adults overwinter in plant debris and emerge in spring as the first spears poke through the soil. Females lay eggs on young spears and stems (later in the season). Larvae feed on plants for 2 weeks, then pupate in the soil. There are two to four generations per year.

Host Plant: Asparagus.

Feeding Habits: Adults and larvae chew spears in spring. In summer, they feed on the fronds of asparagus plants and, if present in high numbers, may defoliate the plants.

Prevention and Control: To prevent damage to early spears, cover them with floating row covers, and harvest often. Hand-pick beetles and larvae as soon as they begin to appear. For serious infestations, spray soap, canola oil, or as a last resort, pyrethrins. In early fall, remove and burn or shred old asparagus fronds so beetles can't overwinter; don't apply mulch to the asparagus bed until late fall so the beetles don't hide out in the mulch.

Insect Predators: Lady beetles (page 49).

Bean Leaf Beetle
Cerotoma trifurcata

Adults and damage

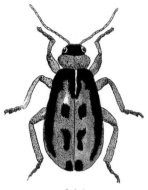

Adult

Adult actual size: ¼ inch ▬

Range: Eastern North America into Canada, especially in the southeastern United States; also Texas, Kansas, and New Mexico.

Description: Adults are reddish orange to yellow, ¼ inch (6.4 mm) long, and shiny; the wing covers have black edges, and three black spots usually dot each wing cover. Larvae are thin, white grubs with darker brown heads and tails. Eggs are orange ovals laid on the undersides of leaves.

Life Cycle: Adults overwinter in leaf litter and emerge in spring. They feed for several days, then lay eggs at the base of plants. Larvae feed for up to 6 weeks on stems or roots, then pupate in the soil. There are two to three generations per year.

Host Plants: Bean, pea, and soybean.

Feeding Habits: Larvae bore into the roots and sometimes girdle the plant stems. Adults feed on leaves throughout the summer. Populations are highest in commercial soybean-growing regions. Adults can spread virus diseases of beans.

Prevention and Control: Full-grown plants tolerate a lot of leaf damage without yields being affected, so controls are usually unnecessary. Plant late (early June) to avoid the first generation of beetles. Cover seedlings with floating row covers. Hand-pick small numbers of beetles. As a last resort, where more than half of the leaves have been eaten, spray plants thoroughly with canola oil or pyrethrins.

Blister Beetles
Epicauta spp.

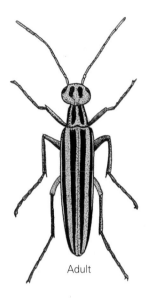

Adult

Adult actual size: ⅜ to ¾ inch ▬▬▬▬▬▬▬

Range: Related species throughout North America.

Description: Adults of most species are ⅜ to ¾ inch (9.5 to 19.1 mm) long and have soft, elongated bodies with long legs and narrow "necks" just behind the head. Colors range from metallic blue-black or dark brown to yellow with black stripes. The larva changes shape as it grows, starting as a tiny, narrow worm with a large head, and eventually becoming a plump, white, C-shaped grub. Eggs are yellow and cylindrical and are laid in clusters in holes dug into the soil.

Life Cycle: Larvae overwinter and pupate in the soil in spring. Adults emerge in midsummer and lay eggs in a burrow in the soil near grasshopper egg burrows. The newly hatched larvae tunnel through the soil to reach grasshopper eggs; they feed for about a month, then overwinter in the burrow. There's one generation per year; in some conditions, pupae may stay in the soil for 2 years.

Host Plants: Bean, beet, melon, pea, potato, tomato, and other vegetable plants.

Feeding Habits: Larvae feed on grasshopper eggs. Adults feed on foliage and fruit.

Prevention and Control: Hand-pick the beetles or knock them into pails of soapy water. Always wear gloves when handling blister beetles because they secrete harmful oil that can blister skin. Spray canola oil to control adults.

Colorado Potato Beetle
Leptinotarsa decemlineata

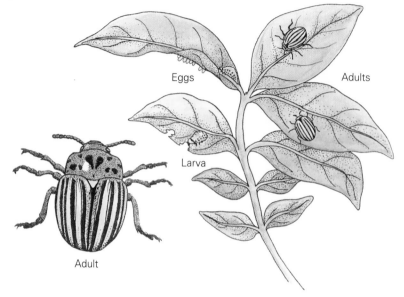

Eggs

Adults

Larva

Adult

Adult actual size: ⅓ inch ▬

Range: Throughout North America, except for some western coastal regions.

Description: Adults are yellowish orange beetles, ⅓ inch (8.5 mm) long, with 10 black stripes on their wing covers and dark spots just behind their heads. Larvae are plump, dark orange grubs with black legs and heads and two rows of black spots on each side. Eggs are yellow ovals, laid in clusters on the undersides of leaves.

Life Cycle: Adults and some pupae overwinter deep in the soil. Adults emerge in spring and walk to host plants to feed until they have the strength to fly. They lay eggs on plants; eggs hatch into larvae, which feed on leaves for up to 3 weeks, then pupate in the soil. There are two to three generations per year.

Host Plants: Eggplant, pepper, potato, tomato, and petunia.

Feeding Habits: Adults and larvae feed on leaves and shoots. Large plants can withstand moderate damage without affecting yields.

Prevention and Control: Plant resistant potato cultivars ('Katahdin', 'Sequoia'). Cover plants with floating row covers until midseason. Plant coriander and dill between rows to attract beneficial insects. In spring, mulch plants with a thick layer of straw to inhibit the movement of beetles, or trap them in steep-sided trenches lined with plastic around the potato patch. Hand-pick egg masses and larvae; knock adults from plants into a bucket of soapy water. For severe infestations, spray kaolin or canola oil. Apply *Bacillus thuringiensis tenebrionis* to control young larvae. In fall, cultivate the soil deeply to kill overwintering beetles.

Insect Predators: Native parasitic wasps (*Edovum puttleri*) and predatory stink bugs (*Perillus bioculatus*) (page 95) are sold commercially.

Corn Rootworms (Northern, Western)
Diabrotica spp.

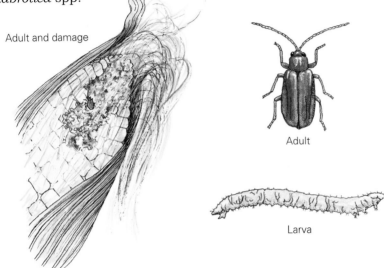

Adult and damage

Adult

Larva

Adult actual size: ⅓ inch ▬

Range: Throughout the United States and into southern Canada.

Description: Adults are yellowish green and up to ⅓ inch (8.5 mm) long with brown antennae and feet; western corn rootworm adults have three black stripes on their wing covers. Larvae are thin, wrinkled, white worms up to ½ inch (12.7 mm) long, with brown heads and feet.

Life Cycle: Females lay eggs near corn roots in fall. Eggs overwinter, and larvae hatch in spring, moving in the soil to corn roots and feeding until early summer, when they pupate. Adults emerge in July and August. There's one generation per year.

Host Plants: Corn, grains, and grasses.

Feeding Habits: Adults chew on corn silks and pollen of corn and other plants. They damage ears and interfere with pollination of kernels. Larvae are most damaging because they burrow into corn roots, stunting growth or causing plants to topple over; they can also spread bacterial wilt and mosaic diseases of corn.

Prevention and Control: Crop rotation, especially with legumes, is very effective. Plant corn patches as far away as possible from where corn was planted the previous year. Pull and compost corn roots in fall to remove overwintering eggs, or cultivate soil well in fall and spring. Plant early so plants have large root systems before rootworms attack. To control larvae in the roots of corn, apply insect parasitic nematodes (*Heterorhabditis bacteriophora*).

Insect Predators: Ground beetles (page 38), rove beetles (page 44), and Pennsylvania leather-wings (page 45).

Similar Insects: Spotted cucumber beetle larvae (page 46) are also known as southern corn rootworms.

Flea Beetles, Striped Flea Beetles
CHRYSOMELIDAE

Adults and damage

Adult

Adult actual size: ¹/₁₀ inch ■

Range: Throughout North America.

Description: Adults of most species are shiny brown or black and ¹/₁₀ inch (2.5 mm) long. Striped flea beetles have a wavy or broken yellowish stripe on each wing cover. All hop quickly when disturbed. Larvae are elongated, thin, white grubs, with brown heads and minute legs.

Life Cycle: Adults overwinter in crop debris, emerging in early spring to feed on seedlings. Females lay eggs at the base of host plants. The larvae feed on plant roots for up to a month before pupating. There are one to four generations per year.

Host Plants: Striped flea beetles attack radishes, turnips, and other cabbage-family plants. Similar species attack corn, eggplant, potatoes, sweet potatoes, and other vegetables.

Feeding Habits: Adults chew tiny shot holes in leaves and can spread some plant diseases. Larvae chew on roots and tubers. Heavy infestations may kill seedlings, but larger plants usually survive and outgrow damage. Large numbers of larvae can heavily damage tuber crops.

Prevention and Control: Plant resistant varieties of broccoli, cabbage, cauliflower, kale, sweet potatoes, and turnips. Cover seedlings with floating row covers or screens. Plant late to avoid the first generation of beetles. Control weeds, and promptly pull and shred or compost crop residues after harvest. For flea beetles attacking cabbage-family plants, plant a trap crop of leafy mustard or radishes between the rows to attract beetles away from crop plants. To control adults, spray kaolin, canola oil or, as a last resort, pyrethrins.

Green June Beetle *Cotinis nitida*
Fig Beetle *Cotinis texana*

Adult

Adult and damage

Adult actual size: 1 inch ▬▬▬▬▬▬▬

Range: Southeastern United States (*C. nitida*); Southwestern United States (*C. texana*).

Description: Adults are stout, somewhat flattened, up to 1 inch (2.5 cm) long, and coppery green, with yellow or bronze edges around the wing covers. Larvae are plump, dirty white grubs, up to 2 inches (5.1 cm) long, with dark heads; they work their way through the soil on their backs. Eggs are laid in soil.

Life Cycle: Larvae overwinter 8 to 24 inches (20.3 to 61 cm) deep in the soil. They pupate in early spring, and adults emerge in summer. They lay eggs in soil that's high in decaying organic matter. The larvae burrow into the soil and feed on the organic matter until winter. There's one generation per year.

Host Plants: Apples, berries, figs, grapes, peaches, and pears; also corn, other vegetables, and melons.

Feeding Habits: Adult beetles chew holes in leaves and ripe fruit. The larvae eat vegetable matter, including roots of grasses and other plants, but are rarely damaging; in large numbers, they can damage plants by tunneling in seed beds.

Prevention and Control: Don't leave piles of compost, grass clippings, or manure near lawns or orchards because they attract beetles to lay eggs; spread and incorporate compost regularly to avoid harboring larvae. Where adults are damaging, knock them into pails of soapy water or onto sheets on the ground and destroy them. To control larvae in turf, flood the soil in spring or late fall to drive them to the surface where they can be squashed.

Similar Insects: June beetles (page 41).

Ground Beetles
CARABIDAE

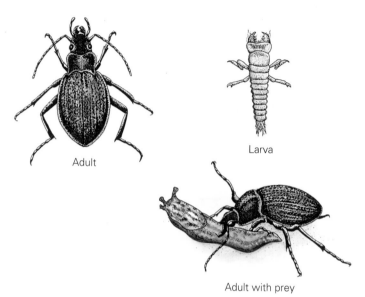

Adult

Larva

Adult with prey

Adult actual size: ¾ to 1 inch

Range: Throughout North America.

Description: Adults are iridescent bluish or purplish black, ¾ to 1 inch (19.1 to 25.4 mm) long, with long legs that enable them to run quickly. They're active at night and hide under rocks or in soil crevices during the day. Larvae are black or brown, up to 1 inch long (25.4 mm), and have large jaws and distinct segments on their bodies.

Life Cycle: Adults overwinter in soil or sheltered sites, emerging in spring to lay eggs. Larvae feed for up to a month, then pupate in the soil. There's one generation per year. Adults live 2 to 3 years.

Feeding Habits: Adults and larvae are beneficial predators of cutworms, fly eggs, maggots, slugs, snails, and other soft-bodied larvae and pupae found in the soil. Larvae may occasionally feed on earthworms, but their beneficial effect far outweighs this drawback.

Attract and Protect: Plant white clover or other groundcovers or use mulches rather than cultivation to control weeds under orchard trees and between garden beds. Mix permanent and annual plantings to provide a stable environment for beetles from year to year.

Similar Insects: Fiery searchers (opposite page).

Ground Beetle, Fiery Searcher
Calosoma scrutator

Adult

Adult stalking prey

Adult actual size: 1 to 1¼ inches ▬▬▬▬▬▬

Range: United States and southern Canada, with similar species found throughout North America.

Description: Adults are blackish purple, 1 inch to 1¼ inches (2.5 to 3.2 cm) long, with metallic green wing covers and golden green on the sides of the head. They run quickly but rarely fly. Larvae are yellowish gray to white and long and narrow, with large jaws.

Life Cycle: Adults overwinter in soil or sheltered sites. Larvae feed for up to a month, then pupate in the soil. There's one generation per year. Adults live for 2 to 3 years.

Feeding Habits: Adults feed at night on soft-bodied grubs and caterpillars, generally traveling up into trees and shrubs to feed on cankerworms, gypsy moth caterpillars, and tent caterpillars. If disturbed, the fiery searcher discharges a foul-smelling juice as a defense.

Attract and Protect: As for other ground beetles (opposite page), provide a stable environment, with ground covers and permanent plantings.

Japanese Beetle
Popillia japonica

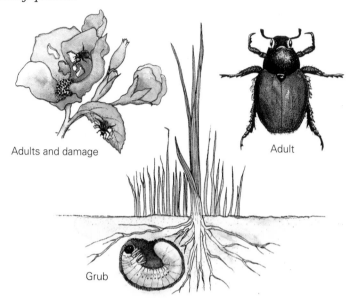

Adults and damage

Adult

Grub

Adult actual size: ½ inch ▬▬▬

Range: Eastern United States and southern Canada, west to Mississippi and Iowa, occasionally in California.

Description: Adults are metallic blue or green, ½ inch (12.7 mm) long, with coppery wing covers. Larvae are plump, grayish white, C-shaped grubs with brown heads that reach up to ¾ inch (19.1 mm) long and are found in sod.

Life Cycle: Beetle larvae overwinter in the soil and feed on plant roots in spring. They pupate in early summer, and adults emerge in late June to July and feed until fall. Females lay eggs in the soil under grasses in late summer. One generation takes 1 to 2 years.

Host Plants: A wide range of fruit, ornamentals, and vegetables.

Feeding Habits: Adults skeletonize leaves and devour flowers; in large numbers they can completely defoliate plants. The larvae chew roots of grasses, leaving patches of dead grass.

Prevention and Control: Cover garden vegetables with floating row covers to keep beetles off. To kill beetle eggs in the sod, allow lawns to thoroughly dry out between waterings or go dormant in summer. In late spring and fall, aerate lawns with spiked sandals to kill larvae. In early morning, hand-pick beetles, vacuum them from plants, or knock them onto a sheet on the ground or into a bucket of soapy water. To prevent adults from feeding, spray kaolin or canola oil on fruit and vegetable crops. Where cost is justified, apply insect parasitic nematodes (*Heterorhabditis bacteriophora, Steinernema glaseri*) to turf to control larvae; use of milky spore disease (*Bacillus popillae*) isn't recommended because results vary.

Insect Predators: Parasitic wasps, tachinid flies (page 91).

June Beetles, May Beetles
Phyllophaga spp.

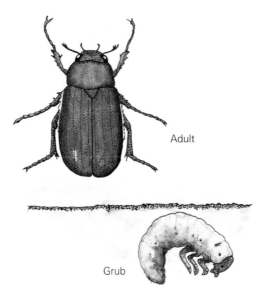

Adult

Grub

Adult actual size: 1 inch ▬▬▬▬▬

Range: Various species found throughout North America.

Description: Adults are reddish brown or black, up to 1 inch (2.5 cm) long. The western species, the 10-lined June beetle (*P. decemlineata*), has white stripes on the wings. Larvae are plump, grayish white, C-shaped grubs, up to 1½ inches (3.8 cm) long with brown heads.

Life Cycle: Females lay eggs in spring soil. Larvae feed on decaying organic matter during summer, then burrow in the soil to spend winter. They feed on plant roots the second summer, overwinter in the soil again, then feed on roots until June of the third summer, when they pupate. Adults remain in the soil until the following spring.

Host Plants: Garden plants, grasses, and ornamentals.

Feeding Habits: Larvae are most damaging in their second year, especially if they occur in high numbers as they feed on roots of corn, grasses, potatoes, strawberries, ornamentals, and other plants. Adult beetles may feed on leaves of deciduous trees and shrubs.

Prevention and Control: Cultivate garden beds before planting and leave soil open to expose grubs to birds. Avoid spreading manure on lawns during the summer because this attracts beetles to lay eggs. Walk over turf wearing spiked, lawn-aerator sandals to kill grubs feeding in the root zone. Where cost is justified, apply insect parasitic nematodes (*Heterorhabditis bacteriophora, Steinernema glaseri*) or the fungus *Beauveria bassiana* to control larvae in lawns.

Insect Predators: Parasitic wasps.

Similar Insects: Fig beetles (page 37). Grubs are similar to Japanese beetle grubs (opposite page).

Lily Leaf Beetle
Lilioceris lilii

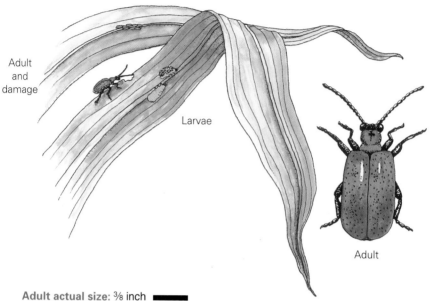

Eggs

Adult and damage

Larvae

Adult

Adult actual size: ⅜ inch ▬▬

Range: Parts of New England, Ontario, and Quebec.

Description: Adults are bright red beetles, ⅜ inch (9.5 mm) long, with black legs, head, antennae, and undersides; they squeak when handled. Larvae are plump, greenish yellow, orange, or brown grubs with black heads; they carry a layer of excrement stuck to their backs. Eggs are orange and laid roughly in a line on undersides of leaves.

Life Cycle: Adults overwinter in the soil in wooded areas or under plant debris. They mate and lay eggs in spring, from late March through June. The eggs hatch in a week and larvae feed on plants for 2 to 4 weeks. They pupate in the soil for up to 3 weeks. When adults emerge, they feed on plants until fall, then crawl away to overwintering sites. There's one generation per year.

Host Plants: Fritillaria, lilies; occasionally potatoes and other plants.

Feeding Habits: Adults and older larvae feed on buds, leaves, and stems of plants; younger larvae feed on the undersides of leaves, causing ragged holes and eventually consuming entire plant parts. Although adults may be found feeding lightly on a variety of plants, they're able to lay eggs and reproduce only on lilies and fritillaria. Larvae cause more damage than adults.

Prevention and Control: Hand-pick adults and larvae, and crush egg masses. To control adults and larvae where numbers are damaging, spray soap, canola oil, or as last resort, pyrethrins. Always inspect lilies before purchasing new plants. Avoid transplanting lilies that come from areas where leaf beetles are established, such as the Boston area.

Mexican Bean Beetle
Epilachna varivestis

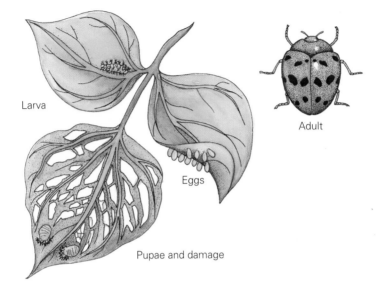

Larva

Adult

Eggs

Pupae and damage

Adult actual size: ¼ inch ▬

Range: Throughout the United States except for West Coast states.

Description: Adults are oval, ¼ inch (6.4 mm) long, yellowish brown to copper-colored with 16 black spots in three rows across their wing covers. Larvae are plump, yellow with spines on each segment, and up to ⅓ inch (8.5 mm) long. Eggs are bright yellow and are laid in clusters on the undersides of leaves.

Life Cycle: Adults overwinter in debris or leaf litter. They emerge in spring over a period of several months. Females lay eggs on the undersides of leaves. Larvae feed for up to 5 weeks, then pupate on the undersides of leaves. Adults emerge in about a week. There are one to four generations per year.

Host Plants: Cowpeas, lima beans, snap beans, and soybeans; also alfalfa, grasses, and weeds, such as devil's beggar-ticks (page 209).

Feeding Habits: Both larvae and adults feed on bean leaves from the underside. They skeletonize leaves in large numbers and can completely defoliate plants.

Prevention and Control: Plant resistant cultivars of snap beans such as 'Royalty Purple Pod'. Plant pollen and nectar plants to attract parasitic wasps. Plant bush beans early in the South or plant them late in the North. Cover plants with floating row covers until mid-season. Remove crop debris, and compost it. Hand-pick adults, larvae, and egg masses. For high populations, spray soap, canola oil, or kaolin, making sure to thoroughly treat undersides of leaves.

Insect Predators: Predatory stink bugs (page 95), assassin bugs (page 93); parasitic wasps (*Pediobius foveolatus*) are sold commercially.

Similar Insects: Lady beetles (page 49).

Rove Beetles
STAPHYLINIDAE

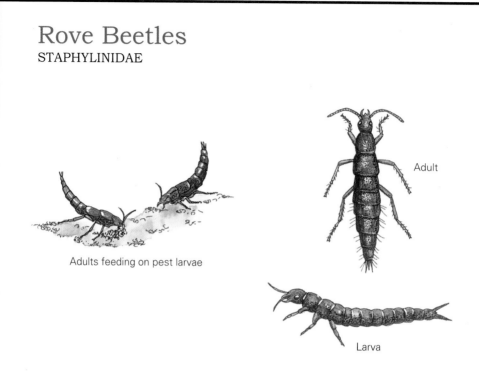

Adults feeding on pest larvae

Adult

Larva

Adult actual size: ⅒ to 1 inch ▬▬▬▬▬▬▬

Range: Throughout North America.

Description: Adults are slender, elongated, fast-moving, and ⅒ to 1 inch (2.5 to 25.4 mm) long, depending on the species. Most species are dark brown or black, and all have very short wing covers that leave most of the abdomen uncovered. When disturbed, they raise the tip of the abdomen as a defense. Most are active at night. Larvae are also dark, elongated, and very fast.

Life Cycle: Most species overwinter in the soil as adults. They lay eggs in the soil, where larvae feed on small insects and other organisms until they pupate.

Feeding Habits: Many species are beneficial predators of fly eggs and maggots, nematodes, slugs, snails, springtails, and other soil-dwelling organisms. Some rove beetles climb plants at night to feed on aphids. Parasitic species of rove beetles are important natural enemies of cabbage maggots and other fly larvae.

Attract and Protect: Maintain permanent plantings among annual crops. Use mulches and cover crops to provide a stable environment.

Soldier Beetle, Pennsylvania Leather-Wing

Chauliognathus pennsylvanicus

Adult

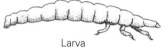

Larva

Adult actual size: ½ inch ▬▬▬

Range: East of the Rocky Mountains; similar species throughout North America.

Description: Adults are ½ inch (12.7 mm) long, and dull yellowish orange, with black head and legs; wing covers are soft and leathery with a large black patch on each tip. Larvae are whitish, elongated, and covered with velvety hairs.

Life Cycle: Larvae overwinter in garden trash or soil and pupate in spring. Females lay clusters of eggs in the soil, and the larvae feed on insects in the soil and on the lower parts of plants. There are two generations per year.

Feeding Habits: Both adults and larvae of soldier beetles feed on grasshopper eggs. Leather-wing larvae also feed on adults and larvae of corn rootworms and cucumber beetles; similar species feed on corn borers, corn earworms, and other caterpillars.

Attract and Protect: Plant pollen and nectar plants to attract adults; Pennsylvania leather-wings are particularly attracted to goldenrod.

Spotted Cucumber Beetle
Diabrotica undecimpunctata howardi

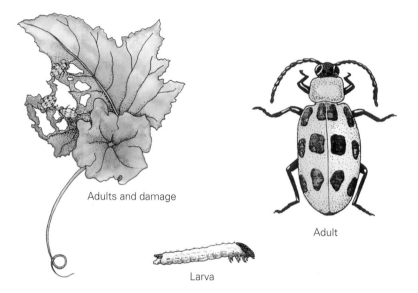

Adults and damage

Adult

Larva

Adult actual size: ¼ inch ▬

Range: Similar species throughout most of North America.

Description: Adults are elongated, greenish yellow, and ¼ inch (6.4 mm) long, with 11 or 12 black spots on wing covers. Larvae are thin white worms, up to ¾ inch (19.1 mm) long, with tiny legs, and brown heads and tails.

Life Cycle: Adults overwinter in southern regions. They emerge in spring to lay eggs in the soil at the base of plants. The larvae feed on the roots and crowns of the plants for up to a month, then pupate in the soil. Some adults migrate north in spring. In northern areas, there are one to two generations per year; in the South, up to three.

Host Plants: Corn, cucumber, peanut, potato, and other plants.

Feeding Habits: The larvae feed on roots and crowns of plants, which can kill young plants and weaken older plants or cause them to topple over. Adults chew holes in leaves and the skin of fruit. They also transmit cucumber mosaic virus and bacterial wilts.

Prevention and Control: Plant mosaic- and wilt-resistant varieties of cucumber ('County Fair'), squash, and melon ('Passmore' muskmelon); grow nonbitter varieties of cucumber. Cover seedlings with floating row covers, which can remain in place for the season if you hand-pollinate flowers or grow partheno-carpic varieties, which don't need to be pollinated by bees. Rotate crops and promptly remove crop residues. Seed squash a week or two earlier than melons to trap beetles. To control larvae in the roots of plants, apply insect parasitic ne-matodes (*Heterorhabditis bacteriophora*). To control adults, spray canola oil, kaolin, or *Beauveria bassiana*.

Predators: Pennsylvania leather-wings (page 45), tachinid flies (page 91).

Striped Cucumber Beetle
Acalymma vittatum

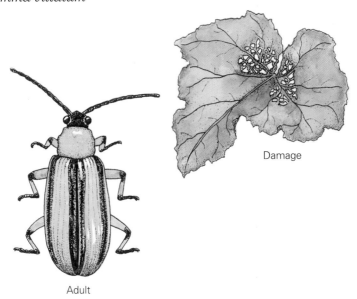

Damage

Adult

Adult actual size: ¼ inch ━━━

Range: Most of North America except far western states.

Description: Adults are ¼ inch (6.4 mm) long, yellow to orange, with black heads and three wide black stripes on wing covers. Larvae are white, slender, up to ¾ inch (19.1 mm) long, each with a brown head and tail. Eggs are orange and are laid in the soil at the base of plants.

Life Cycle: Adults overwinter in wooded or weedy areas. They emerge from April to June, feed for 2 weeks on pollen, then move to host plants to lay eggs at the base of plants. The larvae feed on roots for up to 6 weeks, then pupate in early August. There's usually one generation per year in the North and two or more generations in the South.

Host Plants: Cucumbers, melons, squash; also corn, peas, and blossoms of many plants.

Feeding Habits: Adults chew on leaves and flowers; they can transmit bacterial wilt and cucumber mosaic virus. Larvae feed on roots and crowns of plants, killing seedlings and stunting larger plants.

Prevention and Control: Same as for spotted cucumber beetle (opposite page).

Insect Predators: Pennsylvania leatherwings (page 45).

Wireworms

Limonius spp., *Agriotes* spp.

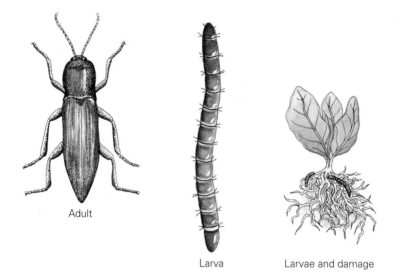

Adult

Larva

Larvae and damage

Adult actual size: ⅓ to ¾ inch ▬▬▬▬

Range: Similar species throughout North America.

Description: Adults are reddish brown or black, elongated, oval, and ⅓ to ¾ inch (8.5 to 19.1 mm) long. When turned upside down, they flip right side up again with a sharp click. Larvae are narrow, leathery worms up to 1 inch (25.4 mm) long, shiny, and yellow or brown; they appear jointed.

Life Cycle: Adults and partly grown larvae overwinter in the soil. Adults emerge in early spring, and females lay eggs at the base of plants. The larvae feed on small soil organisms and plant roots for 2 to 6 years before completing development and pupating.

Host Plants: Carrots, corn, potatoes, sweet potatoes, and other vegetables; tubers and corms of ornamentals.

Feeding Habits: Larvae burrow into seeds, crowns, tubers, and roots of plants,

killing seedlings and hollowing out tubers. Plants may also die of diseases that enter through wounds. Larvae of some species also eat other insects in the soil.

Prevention and Control: Avoid planting susceptible plants after turning sod and for several years thereafter. Cultivate soil several times before seeding to expose wireworms to birds or chickens. Delay planting until the soil is very warm. In bare soil, trap wireworms in pieces of carrots or potatoes buried in the soil; check every few days, and destroy wireworms. About 7 to 10 days before planting susceptible crops, sow thickly seeded rows of wheat, 2 feet (61 cm) apart, as a trap crop; after a few weeks, pull the wheat and destroy the wireworms among the roots. Correct poorly drained soil.

Similar Insects: Millipedes and centipedes (page 120).

Insect Predators: Braconid wasps (page 26), parasitic flies.

Lady Beetles, Convergent

Hippodamia convergens and others

Larva with prey

Adult

Adult actual size: ⅜ inch ▬▬▬

Range: Found throughout North America; convergent lady beetles are sold commercially.

Description: Convergent lady beetle adults are orange or red and ⅜ inch (9.5 mm) long, usually with 12 black spots on wing covers; the thorax is black with two white stripes and white rims. Other species are gray, pale yellow, orange, or red with or without black spots on wing covers. Larvae are alligator-shaped and dark-colored, with orange, yellow, or violet spots on their sides and short spines on each segment. Eggs are orange ovals, laid in clusters.

Life Cycle: Adults of most species overwinter in garden trash and protected sites; in the West, convergent lady beetles migrate to the mountains in fall to hibernate. Beetles resume feeding in spring and lay eggs. Larvae feed for up to 3 weeks, then pupate on a plant stem or leaf for up to 10 days. There are two to four generations per year.

Feeding Habits: Adults and larvae are important predators of aphids, insect eggs, and small, soft-bodied insects, such as mealybugs, scales, small caterpillars, and whitefly nymphs.

Attract and Protect: Plant pollen and nectar flowers for adults, or allow weeds—such as dandelion, Queen-Anne's-lace, and yarrow—to grow among garden plants. Avoid harming eggs and larvae by spraying water to control aphids, rather than using soap or other insecticides. Attract beetles by spraying sugar water (5 ounces [141.7 g] sugar and 1 quart [0.9 l] water) on the plants that aphids usually attack.

Similar Insect: Mexican bean beetle (page 43).

Multicolored Asian Lady Beetle
Harmonia axyridis

Adult and larva
feeding on aphids

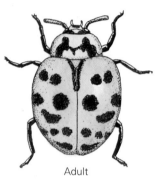

Adult

Adult actual size: ¼ inch ▬

Range: An introduced species throughout the United States and southern Canada; also sold commercially.

Description: Adults are oval and ¼ inch (6.4 mm) long. They range from yellow-orange to reddish orange, with or without 10 black spots on each wing cover; some are black with red spots on wing covers. They emit an orange fluid as a defense when disturbed. Larvae are alligator-shaped and black, with orange patches on their sides and short spines on each segment. Eggs are yellow ovals, laid upright in clusters on leaves.

Life Cycle: Adults congregate in large swarms in fall on the south sides of buildings, rock outcrops, and other light-colored surfaces before moving to over-wintering sites. Beetles resume feeding in spring and lay eggs. Larvae feed for up to 3 weeks, then pupate on a plant stem or leaf for up to 10 days. There are two to four generations per year.

Feeding Habits: Both adults and larvae feed on aphids and other soft-bodied insects. They appear to prefer feeding on aphids in trees, but they're also found on various crop and ornamental plants.

Attract and Protect: See "Convergent Lady Beetles" on page 49. Fall swarms of beetles get attention when they find their way inside homes looking for hibernation sites. To preserve beetles, gently sweep or vacuum them up with a handheld vacuum and release outdoors. Caulk or seal cracks around windows and other entry points to keep them out; those that remain inside for the winter usually die. A blacklight trap that USDA scientists invented to attract beetles without harming them can be used indoors to collect beetles for release outdoors.

Lady Beetles, Spider Mite Destroyers
Stethorus spp.

Adult

Larva

Adult actual size: ¹⁄₁₆ inch ■

Range: Similar species throughout North America.

Description: Adults are round, black, and shiny, and up to ¹⁄₁₆ inch (1.6 mm) long; they're good fliers. Larvae are gray to black grubs with black patches; each segment has long, branched spines. Eggs are minute, white ovals, laid singly on the undersides of leaves.

Life Cycle: Adults overwinter in fallen leaves under fruit trees, in fencerows, and in other protected sites. They emerge while trees are blooming and remain active until fall, laying eggs all summer. Larvae feed on mites for up to 2 weeks, then pupate on a leaf. There are two to four overlapping generations per year.

Feeding Habits: Both adults and larvae are important predators of plant-feeding mites, particularly spider mites, found on avocados, fruit trees, strawberries, and other berry crops.

Attract and Protect: Avoid harming eggs and larvae by using only water sprays to control spider mites, rather than soap or other insecticides. Avoid disturbing leaf litter under fruit trees between November 1 and mid-April because this is where most beetles spend the winter.

Lady Beetle, Vedalia
Rodolia cardinalis

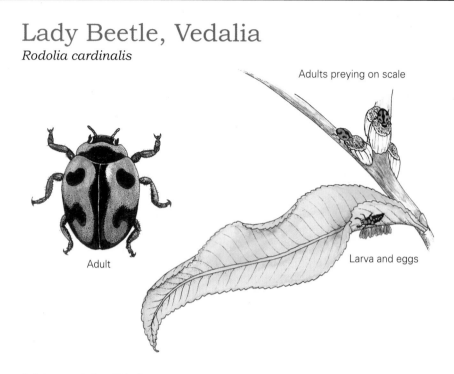

Adults preying on scale

Adult

Larva and eggs

Adult actual size: ⅓ inch ━━

Range: California, Florida.

Description: Adults are ⅓ inch (8.5 mm) long. Females are red with irregular black marks, whereas males are predominantly black with some red markings. Both sexes are covered with fine hairs that obscure the markings and give them a grayish look. Eggs are red and oval, laid singly or in small groups on the egg sac of the scale insect. Larvae are reddish with black markings and spindle-shaped, with many soft spines, and up to ⅓ inch (8.5 mm) long.

Life Cycle: The pupae overwinter on the branches and leaves of citrus trees. Adults emerge to lay eggs underneath scales or on scale egg sacs. Larvae feed for 1 to 2 weeks, then pupate on trees. There are 8 to 12 generations per year.

Feeding Habits: Adults and mature larvae feed on all stages of cottony cushion scale. Young larvae feed on the scale eggs.

Attract and Protect: Avoid using sprays.

Mealybug Destroyer
Cryptolaemus montrouzieri

Adult

Larva

Adult actual size: ⅓ inch ▬

Range: California and the West Coast; also sold commercially.

Description: Adults are oval, ⅓ inch (8.5 mm) long, and black, with an orange head and tail. Larvae are cream-colored, alligator-shaped, and up to ⅓ inch (8.5 mm) long and covered with long, white, waxy hairs. Eggs are yellow ovals, laid singly among mealybugs.

Life Cycle: Females lay eggs among mealybugs. The larvae feed on mealybug eggs and nymphs for up to 3 weeks, then pupate on the plants. Adults emerge in 3 weeks. The beetles overwinter as adults, but only in mild climates. There are about four overlapping generations per year.

Feeding Habits: Both larvae and adults feed on all stages and species of mealybugs, except for root-feeding mealybugs. They're particularly valuable predators on citrus plants, greenhouse ornamentals, and grapes. They also feed on some types of scale.

Attract and Protect: Where beetle numbers are low after an unusually cold winter and mealybug populations are high, it may be worthwhile to release purchased beetles in spring.

Similar Insects: Mealybug destroyer larvae look similar to mealybugs (page 106), but are larger and more active than their prey.

Apple Curculio
Tachypterellus quadrigibbus

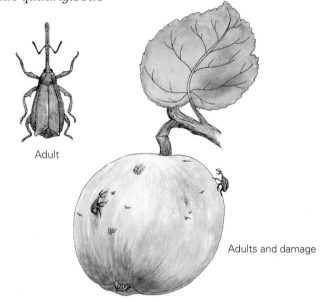

Adult

Adults and damage

Adult actual size: ¹⁄₁₀ inch ▬

Range: Eastern North America.

Description: Adults are brownish red and ¹⁄₁₀ inch (2.5 mm) long, with hard, warty wing covers; they have a long, curved "snout" with antennae attached in the middle. Larvae are white, legless grubs that have humped backs. Eggs are white and oval and are laid in tiny punctures close together in young fruit.

Life Cycle: Adults overwinter in the soil or leaf litter near host trees. In spring, they start laying eggs in developing fruit shortly after the flower petals fall. Upon hatching, the larvae tunnel into the fruit core and feed on the developing seeds. They pupate inside the fruit, and in late summer when the fruit drops, the adult curculios emerge and crawl into the nearby soil to spend winter. There's one generation per year.

Host Plants: Apples, pears, quince, and related ornamentals.

Feeding Habits: Adults feeding on developing fruit leave brown woody scars and distorted fruit. Fruit is also scarred where the curculio lays eggs. Larvae feeding in fruit leave thin brown streaks in the flesh and cause infested fruit to drop prematurely.

Prevention and Control: Curculios drop readily when startled and can be knocked onto sheets on the ground by striking branches with a padded stick; destroy the collected weevils. Most damage occurs to fruit so early that infested fruit can be easily seen and removed during thinning early in the season. Starting at petal fall, spray kaolin to prevent egg laying and feeding. Collect and destroy dropped fruit daily to kill adults before they emerge and burrow into the soil.

Similar Insects: Plum curculios (page 58).

Bean Weevil
Acanthoscelides obtectus

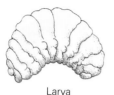

Larva

Pupa

Adult

Adults and damage

Adult actual size: ⅛ inch ▬

Range: Throughout North America.

Description: Adults are teardrop-shaped, light olive-brown with darker mottling, and ⅛ inch (3.2 mm) long. Larvae are small, hairy, white grubs with legs, found inside dried seeds. Eggs are white and laid on pods or shelled beans.

Life Cycle: Adult beetles overwinter outdoors in garden debris or in stored beans. In spring, adults escape from storage areas or emerge from hibernation and move to plants. They lay eggs in small holes that they chew in pods along the seam or other cracks. The eggs hatch in 3 to 30 days, and the larvae move to the seeds and bore inside. The larvae feed from 2 weeks to 6 months, depending on the temperature, then pupate inside the seeds. Adults emerge from the seeds and, if they're outdoors, lay eggs on nearby beans. There are up to seven generations per year; more in stored beans.

Host Plants: Beans, lentils, peas; occasionally other seeds.

Feeding Habits: The larvae feed inside bean seeds, drilling many round holes and leaving behind fine, powdery excrement. Larvae are so small that entry points into seeds are hard to see. There can be a dozen or more larvae in one seed. They attack the seeds of beans growing in the field as well as dry seeds in storage.

Prevention and Control: Dry seeds thoroughly, then freeze them for 48 hours after harvesting, or spread the dry beans out and heat them at 135°F (57°C) for ½ hour (this does not affect germination). Promptly plow under or shred and compost crop residue to kill larvae and adults on plants and immature beans. Treat seed with mint oil or diatomaceous earth to prevent adults from laying eggs on seed.

Black Vine Weevil

Otiorhynchus sulcatus

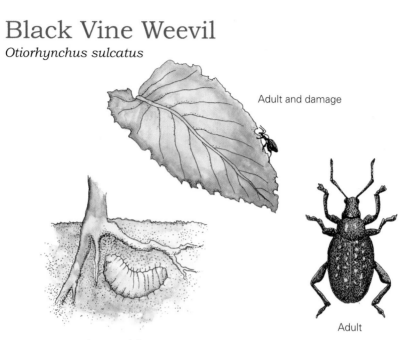

Adult and damage

Larva and damage

Adult

Adult actual size: ½ inch ▬▬▬

Range: West Coast from California to British Columbia; also East Coast.

Description: Adults (only females exist) are brownish gray or black and ½ inch (12.7 mm) long with a prominent "snout." Larvae are fat, white grubs, up to ½ inch (12.7 mm) long, with yellowish brown heads.

Life Cycle: Larvae overwinter in the soil among plant roots. They resume feeding in spring, then pupate. Adults emerge in early summer and feed on leaves for several weeks before laying eggs in the soil around host plants. They hatch in 10 days, and the larvae burrow into the roots to feed. They remain in the soil until the following spring. There's one generation per year.

Host Plants: Blackberries, blueberries, cranberries, grapes, strawberries; also azaleas, laurels, rhododendrons, yews, and other evergreens.

Feeding Habits: Adults chew neat, scalloped bites out of the edges of leaves, detracting from the appearance of ornamentals. The larvae feed in the crowns and roots of host plants, which can stunt or kill plants. Plants may die of diseases that enter through the wounds in the roots.

Prevention and Control: Plant resistant azalea and rhododendron cultivars. Rotate plantings of strawberries. In the evening, shake plants over a ground sheet and collect and destroy weevils. Lay boards around host plants and check under them during the day for hiding adults. Set out stakes wrapped with 12-inch (31 cm)-wide layers of corrugated cardboard; check every few days and destroy weevils. Wrap trunks of single-stemmed plants with bands of plastic, painted with sticky trap glue to catch adults. Drench the soil around the roots with insect parasitic nematodes (*Heterorhabditis bacteriophora, H. megidis*) in early fall or late spring. As a last resort, control adults by spraying plants with *Beauveria bassiana* or pyrethrins.

Carrot Weevil

Listronotus oregonensis

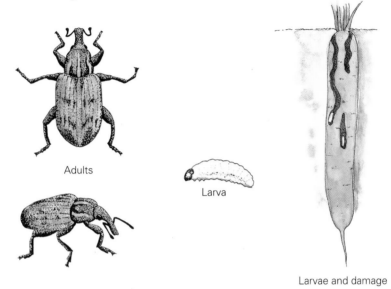

Adults

Larva

Larvae and damage

Adult actual size: ⅕ inch ▬

Range: Eastern and central North America.

Description: Adults are dark brown to black and ⅕ inch (5.1 mm) long, with a pattern of lengthwise grooves on the back and a prominent "snout"; they rarely fly. Larvae are legless, curved, white grubs with amber heads. Eggs are inserted in the stalks of leaves.

Life Cycle: Adults overwinter under crop debris. They emerge in early spring to feed and lay eggs on the foliage of young carrots. When the larvae hatch, they tunnel into the main root to feed for 3 weeks or more. They leave the root to pupate in the soil nearby, and the next generation of adults emerges in 2 weeks. There are one or two generations per year.

Host Plants: Carrots, celery, dill, and parsley.

Feeding Habits: Larvae burrow into the crowns and upper one-third of carrot roots and into hearts of celery. Young plants may collapse from the feeding damage or die of diseases entering the wounds.

Prevention and Control: Grow pollen and nectar plants, or leave flowering weeds to attract parasitic wasps, which attack the eggs. Protect ground beetles. Sow carrots late to avoid the main egg-laying period; this measure is very successful at preventing damage. Rotate crops and cover seed beds with floating row covers to prevent weevils from laying eggs on plants. Shred and compost crop debris, and remove broken carrots from soil after harvest to reduce the number of overwintering weevils.

Similar Insects: Vegetable weevils (page 60).

Predator Insects: Ground beetles (page 38), parasitic wasp (*Anaphes sordidatus*).

Plum Curculio

Conotrachelus nenuphar

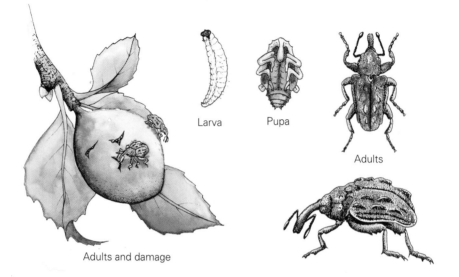

Larva   Pupa

Adults

Adults and damage

Adult actual size: ⅕ inch ▬

Range: Eastern North America.

Description: Adults are dark brownish gray and ⅕ inch (5.1 mm) long with warty wing covers and a strong, curved "snout." Larvae are fat, grayish white, ⅓-inch (8.5 mm)-long grubs. Eggs are round, white to gray, and laid singly under crescent-shaped slits in the skin of fruit.

Life Cycle: Adults overwinter in wooded areas or leaf litter, emerging in spring to move to fruit trees to lay eggs when flowers and first leaves appear. Eggs hatch in up to 10 days, and the larvae burrow into the fruit to feed for up to 3 weeks. When the fruit drops, the larvae exit and pupate in the soil. Adults emerge from late July to late October, feeding on ripe or fallen fruit until they migrate to hibernation sites. There's one generation per year in the North and two in the South.

Host Plants: Apples, blueberries, cherries, peaches, pears, plums, and quince.

Feeding Habits: Adults damage fruit by laying eggs and by feeding, which scars the fruit and allows diseases to enter. Larvae burrow within fruit, causing the fruit to drop early.

Prevention and Control: Use thick mulches or grow clover under orchard trees to attract ground beetles. Overwintering curculios are attracted first to plums and early-blooming apples; use these as trap trees or monitoring trees, to tell when adults are appearing. In early morning, knock adults from the trees onto a sheet on the ground, using a padded stick to beat limbs and trunks. Starting at petal fall, spray kaolin to prevent egg laying and feeding. Collect and destroy dropped fruits daily.

Similar Insects: Apple curculios (page 54).

Predator Insects: Ground beetles (page 38), braconid wasps (page 26), and other parasitic wasps.

Strawberry Root Weevils

Otiorhynchus ovatus, O. rugostriatus

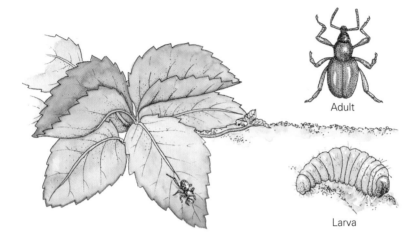

Adult

Larva

Adult actual size: ¼ inch ▬

Range: Throughout the United States and southern Canada.

Description: Adults are brown to black and ¼ inch (6.4 mm) long with short, blunt "snouts." Larvae are fat, dirty white, legless grubs, up to ¼ inch (6.4 mm) long, with light brown heads. Eggs are oval and white to amber.

Life Cycle: Larvae and some adults overwinter in roots; most adults overwinter in leaf litter or weedy areas nearby. Overwintering larvae pupate in spring. Adults emerge from late May through June and feed on leaves for up to 3 weeks before laying eggs around the crowns of plants. The larvae feed on roots, remaining in them over winter in northern areas. There's one generation per year.

Host Plants: Strawberries, raspberries, and other small fruits; also tree fruit, nursery seedlings, and ornamentals.

Feeding Habits: The adults clip notches out of leaf edges and cut off flower stems, reducing the number of berries on plants. Larvae feeding in crowns and roots can stunt or kill plants, typically from diseases that enter through wounds.

Prevention and Control: Rotate strawberry plantings with nonhost plants. Avoid newly turned sod and plant as far from previous beds as possible. Knock adults from taller plants at night by shaking or tapping branches over a ground sheet. In new beds cover plants with floating row covers until blossoms require pollination. Apply insect parasitic nematodes (*Heterorhabditis bacteriophora*) in spring or late summer to control larvae. As a last resort, spray pyrethrins.

Similar Insects: Black vine weevils (page 56).

Predator Insects: Ground beetles (page 38), rove beetles (page 44).

Vegetable Weevil
Listroderes difficilis

Larvae and damage

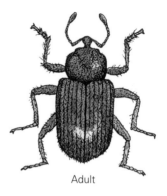

Adult

Adult actual size: ⅓ inch ▬▬▬

Range: Southern United States.

Description: Adults (only females exist) are dull gray to brown and ⅓ inch (8.5 mm) long, with a light V-shaped mark near the tips of their wing covers; they have a short, blunt "snout." Larvae are light green, legless, and up to ⅓ inch (8.5 mm) long, with a dark mottled head. Eggs are white, turning dark before hatching, and are laid on stems and crowns of plants.

Life Cycle: These subtropical insects are active in fall, winter, and spring. They go into dormancy during summer, which they spend under garden litter and in weeds. After adults emerge in late summer, they feed for up to a month. They start laying eggs on plants in September. The larvae feed for up to a month and a half, then burrow into the soil to pupate for 2 weeks. Adults emerge from January to June. There's one generation per year.

Host Plants: Cabbage, carrots, collards, mustard, potatoes, radishes, spinach, tomatoes, turnips; also some weeds.

Feeding Habits: Both adults and larvae chew on roots and foliage of host plants, leaving large, irregular holes in leaves. Their feeding can damage or kill small plants or seedlings. Root crops may be attacked underground.

Prevention and Control: Weevils drop from plants when startled; knock them from plants at night by shaking or tapping foliage over a sheet on the ground. Rotate crops and cover plants with floating row covers to prevent adults from reaching the crop. Promptly shred and compost crop residues after harvest. As a last resort, spray pyrethrins on plants to control adults.

Similar Insects: Carrot weevils (page 57).

European Corn Borer
Ostrinia nubilalis

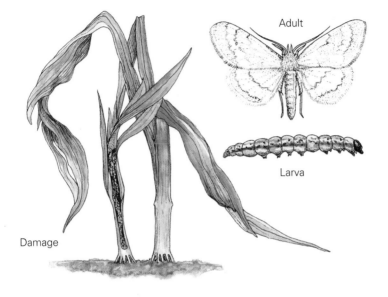

Adult

Larva

Damage

Adult actual size: 1 inch ▬▬▬▬▬▬

Range: Northern and central United States and southern Canada.

Description: Adults are yellowish brown moths, with 1-inch (2.5 cm) wingspans and dark zigzag bands on their wings. Larvae are grayish pink caterpillars, up to 1 inch (2.5 cm) long, with brown heads and small spots on each segment. Eggs are white to tan and are laid in masses on the undersides of leaves.

Life Cycle: Larvae overwinter in stalks left in the garden. They pupate in spring, and adults emerge in June. Eggs are laid from late June to mid-July, and larvae feed for up to a month. Depending on the strain of European corn borer, there are one to three generations per year.

Host Plants: Mainly corn; in some areas beans, peppers, potatoes, tomatoes, and other garden crops and flowers.

Feeding Habits: Young larvae chew on corn leaves, tassels, and beneath husks. Older larvae bore into corn stalks and ears or into the stems of other garden crops. Damaged stalks break easily.

Prevention and Control: Plant corn varieties with strong stalks and tight husk covers. Where corn borer numbers are high, remove the tassels from up to two-thirds of the plants before pollen sheds; this leaves enough tassels for pollination. Dig larvae out of developing ears, or squirt liquid or granular BTK (*Bacillus thurinigiensis* var. *kurstaki*) or mineral oil into tips of the ears. Remove old stalks; shred and compost or bury them. Hand-pick larvae feeding on leaves or spray BTK.

Insect Predators: Braconid wasps (page 26) and other parasitic wasps, and tachinid flies (page 91).

Similar Insects: Corn earworms (page 70).

Peachtree Borers

Synanthedon exitiosa and related species

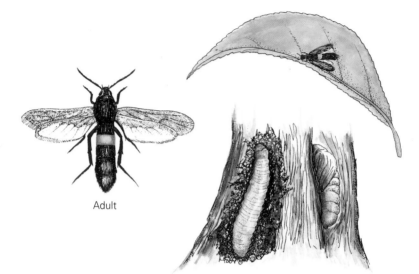

Adult

Larva, pupa, and damage

Adult actual size: 1 inch ▬▬▬▬▬

Range: Throughout North America.

Description: Adults are steel blue, clear-winged moths with yellow stripes (in males) or a wide orange band (in females) around their abdomens. Larvae are pale yellow or whitish caterpillars, up to 1 inch (2.5 cm) long, with brown heads. Eggs are brown or gray, laid in small groups near the base of trees.

Life Cycle: Larvae overwinter in a burrow under bark or in the soil at the base of the tree. They resume feeding in spring and pupate in the soil by mid-summer. Adults emerge in 3 weeks, and the females lay eggs on trees or in the soil close to the trunk. When the eggs hatch, the larvae bore under the bark. There's one generation per year; some have a two-year life cycle.

Host Plants: Peaches; occasionally apricots, cherries, plums, and nectarines.

Feeding Habits: Larvae bore beneath the bark at the base of the tree and in the upper roots, leaving a mass of gummy sawdust at the base of injured trees. Young trees may be seriously injured or killed; older trees are less affected.

Prevention and Control: Grow vigorous trees and take care not to mechanically injure the bark, which gives the borers a place to enter. In fall, check for borer holes in tree trunks from about 12 inches (30 cm) above ground to 3 inches (8 cm) below ground level; dig out larvae with a knife or kill them by pushing a length of flexible wire into entry holes. Cultivate soil shallowly around the base of trees to destroy pupae. Where cost is justified, inject *Beauveria bassiana* or insect parasitic nematodes (*Steinernema carpocapsae*) into borer holes.

Similar Insects: Codling moths (page 69), oriental fruit moths (page 80).

Pickleworm
Diaphania nitidalis

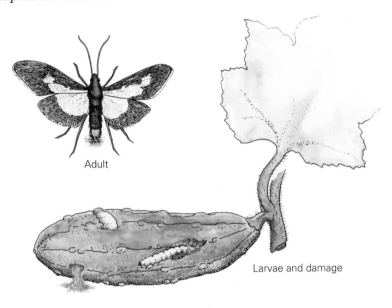

Adult

Larvae and damage

Adult actual size: 1 inch ▬▬▬▬▬

Range: Southeastern United States; sometimes found north to New York and west to Nebraska.

Description: Adults are yellowish brown moths with a purplish sheen and 1-inch (25.4 mm) wingspan and long, brown hairs on the tips of their abdomens. Younger larvae are pale yellow with dark spots; older larvae are green or pinkish, without spots; they're up to ¾ inch (19.1 mm) long with a brown head. Eggs are pale, laid singly or in small groups.

Life Cycle: Pickleworm pupae overwinter inside rolled leaves in semitropical areas, such as southern Florida and Texas. Adults emerge in late spring and lay eggs on plants. The larvae feed for up to 2 weeks, then pupate while rolled in a wilted leaf or other debris. There are one to four generations per year. Adults migrate farther north as temperatures rise over the season.

Host Plants: Cucumber, melon, pumpkin, and squash.

Feeding Habits: Larvae feed on leaf and flower buds, later moving into fruit and stems. North of Florida, they seldom become a problem until July, after migrating moths arrive.

Prevention and Control: Plant as early as possible. Cover young plants with floating row covers to keep moths from laying eggs on plants (hand-pollinate the blossoms or grow parthenocarpic varieties, which don't require pollination). Slit infested stems and remove the worms, then heap dirt over the injured stem to encourage rooting. After harvest, promptly shred or compost vines, weeds, and crop debris. Grow a border of squash around cucumber patches, and check weekly in buds for larvae; when squash has become infested, destroy the plants. Cultivate in early fall to bury pupae.

Potato Tuberworm
Phthorimaea operculella

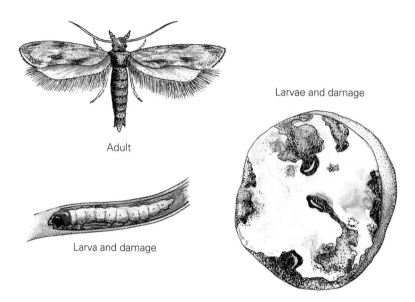

Adult

Larvae and damage

Larva and damage

Adult actual size: ½ inch ▬▬▬

Range: Southern United States from Florida to California.

Description: Adults are small, narrow-winged moths, with ½-inch (12.7 mm) wingspans; they're grayish brown mottled with darker brown, and they're active at night. Larvae are pale pink or greenish and up to ¾ inch (19.1 mm) long, with dark brown heads. Eggs are laid singly or in groups on the undersides of leaves or on exposed potatoes.

Life Cycle: Larvae and pupae overwinter in potatoes that are in storage or left in the soil, and in garden trash. Adults emerge in spring and lay eggs on exposed potatoes or work their way into cracks in the soil to lay eggs; later generations lay eggs on exposed tubers. Larvae feed for up to 3 weeks, then spin a cocoon in dead leaves or debris on the ground or in the storage area and pupate. Adults emerge in 7 to 10 days. There are up to six generations per year.

Host Plants: Primarily potato; also eggplant, tomato, and related weeds, such as black nightshade (page 200).

Feeding Habits: Early larvae mine leaves, then work their way into the stems. Later larvae migrate from stems to tubers, usually entering through an eye to feed and spin silk-lined burrows in the potatoes. They're most damaging in unusually hot, dry years.

Prevention and Control: Mulch soil to prevent cracking, and keep potatoes well hilled with soil. At harvest, cut off and destroy infested plants a few days before digging up potatoes to prevent larvae in the plants from infesting the tubers. Thoroughly dig up all potatoes, and don't leave them out overnight where moths could lay eggs on them. Thoroughly clean storage bins.

Insect Predators: Braconid wasps (page 26).

Southwestern Corn Borer
Diatraea grandiosella

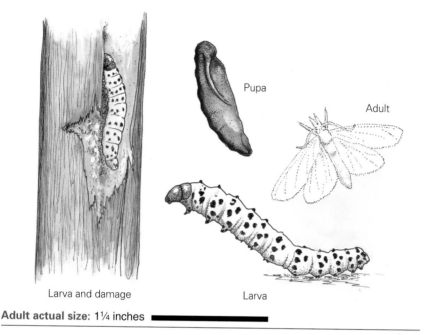

Pupa

Adult

Larva and damage

Larva

Adult actual size: 1¼ inches ▄▄▄▄▄▄▄

Range: Southern United States and corn-belt states.

Description: Adults are light beige (females) or darker (males) moths with 1¼-inch (3.2 cm) wingspans and light markings on wings. Larvae are white caterpillars with brown heads and black dots on every segment; overwintering larvae don't have dots. Eggs are pale yellow with three reddish crosswise lines that are laid in overlapping rows on leaves.

Life Cycle: Larvae overwinter in the roots of corn plants and pupate in early June. Moths emerge to lay eggs on leaves of young plants. First-generation larvae bore into developing leaf whorls; later they bore into stalks, where they pupate. Adults emerge in early August and lay eggs. The second generation of larvae bore into ears, into stalks, and later into roots to spend the winter. There are two or more generations per year.

Host Plants: Corn, grasses, and sorghum.

Feeding Habits: Larvae feeding in leaf whorls can kill the growing points of plants. Later larvae are more damaging as they bore under husks and into stalks, which causes them to break off easily.

Prevention and Control: Choose varieties with strong stalks. Plant early. To control larvae on leaves, spray *Beauveria bassiana*, canola oil, or as a last resort, pyrethrins. Shred and compost corn stalks and roots promptly after harvest to destroy larvae. Cultivate soil in fall.

Insect Predators: Braconid wasps (page 26) and other parasitic wasps. Birds and naturally occurring diseases are also important controls.

Similar Insects: European corn borers (page 61).

Squash Vine Borer
Melittia cucurbitae

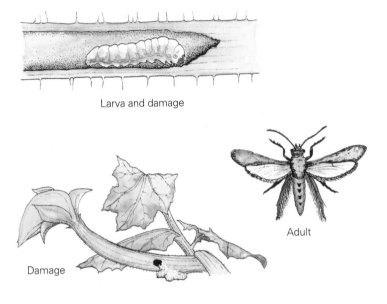

Larva and damage

Damage

Adult

Adult actual size: 1 to 1½ inches ▬▬▬▬▬▬▬▬

Range: East of the Rocky Mountains in the United States and southern Canada, and south to Mexico.

Description: Adults are narrow-winged moths with 1- to 1½-inch (2.5 to 3.8 cm) wingspans. They have olive-brown fore-wings and clear hind wings; their abdomen is red with black rings, and their hind legs have long red fringes. Larvae are fat, white, wrinkled, and up to 1 inch (2.5 cm) long, with brown heads. Eggs are brown, flat, and oval, and are laid singly on the stems near the base of the plant.

Life Cycle: Larvae and pupae overwinter in cocoons in soil 1 inch (2.5 cm) deep. Adults emerge as squash vines start to spread, laying eggs on stems and stalks. Larvae burrow into stems for up to 6 weeks, then pupate in the soil. There's one generation a year in most areas and two generations in the Gulf states.

Host Plants: Cucumber, gourd, melon, pumpkin, and squash.

Feeding Habits: Larvae chew on the base of stems, causing vines to wilt suddenly. As they feed, larvae push masses of greenish excrement out of their entry holes in the stems.

Prevention and Control: Plant early. As a precaution in case vines are girdled at the base, cover vines with soil a few feet away from the base so they can grow additional roots. Cover plants from the seedling stage onward with floating row covers or screens, and grow parthenocarpic varieties, which don't need pollination, or hand-pollinate flowers. On wilting vines, look for frass at entry holes, slit the stem, remove the borer, and heap dirt over the damaged stalk to promote rooting. Eggs can be controlled by spraying or wiping the lower 4 feet (1.2 m) of stems with insecticidal soap spray twice a week. After harvest, promptly shred and compost or bury crop residue, and cultivate soil.

Beet Armyworm
Spodoptera exigua

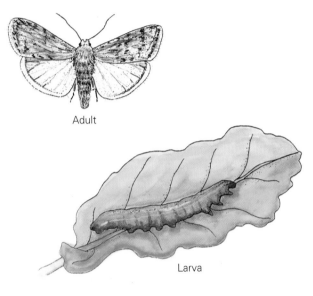

Adult

Larva

Adult actual size: 1¼ inches ▬▬▬▬▬▬▬

Range: Southern half of the United States; related species throughout North America.

Description: Adults are mottled gray moths with 1¼-inch (3.2 cm) wingspans; each forewing has a pale yellow spot near the middle of the front edge; hind wings are white with a dark border. Larvae are green, up to 1¼ inches (3.2 cm) long, with dark green and yellow stripes along the sides. Eggs are laid in masses and are covered with fine, white hairs.

Life Cycle: Pupae overwinter in soil or leaf litter around roots. In spring females lay eggs on host plants. Larvae feed for up to 3 weeks, spinning fine webs on leaves as they feed. They pupate just under the surface of the soil. There are four or more generations per year.

Host Plants: Asparagus, beets, sugar beets, corn, lettuce, onions, peas, potatoes, and tomatoes; also grasses, plantain, and other weeds.

Feeding Habits: The larvae attack leaves, stems, and roots of crops. At times they appear in very large numbers, traveling together from field to field.

Prevention and Control: In light infestations, hand-pick caterpillars. Attract and protect parasitic wasps and flies. In serious infestations, spray *Beauveria bassiana,* canola oil, or kaolin, or spray *Bacillus thuringiensis* var. *azaiwi* (brand name Agree, Javelin, or Xentari) while larvae are still small. To kill eggs, spray narrow-range oil on plants that tolerate it. After harvest is over, promptly cultivate the soil.

Insect Predators: Many species of parasitic wasps, including braconid wasps (page 26); also ground beetles (page 38), lacewings (page 92), minute pirate bugs (page 94), spiders, and tachinid flies (page 91).

Similar Insects: Fall armyworms (page 73).

Cabbage Looper
Trichoplusia ni

Larva

Adult

Adult actual size: 1½ inches ▬▬▬▬▬▬

Range: Throughout North America.

Description: Adults are grayish brown moths with 1½-inch (3.8 cm) wingspans; each forewing has a small silvery spot in the middle, and hind wings are pale brown to bronze. These insects fly at night. Larvae are green caterpillars, 1½ inches (3.8 cm) long, with pale stripes down their backs. They raise their bodies up into a loop as they crawl. Eggs are light green and dome-shaped; they're laid singly on the upper surface of leaves.

Life Cycle: Pupae overwinter in thin silken cocoons that are attached along one side to a leaf or stem of a host plant. The moths emerge in spring and fly to plants to lay eggs. The larvae feed for up to 4 weeks, then pupate in cocoons on the plants. There are three to four generations per year in most areas.

Host Plants: Mainly cabbage-family plants; also beans, beets, celery, lettuce, peas, spinach, tomatoes,

and flowers, including carnations, mignonettes, and nasturtiums.

Feeding Habits: Larvae chew holes in leaves, leaving behind green excrement. Seedlings and small plants may be destroyed in severe infestations.

Prevention and Control: Many native beneficial insects feed on eggs and larvae; plant pollen and nectar plants to attract them. Several times a week, inspect plants and hand-pick larvae and crush eggs on leaves. Spray *Bacillus thuringiensis* var. *kurstaki*, insecticidal soap, or canola oil to control larvae in serious infestations.

Insect Predators: Braconid wasps (page 26) and other parasitic wasps, yellow jackets (page 27).

Similar Insects: Garden webworms (page 76), imported cabbageworms (page 79).

Codling Moth
Cydia pomonella

Adult

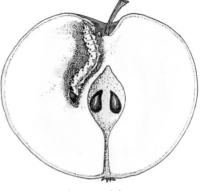

Larva and damage

Adult actual size: ¾ inch ■■■■■

Range: Throughout North America.

Description: Adults are grayish brown moths with ¾-inch (19.1 mm) wingspans; the wings have a fine wavy pattern of coppery brown lines, with a darker band across the forewing tips. Larvae are white to pale pink caterpillars up to ¾ inch (19.1 mm) long, with brown heads. Eggs are very difficult to see and are laid singly on fruit buds, leaves, and twigs.

Life Cycle: The larvae overwinter in cocoons beneath bark or in leaf litter, then pupate in spring. The adults emerge around the time apple trees bloom. Females lay eggs on the fruit or upper sides of leaves. Larvae feed on fruit for up to 5 weeks, then exit the fruit and travel down the trunk to spin cocoons under bark or leaf litter. There are two or three generations per year.

Host Plants: Apples, crabapples, pears; occasionally other fruits and walnuts.

Feeding Habits: Larvae enter developing fruit, usually at the blossom end, and tunnel into the core. As they feed, they push crumbly brown excrement out of the entry holes. When ready to pupate, they tunnel out of the fruit and spin cocoons.

Prevention and Control: To kill overwintering larvae, scrape loose bark from trees to remove cocoons in late winter, then spray with narrow-range oil. During the growing season wrap 6-inch (15.2 cm)-wide bands of corrugated cardboard around tree trunks; check bands every 1 to 2 weeks and destroy larvae and cocoons in the crevices, or burn and replace the bands. Starting at petal fall, spray kaolin to prevent moths from laying eggs on developing fruit. Pick up early dropped fruit daily, and compost or bury them because these may contain codling moth larvae.

Similar Insects: Oriental fruit moths (page 80), peachtree borers (page 62).

Corn Earworm, Tomato Fruitworm

Heliocoverpa zea

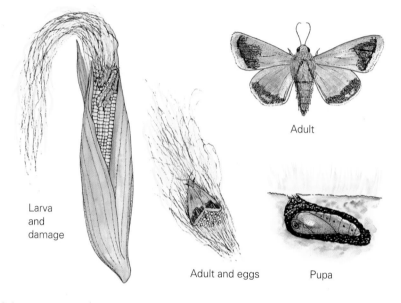

Larva
and
damage

Adult

Adult and eggs

Pupa

Adult actual size: 1½ inches ▬▬▬▬▬▬▬▬▬▬

Range: Throughout North America, but most common in the South.

Description: Adults are yellowish tan to olive brown moths with 1½-inch (3.8 cm) wingspans. Larvae are 1 to 2 inches (2.5 to 5.1 cm) long, and light yellow or green, pink, or dark reddish brown, with stripes. Eggs are pale green, domed with a ridged pattern, and laid singly on leaves.

Life Cycle: Pupae overwinter 2 to 6 inches (5.1 cm to 15.2 cm) deep in the soil, and adults emerge in early spring to lay eggs. The larvae feed on a plant for up to 4 weeks, then crawl down to pupate in the soil. Moths emerge in 10 to 25 days. There can be four or more generations per year. Infestations north of 40° latitude usually come from moths migrating from the South.

Host Plants: Corn, peppers, and tomatoes; also beans, cabbage, okra, peas, potatoes, squash, and other vegetables.

Feeding Habits: Larvae chew large holes in leaves and fruit. On corn, they feed on the kernels.

Prevention and Control: Choose corn varieties with tight husks and plant as early as possible so that corn silks dry up before moths emerge. Hand-pick larvae on plants; spray BTK (*Bacillus thuringiensis* var. *kurstaki*) for serious infestations. On corn, use a dropper to apply 5 drops of vegetable oil or an oil-and-BTK mixture into the tip of each ear after the silk has wilted; granular BTK may be used instead. In fall, till under cornstalks. Spray kaolin on tomato plants to prevent moths from laying eggs.

Similar Insects: European corn borers (page 61).

Insect Predators: Braconid wasps (page 26) and other parasitic wasps, lacewings (page 92), tachinid flies (page 91), and minute pirate bugs (page 94).

Cutworms
NOCTUIDAE

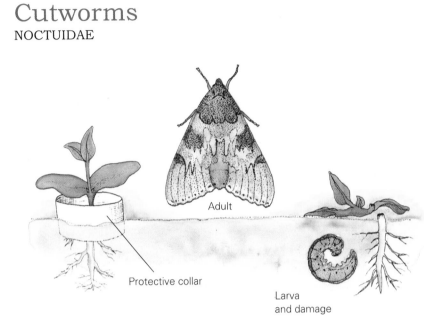

Adult

Protective collar

Larva
and damage

Adult actual size: 1 to 1½ inches

Range: Various species throughout North America.

Description: Adults are gray or brownish moths with pale hind wings and 1- to 1½-inch (2.5 to 3.8 cm) wingspans. Larvae are smooth, fat, greasy gray or brown caterpillars, 1 to 2 inches (2.5 to 5.1 cm) long. They curl up when disturbed.

Life Cycle: Most species overwinter as larvae among roots, garden trash, or leaf litter; others overwinter in the egg stage on weeds. Larvae feed on roots, stems, and leaves in spring for 3 weeks to several months, then pupate in the soil. Moths emerge from late August to early September and lay eggs on plant stems and in grasses. Most species have one generation a year, but some have more.

Host Plants: All garden vegetables, particularly seedlings and transplants.

Feeding Habits: Larvae of several species attack roots and stems just below or above the soil surface. Transplants look like they've been cut off, whereas seedlings may disappear entirely. Climbing species travel up plants at night and chew large holes in leaves.

Prevention and Control: Set out transplants with a collar of stiff paper, cardboard, or a tin can around the stem, pushed 1 inch (2.5 cm) into the soil. Where many cutworms are seen during spring cultivation, leave the soil open for a couple of weeks to allow birds to eat them. Treat the soil with insect parasitic nematodes (*Steinernema carpocapsae*) or apply *Beauveria bassiana*. In fall, cultivate soil 6 to 8 inches (15 to 20 cm) deep to kill pupae. Keep weeds pulled from late summer until spring to prevent moths from laying eggs. To combat climbing cutworms, spray pyrethrins as a last resort.

Insect Predators: Braconid wasps (page 26) and many other parasitic wasps, and tachinid flies (page 91).

Tent Caterpillars

Malacosoma spp.

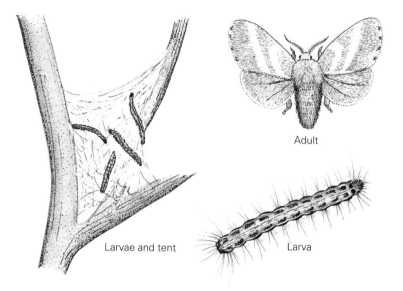

Adult

Larvae and tent

Larva

Adult actual size: 1 to 1½ inches

Range: Various species throughout North America.

Description: Adults are yellowish to reddish brown moths, with 1- to 1½-inch (2.5 to 3.8 cm) wingspans. Larvae are black caterpillars, up to 2 inches (5.1 cm) long, with a white stripe or row of dots down their backs; fine lines and patterns of brown, blue, red, or yellow are visible along the sides. Eggs are laid in masses circling small branches.

Life Cycle: The eggs overwinter on tree branches, hatching in early spring about the time apples bloom. The larvae spin silk webs in a crotch of a branch and hide in the tent by day, coming out to feed at night. After feeding for up to 8 weeks, they pupate in leaf litter. Adult emerge in 10 days and lay eggs on the trees in mid- to late summer. There is one generation per year.

Host Plants: Apples, pears, and other deciduous fruit, and ornamental trees.

Feeding Habits: The larvae feed on tree leaves and make large, unsightly web tents in the forks and crotches of trees. In years when caterpillar numbers are high, trees may be defoliated.

Prevention and Control: Prune out or scrape off egg masses in winter and remove hatching egg masses in April. Prune out nests of caterpillars and drop them in soapy water or crush them. When populations are very high, thoroughly cover leaves with a spray of *Bacillus thuringiensis* var. *kurstaki* while larvae are still small, or spray canola oil.

Insect Predators: Ground beetles (page 38), braconid wasps (page 26) and other parasitic wasps, and tachinid flies (page 91).

Similar Insects: Fall webworms (page 74).

Fall Armyworm
Spodoptera frugiperda

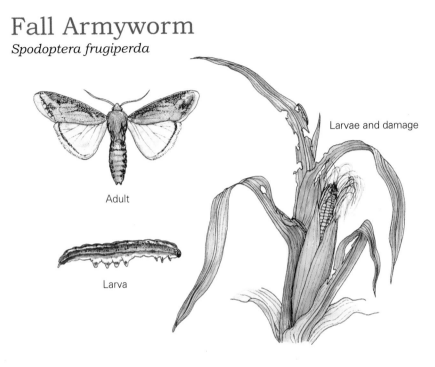

Adult

Larva

Larvae and damage

Adult actual size: 1½ inches ▬▬▬▬▬

Range: Most of the United States east of the Rocky Mountains.

Description: Adults are dark gray moths with mottled markings on wings and 1½-inch (3.8 cm) wingspans. Larvae are green, brown, or black caterpillars with a wide yellow stripe down their backs, a black stripe along each side, and a pale inverted Y-shaped mark on the head. Eggs are laid in clusters with a fuzzy gray covering.

Life Cycle: Fall armyworm overwinters in the Gulf states. The moths lay eggs on leaves of host plants; the young larvae feed for up to 4 weeks, then pupate in leaf litter just below soil surface. During the growing season the moths migrate north. There are one to six generations per year.

Host Plants: Corn and other grasses; also beans, cabbage, cucumbers, potatoes, spinach, sweet potatoes, tomatoes, turnips, and others; weeds.

Feeding Habits: Larvae eat the leaves of corn and other plants, leaving large, ragged holes. Young larvae feed in whorls of corn leaves; older larvae may eat so much of the plant that only the ribs or stalks remain. They also burrow into ears of corn through the side of the husk.

Prevention and Control: Plant corn as early as possible and use early maturing varieties to avoid the larger numbers of armyworms present in late summer. Hand-pick caterpillars and egg masses. For larger infestations, spray *Bacillus thuringiensis* var. *kurstaki* while larvae are still very small, or spray *Beauveria bassiana*, canola oil, or kaolin. As a last resort, spray neem.

Insect Predators: Braconid wasps (page 26), ground beetles (page 38), minute pirate bugs (page 94), predatory stink bugs (page 95), and tachinid flies (page 91).

Similar Insects: Beet armyworms (page 67).

Fall Webworm
Hyphantria cunea

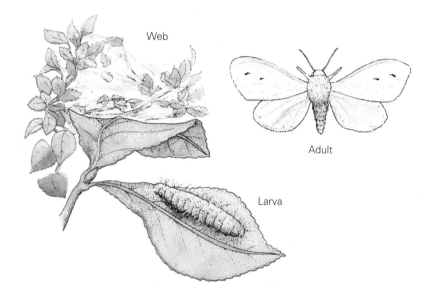

Web

Adult

Larva

Adult actual size: 2 to 2½ inches ▮▮▮▮▮▮▮

Range: Throughout the United States and southern Canada.

Description: Adults are pure white moths with 2- to 2½-inch (5.1 to 6.4 cm) wingspans; the forewings have black dots and the abdomen is yellow with black spots. Larvae are pale, hairy caterpillars, up to 1 inch (2.5 cm) long, with dark spots and tufts of longer white hairs on their sides. Eggs are laid in masses protected by a covering of yellowish hair.

Life Cycle: Pupae overwinter in cocoons under leaf litter or attached to tree bark. Adults emerge from May to June and lay eggs on host plants. Larvae feed together in groups inside large, loose webs they spin over leaves and branch tips; they feed for up to 6 weeks, expanding the web as they eat the leaves inside. Mature larvae wander away from the web to pupate in crevices in bark or in leaf litter. There are one or two generations per year.

Host Plants: Many fruit trees, and other deciduous trees and shrubs.

Feeding Habits: Larvae feed on leaves, which they enclose in large silken webs over the ends of branches. Trees are rarely harmed by the feeding, but the webs are unsightly.

Prevention and Control: Grow pollen and nectar plants to attract beneficial insects. Prune out developing webs and drop larvae in soapy water or crush them. In unusually large infestations, spray *Bacillus thuringiensis* var. *kurstaki* or canola oil while larvae are very small or when older larvae have started to leave the webs to feed (because most feeding is inside the web, sprays aren't very effective).

Insect Predators: Braconid wasps (page 26) and other parasitic wasps.

Similar Insects: Tent caterpillars (page 72).

Fruittree Leafroller

Archips argyrospila

Adult

Larva
and
damage

Rolled leaf

Adult actual size: ¾ to 1 inch ▬▬▬▬▬

Range: Similar species throughout North America.

Description: Adults are small, brownish moths with ¾- to 1-inch (19.1 to 25.4 mm) wingspans; forewings are mottled with gold and have light-colored patches on the front edge. Larvae are green caterpillars, up to ¾ inch (19.1 mm) long with dark brown or black heads. Eggs are greenish brown, but they're well camouflaged by a grayish coating and are laid in masses on bark.

Life Cycle: The eggs overwinter on trees and begin hatching about the time apple buds start to show in spring. The larvae feed on leaves and buds for up to 6 weeks, then spin a cocoon and pupate in a rolled-up leaf. Adult moths emerge in early summer and lay eggs in July, which remain on trees until the following spring. There's one generation per year.

Feeding Habits: Larvae feed on leaves, flowers, and small developing fruit.

They usually spin a fine web to pull together several leaves over a flower or branch tip and feed inside. They move between trees by spinning a line of silk and floating on the wind. Leaf damage is rarely a problem; however, fruit may be deeply scarred or malformed.

Host Plants: Apples, apricots, berries, cherries, pears, and others.

Prevention and Control: Spray narrow-range oil during the winter to kill overwintering eggs. Hand-pick rolled leaves where larvae and pupae are hiding. Where fruit requires thinning, concentrate on removing damaged fruit. For severe infestations, spray *Bacillus thuringiensis* var. *kurstaki* before petal fall while larvae are still small, or spray canola oil or kaolin.

Insect Predators: Braconid wasps (page 26) and many other parasitic wasps, and tachinid flies (page 91).

Garden Webworm
Achyra rantalis

Adult

Larva and web

Adult actual size: ¾ inch ▬▬▬▬

Range: Throughout North America.

Description: Adults are brownish yellow moths with ¾-inch (19.1 mm) wingspans; forewings have gray, gold, and brown markings. Larvae are light green to almost black caterpillars, up to ¾ inch (19.1 mm) long, with a light or dark stripe down the back and small dark spots on each segment. Eggs are laid in clusters on the leaves.

Life Cycle: Pupae overwinter in cocoons in the soil. Adult moths emerge from March to June and lay eggs on host plants. Larvae feed for up to 4 weeks, then pupate in the soil. There are two to five generations per year.

Host Plants: Beans, peas, and other vegetables; strawberries; and weeds.

Feeding Habits: Larvae spin light webs around leaves and feed inside the webs, chewing holes in the leaves. When disturbed, the larvae drop quickly to the ground on a fine silk thread. In severe infestations, plants may be covered with webs and completely defoliated.

Prevention and Control: Control weeds, especially pigweed and lamb's-quarters, in garden beds. Knock larvae from plants into a pail of soapy water; pull webbing off of leaves. For serious infestations, spray *Bacillus thuringiensis* var. *kurstaki* while larvae are small, or spray canola oil. After harvest, promptly cultivate the soil to destroy pupae and expose them to predators.

Similar Insects: Cabbage loopers (page 68), imported cabbageworms (page 79).

Grapeleaf Skeletonizers

Harrisina spp.

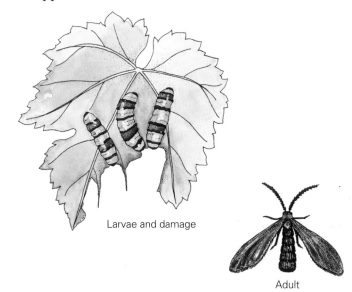

Larvae and damage

Adult

Adult actual size: 1 inch ▬▬▬▬▬

Range: Related species throughout the United States and southern Canada.

Description: Adults are dark gray or metallic blue moths, with narrow wings and 1-inch (25.4 mm) wingspans. Larvae are cream to yellow colored and up to ¾ inch (19.1 mm) long, with purple and black bands just behind the head (eastern species have an orange collar); they have tufts of long, poisonous black hairs on each segment. Eggs are pale yellowish capsules, laid in clusters on leaves.

Life Cycle: Pupae overwinter in cocoons under loose bark or leaf litter. Adults emerge from early spring to June and lay eggs on grape leaves. Eggs hatch in 2 weeks; larvae feed on undersides of leaves, lining up side-by-side on the leaf as they feed. They pupate in cocoons under bark or in the soil. There are two or three generations per year.

Host Plants: Grapes.

Feeding Habits: Larvae feed together in colonies on the undersides of leaves between the veins, leaving a papery appearance. Eastern species are rarely damaging. Western grape skeletonizer (*H. brillians*) is a more serious problem and in large numbers can defoliate vines and feed on grape clusters.

Prevention and Control: Grow pollen and nectar plants to attract parasitic wasps and flies. Where natural enemies and diseases don't provide sufficient control, spray *Bacillus thuringiensis* var. *kurstaki* to control larvae, or spray canola oil or kaolin.

Insect Predators: Braconid wasp (*Apanteles harrisiniae*) (page 26), tachinid flies (page 91), and other parasitic insects.

Gypsy Moth
Lymantria dispar

Adult

Larva and damage

Adult actual size: 1½ to 2 inches

Range: Eastern half of the United States and into southern Canada.

Description: Adults are gray (male) or white (female) moths, with thick, furry bodies and 1½- to 2-inch (3.8 to 5.1 cm) wingspans. Females are unable to fly. Larvae are gray, up to 2 inches (5.1 cm) long, with tufts of long brown hairs, five pairs of blue dots, and six pairs of red dots. Eggs are laid in masses on tree trunks and are protected by a yellowish covering of hairs.

Life Cycle: The eggs overwinter and hatch in late April to May. The tiny larvae crawl up trees or spin fine silk threads, which blow onto trees. They feed on leaves for up to 8 weeks, then pupate for 2 weeks in loosely spun cocoons. Adults emerge in late July to early August and lay eggs. There's one generation per year.

Host Plants: Many shrubs and trees, including conifers; also garden plants and cranberries.

Feeding Habits: The youngest caterpillars feed on leaves of deciduous trees and shrubs; larger larvae may also move to conifers. In areas with high populations, the caterpillars may completely defoliate trees. Repeated defoliation may kill some trees.

Prevention and Control: In fall and winter, look for egg masses on lower sections of tree trunks, fence posts, outbuildings, and outdoor equipment, and scrape them off. When caterpillars are small, spray *Bacillus thuringiensis* var. *kurstaki* two or three times at 1- to 2-week intervals. Wrap burlap tree bands around trunks and check daily to destroy cocoons and caterpillars.

Insect Predators: Ground beetles (page 38), parasitic wasps, and tachinid flies (page 91). Naturally occurring fungal diseases also wipe out local populations.

Imported Cabbageworm
Pieris rapae

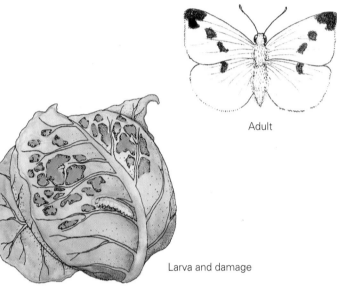

Adult

Larva and damage

Adult actual size: 1½ inches

Range: Throughout North America.

Description: Adults are common white butterflies with 1½-inch (3.8 cm) wingspans; forewings have a black tip with two or three small black spots. Larvae are velvety, pale green caterpillars, up to 1 inch (2.5 cm) long, with a fine yellow stripe down the back. Eggs are yellow, shaped like bullets standing on end, and are laid singly on leaves.

Life Cycle: The pupae overwinter attached by a loop of silk to plant stalks or objects near the garden. The adults emerge in early spring and lay eggs on a wide range of host plants. The larvae feed for up to 3 weeks, then pupate on plants or other objects. Pupation takes up to 2 weeks. There are three to five overlapping generations per year.

Host Plants: Broccoli, cabbage, cauliflower, and other cabbage-family plants; also related weeds (shepherd's purse, wild mustard) and some flowers (nasturtium, sweet alyssum).

Feeding Habits: Caterpillars chew large holes in leaves and also chew on florets. They produce dark green excrement that falls between leaves of cabbage and other plants. Although many butterflies and eggs may be seen, there's usually little leaf damage because wasps and other predators control the caterpillars.

Prevention and Control: Grow plants to attract beneficials, and interplant cabbage crops with clover. Hand-pick caterpillars and crush eggs. Where populations are high, spray *Bacillus thuringiensis* var. *kurstaki* or canola oil.

Insect Predators: Braconid wasps (page 26) and other parasitic wasps, and yellow jackets (page 27).

Similar Insects: Cabbage loopers (page 68), garden webworms (page 76).

Oriental Fruit Moth

Grapholitha molesta

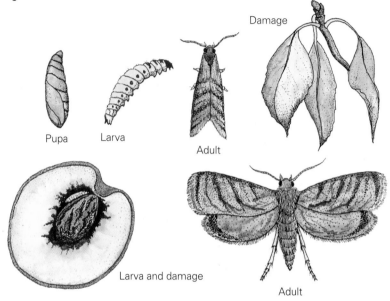

Pupa Larva

Adult

Damage

Larva and damage

Adult

Adult actual size: ½ inch ▬▬▬

Range: Eastern North America and the Pacific Northwest.

Description: Adults are gray moths with ½-inch (12.7 mm) wingspans; the wings have mottled brown markings. Larvae are grayish white to pink caterpillars, up to ½ inch (12.7 mm) long, with brown heads. Eggs are white and flat, and they're laid on undersides of leaves or on twigs.

Life Cycle: Larvae overwinter in cocoons spun on tree bark or weeds or in soil debris. They pupate in spring, and adults emerge in early May to mid-June and lay eggs on leaves and twigs. Larvae feed for up to 3 weeks and then pupate on bark or debris. There are three to seven generations per year.

Host Plants: Peaches and most tree fruit; also almonds.

Feeding Habits: Early larvae bore into young twigs; later generations enter fruits at the stem end to feed. The damage resembles that of the codling moth (page 69), but there's no external damage to leaves and less excrement in the tunnels in fruit.

Prevention and Control: Plant early peach and apricot varieties so that the harvest is over by midsummer. Grow pollen and nectar plants to attract beneficial insects. Before trees bloom, cultivate the soil 4 inches (10.2 cm) deep around trunks to kill overwintering larvae and pupae. Starting at petal fall, spray kaolin to prevent moths from laying eggs, or spray canola oil or narrow-range oils to control eggs and larvae on leaves. Promptly destroy early dropped fruit and culled fruit.

Insect Predators: Braconid wasps (page 26) and many other parasitic wasps.

Similar Insects: Codling moths (page 69).

Parsleyworm, Black Swallowtail Butterfly *Papilio polyxenes*
Western Parsleyworm *Papilio zelicaon*

Chrysalis

Larva

Adult

Adult actual size: 3 inches

Range: Related species throughout North America.

Description: Adults are large, black or black-and-yellow butterflies, with 3-inch (7.6 cm) wingspans; each hind wing has a tail and a peacocklike eye spot. Younger larvae are small brown or black caterpillars with white marks on their backs; mature caterpillars (parsleyworms) are up to 1½ inches (3.8 cm) long and green, with a black band on each segment and yellow or orange spots on the bands. When disturbed, they stick out fleshy, orange, scent horns from behind the head to give off an unpleasant odor. Eggs are white and are laid singly on leaves of host plants.

Life Cycle: The pupae overwinter attached to stems or debris. The adults emerge in April or early May and lay eggs on host plants. The larvae feed for up to 4 weeks, then pupate for up to 2 weeks. There are two to four generations per year.

Host Plants: Carrots, celery, fennel, lovage, parsley, and parsnips as well as dill and related weeds, such as wild carrot and wild parsley.

Feeding Habits: Larvae eat leaves of host plants. Although noticeable due to their size and striking colors, the larvae are usually few in number and cause little damage. Adults are beautiful butterflies.

Prevention and Control: In the extremely rare case that larvae are damaging, hand-pick caterpillars. To preserve butterfly populations, rather than killing caterpillars, move them gently to a more robust host plant to continue feeding.

Tomato Hornworm
Manduca quinquemaculata

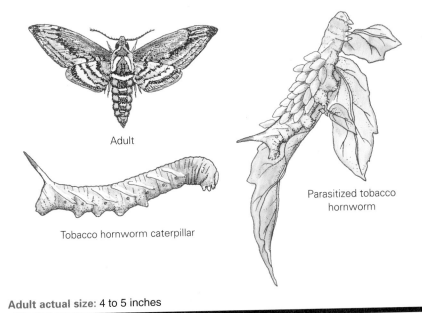

Adult

Tobacco hornworm caterpillar

Parasitized tobacco hornworm

Adult actual size: 4 to 5 inches

Range: Related species throughout North America.

Description: Adults are mottled gray moths with 4- to 5-inch (10.2 to 12.7 cm) wingspans; wings are narrow in proportion to the large body. The hind wings have light and dark zigzag patterns; the body is furry, with orange spots on the sides of the abdomen. Larvae are huge green caterpillars, up to 4 inches (10.2 cm) long, with seven or eight diagonal white marks on each side and a large black horn on their tail. A similar species, the tobacco hornworm (*M. sexta*), has a red horn. Eggs are greenish yellow and are laid on the undersides of leaves.

Life Cycle: The large pupae overwinter in dark brown cocoons in the soil. Adult moths, which resemble hummingbirds in their behavior, emerge in spring and lay eggs on host plants. The caterpillars feed for up to 4 weeks, then pupate in the soil. There's only one generation in most areas; two generations in the South.

Host Plants: Eggplants, peppers, potatoes, and tomatoes.

Feeding Habits: The larvae chew on leaves and gnaw holes in fruit. They produce large, dark green droppings as they feed. Although the large caterpillars are alarming, they usually aren't present in large enough numbers to be damaging.

Prevention and Control: Grow pollen and nectar plants to attract beneficial insects. Hand-pick caterpillars, but be careful to preserve any with white or tan cocoons stuck to their backs—those cocoons are of beneficial parasitic wasps. Where large numbers of hornworms are defoliating plants, spray *Bacillus thuringiensis* var. *kurstaki*, which is very effective for caterpillars.

Insect Predators: Braconid wasps (page 26) and other parasitic wasps.

Aphid Midge
Aphidoletes aphidimyza

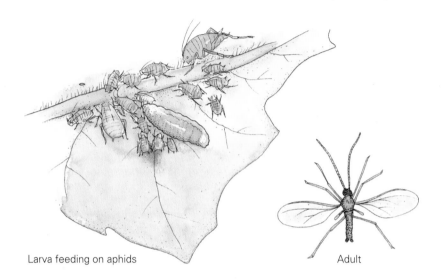

Larva feeding on aphids   Adult

Adult actual size: ¹⁄₁₆ inch ■

Range: Throughout North America; also sold commercially.

Description: Adults are delicate, ¹⁄₁₆-inch (1.6 mm)-long flies, with long legs and clear wings. Larvae are light to dark orange maggots, up to ⅛ inch (3.2 mm) long. Eggs are pinpoint-sized orange capsules laid on leaves among aphids.

Life Cycle: Larvae overwinter in cocoons in the soil. Adults emerge in spring and lay eggs among aphid colonies. Larvae feed for up to a week, then drop to the soil and burrow just under the surface to pupate. Adults emerge after 2 to 3 weeks. There are three or more overlapping generations per year.

Feeding Habits: Larvae feed on most species of aphids. Adults feed on nectar and on aphid honeydew.

Attract and Protect: Plant insect-attracting flowers and herbs—such as coriander, dill, and fennel—or leave weeds such as Queen-Anne's-lace and wild mustard to grow. In dry, dusty periods, provide a source of water, such as a shallow tray of water filled with pebbles. It may be worthwhile to release commercially reared aphid midges to control aphids in greenhouses and on trees and vegetables when native populations of aphid predators are low.

Apple Maggot
Rhagoletis pomonella

Adult

Maggot and damage

Adult actual size: ¼ inch ▬

Range: Eastern United States and southeastern Canada.

Description: Adults are black, ¼-inch (6.4 mm)-long flies, with white bands on the abdomen and yellow legs; they have dark zigzag bands across their wings. Larvae are white or yellow, legless maggots, up to ¼ inch (6.4 mm) long, found inside fruit. Eggs are laid singly in punctures in the skin of apples.

Life Cycle: The pupae overwinter 1 to 6 inches (2.5 to 15.3 cm) deep in the soil. Adults emerge from mid-June to July and lay eggs on fruit. Larvae develop slowly, tunneling inside the fruit until it drops. They then leave the fruit to pupate in the soil. There's usually one generation per year. Some pupae remain in the soil for several years before adults emerge.

Host Plants: Apples, blueberries; occasionally cherries and plums.

Feeding Habits: Larvae bore through fruit, leaving winding tunnels in the flesh; this usually causes the fruit to drop early and rot.

Prevention and Control: Plant late-ripening apple cultivars that develop after most of the flies lay eggs. Collect and destroy early dropped fruit every day until September to control larvae before they enter the soil to pupate. Plant clover groundcovers in orchards to attract ground beetles (they prey on the pupae). Trap female flies by hanging sticky red ball traps in trees from mid-June until harvest, or make traps by covering red balls with plastic bags spread with insect glue, such as Tanglefoot. Replace commercial traps or plastic covers as they become coated with dust and debris. Starting before bloom, spray kaolin to prevent flies from laying eggs on fruit.

Cabbage Maggot
Delia radicum

Maggots
and damage

Adult

Maggot

Adult actual size: ¼ inch ▬

Range: Throughout North America.

Description: Adults are gray, ¼-inch (6.4 mm)-long flies, with black stripes on their thoraxes. Larvae are white maggots, up to ¼ inch (6.4 mm) long.

Life Cycle: Pupae overwinter in the soil and adults emerge from late March onward. Eggs are laid in the soil beside plant stems. The larvae tunnel into roots for up to 4 weeks, then pupate in the soil for up to 3 weeks. There are two to four generations per year.

Host Plants: Broccoli, brussels sprouts, cabbage, cauliflower, radishes, and turnips.

Feeding Habits: Larvae tunnel into roots and stems, causing plants to wilt in the sun and eventually stunting growth. Plants may die, or may become infected by diseases entering the wounds that the larvae made. They're rarely a problem south of 40° latitude.

Prevention and Control: Plant radishes very early and cabbages late to avoid the first generation of flies. Cover seedbeds and seedlings with floating row covers to prevent egg laying. Protect transplants by setting them out with a 6-inch (15 cm) square of tar paper around the stem and laid flat on the ground. Prevent flies from laying eggs on plants by fencing plots of cabbage-family plants with 4-foot (1.2 m)-wide nylon window screen; leave the top 10 inches (25 cm) loose and folded over to the outside; crop rotation is essential because no adults must emerge from the soil inside the fences. Where cabbage maggot populations are usually low, mounding diatomaceous earth, wood ashes, hot pepper, or ginger powder around the bases of transplants may provide control. After harvest, promptly pull and destroy roots of cabbage-family plants.

Insect Predators: Ground beetles (page 38), rove beetles (page 44).

Carrot Rust Fly
Psila rosae

Adult

Maggot

Maggots and damage

Adult actual size: ¼ inch ▬

Range: Throughout most of North America.

Description: Adults are shiny, metallic greenish black flies, ¼ inch (6.4 mm) long, with yellow head and legs. Larvae are cream-colored maggots, up to ⅓ inch (8.5 mm) long.

Life Cycle: Larvae overwinter in roots and pupae overwinter in the soil. Adults emerge in spring and lay eggs beside the crowns of plants. The larvae burrow down to feed on root hairs, then move into the tip of the root. After feeding for up to 4 weeks, the larvae pupate in the soil. There are two or three generations per year.

Host Plants: Carrots, celery, parsley, parsnips, and related weeds.

Feeding Habits: Young larvae feed on root hairs, then tunnel into roots. They leave behind reddish brown excrement in the tunnels. In heavy infestations,

plants are stunted and may also die of soft-rot bacteria that enter wounds. Larvae continue to feed on carrots in storage. Rust flies are most damaging north of 40° latitude.

Prevention and Control: Plant 'Fly Away' carrot. Sow midseason carrots after mid-May to avoid the first flies; harvest before early October. For reliable control, cover seed beds with floating row covers from seeding to harvest; crop rotation is essential to make sure no adults emerge from the soil under the fabric. Prevent flies from laying eggs on plants by fencing plots of carrots with 4-foot-wide (1.2 m) nylon window screen; leave the top 10 inches (25 cm) loose and folded over to the outside. Where rust fly numbers are high, controlling Queen-Anne's-lace (wild carrot) may help reduce populations.

Insect Predators: Rove beetles (page 44).

Cherry Fruit Flies
Rhagoletes spp.

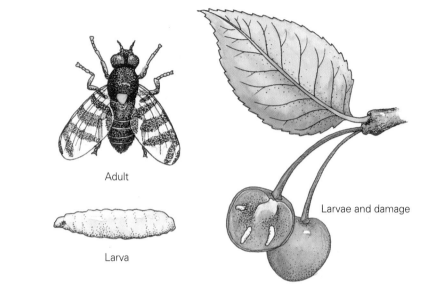

Adult

Larva

Larvae and damage

Adult actual size: 1/5 inch ▬

Range: Related species throughout North America.

Description: Adult cherry fruit flies (*R. cingulata*) are black, shiny, and 1/5 inch (5.1 mm) long; they have four white bands across their abdomen, and their wings have black bands. Black cherry fruit fly (*R. fausta*) is similar but slightly larger and with a solid black abdomen. Larvae of all species are yellowish white maggots and up to 1/5 inch (5.1 mm) long, and are found in the flesh of fruit. Eggs are creamy white and are laid in small slits in the fruit.

Life Cycle: Pupae overwinter in the soil and adults emerge from mid-May to mid-July. Females lay eggs on developing fruit for a month. Larvae burrow in the fruit for up to 3 weeks. They drop to the ground to pupate. Some adults emerge in September, but most pupae remain in the soil for the winter. There's one generation per year.

Host Plant: Cherries, wild cherries; also plums and pears.

Feeding Habits: Young larvae first feed near the pit, then they move out to feed on the flesh of the fruit, causing the infested cherry to shrivel up. Early signs of infestation are cherries that are misshapen or turning red prematurely.

Prevention and Control: Where populations are high, plant early maturing cherries, which are less damaged than later varieties. Grow plants to attract beneficial insects. Spray kaolin at 10- to 14-day intervals during egg-laying periods to prevent females from laying eggs on fruit. Pick off and destroy any fruit that's misshapen or shriveled or that's turning red unusually early.

Insect Predators: Braconid wasps (page 26) and other parasitic wasps, ground beetles (page 38), rove beetles (page 44).

Flower Flies, Hoverflies
SYRPHIDAE

Larva

Adult fly

Adult fly

Adult actual size: ⅜ to ⅝ inch ▬▬▬▬▬

Range: Various species throughout North America.

Description: Adults are shiny flies, ⅜ to ⅝ inch (9.5 to 15.9 mm) long, with black abdomens with yellow or white bands; they have large, reddish eyes and clear wings. They're strong fliers and hover over flowers like tiny hummingbirds. Larvae are greenish, gray, or light brown maggots, somewhat translucent, and up to ½ inch (12.7 mm) long. Eggs are white ovals, laid singly or in groups among aphids on leaves.

Life Cycle: Pupae overwinter in the soil, and adults are among the first insects to emerge in spring. Females lay their eggs among aphid colonies, and the larvae feed on the aphids for up to 2 weeks. They drop to the soil to pupate, and the next generation of adults emerges in 2 weeks. There are three to seven overlapping generations per year.

Feeding Habits: Adults feed on pollen and nectar and are attracted to various cultivated flowers and weeds. The larvae of many species feed on aphids; one larva can eat 400 aphids during its lifetime.

Attract and Protect: Plant flowers to attract adults, such as ajuga, feverfew, golden marguerite, lavender, speedwell, sweet alyssum, wild bergamot, and yarrow. Flower flies are also attracted to herbs, such as coriander, dill, and fennel, and weeds, including prickly sow thistle, Queen-Anne's-lace, scentless mayweed, white campion, and wild chamomile.

Similar Insects: Honeybees (page 29), yellow jackets (page 27).

Leafminers *Liriomyza* spp.
Spinach Leafminer *Pegomya hyoscyami*

Adults

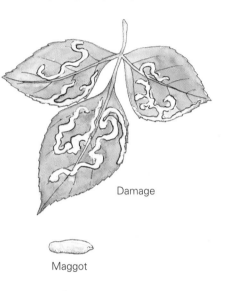

Damage

Maggot

Adult actual size: 1/10 inch ▪

Range: Various species throughout North America.

Description: Adults are black or black-and-yellow flies, 1/10 inch (2.5 mm) long. Larvae are pale green or yellowish maggots, found in tunnels between upper and lower surfaces of leaves. Eggs are white ovals or cylinders, laid on leaves.

Life Cycle: Pupae overwinter in the soil and adults emerge to lay eggs in spring. Upon hatching, the larvae burrow into the leaf tissue, carving out curving mines between the upper and lower leaf surfaces. There are two to three generations per year for most species.

Host Plants: Beans, blackberries, cabbage, celery, lettuce, peppers, potatoes, spinach, and turnips.

Feeding Habits: Larvae mine in leaves, leaving grayish tunnels. Depending on the species, mines may be long and curving, or they may appear as whitish or gray blotched areas in the leaves.

Prevention and Control: For reliable control, cover plants with floating row covers. Remove and destroy infested leaves when the first mines are seen; this usually provides sufficient control. Grow pollen and nectar plants to attract beneficial insects. Where spinach leafminer is a problem, remove nearby host weeds, including dock and lamb's-quarters. To kill eggs, spray canola oil; as a last resort, spray neem to control larvae.

Insect Predators: Many species of braconid wasps (page 26) and other parasitic wasps.

Onion Maggot
Delia antiqua

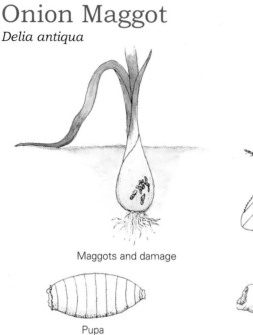

Maggots and damage

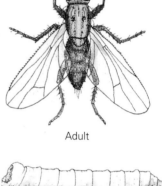

Adult

Pupa

Maggot

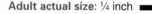

Adult actual size: ¼ inch ▬

Range: Northern United States and southern Canada.

Description: Adults are gray flies, ¼ inch (6.4 mm) long, with humped backs and clear wings. Larvae are white maggots, up to ⅓ inch (8.5 mm) long, that burrow into onions. Eggs are white and cylindrical.

Life Cycle: Pupae overwinter in the soil, and adults emerge from mid-May to late June. Females lay eggs at the base of plants; upon hatching, the larvae burrow into the roots. They feed for up to 3 weeks, then pupate in the soil. Adults emerge in up to 2 weeks. There are two or three generations per year.

Host Plants: Onions.

Feeding Habits: Larvae tunnel into onion bulbs, killing young onions and stunting larger onions. Bulbs may rot from diseases that enter wounds. Larvae can continue to feed on bulbs in storage.

Prevention and Control: Plant onion sets late. Red onions and Japanese bunching onions are somewhat less susceptible than white onions. Cover beds with floating row covers from planting to harvest; crop rotation is essential to make sure no adults emerge from the soil under the fabric. Prevent flies from laying eggs on plants by fencing plots of onions with 4-foot (1.2 m)-wide nylon window screen; leave the top 10 inches (25 cm) loose and folded over to the outside (crop rotation is essential). Plant trap rows of cull onions among rows of seedlings; at the same time treat seedlings with chili powder, dill, ginger, or hot peppers to drive the flies to the cull onions. Pull and destroy cull onions 2 weeks after they sprout.

Insect Predators: Braconid wasp (*Aphaereta pallipes*) (page 26) and other parasitic wasps, ground beetles (page 38), and rove beetles (page 44).

Tachinid Flies
TACHINIDAE

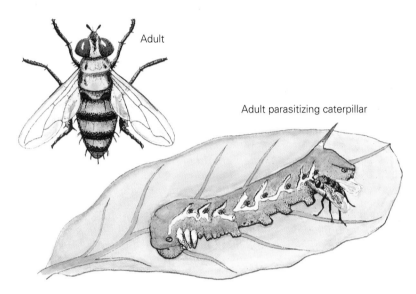

Adult

Adult parasitizing caterpillar

Adult actual size: ⅓ to ½ inch ▬▬▬▬

Range: Various species throughout North America.

Description: Adults are gray, brown, or black flies, ⅓ to ½ inch (8.5 to 12.7 mm) long, with big, reddish eyes and pale markings; some look like house-flies. Larvae are plump, white maggots, found inside host insects.

Life Cycle: Larvae overwinter in the body of the host in some species; others overwinter as pupae in the soil. Adult flies emerge in spring and lay eggs on host insects or on nearby leaves where the host will swallow the eggs; females of some species lay newly hatched larvae on the host insect. The fly larvae burrow into the host and feed inside, eventually killing it. They pupate in the host body or in the soil. Most species have one to three generations per year.

Feeding Habits: Larvae are internal parasites of many species of beetles, bugs, caterpillars, grasshoppers, and sawflies. Adult flies feed on flower nectar and pollen as well as on the honeydew that aphids and other sucking insects produce.

Attract and Protect: Plant pollen and nectar flowers that attract adult flies, such as alyssum, calendula, caraway, coriander, daisies, dill, and fennel. Allow some flowering weeds, such as Queen-Anne's-lace and wild mustard, to grow nearby.

Lacewings

Chrysopa spp., *Chrysoperla* spp.

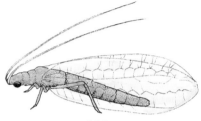

Adult

Larva and prey

Adult actual size: ½ to ¾ inch ▬▬▬▬▬

Range: Various species throughout North America; two species are sold commercially.

Description: Adults are pale green or beige, ½ to ¾ inch (12.7 to 19.1 mm) long, with slender bodies and small heads with large eyes; their wings are translucent with many fine veins. Larvae are tan or gray and alligator-shaped, with prominent curved jaws; they move very quickly. Eggs are white and each is laid on the end of a hairlike stalk attached to a leaf.

Life Cycle: Adults or pupae overwinter, and adults emerge in spring to lay eggs among host insects on leaves. Larvae feed on soft-bodied insects for up to 3 weeks, then spin round, white cocoons and pupate for up to a week. There are three to six overlapping generations per year.

Feeding Habits: Larvae prey on aphids, mites, scales, small caterpillars, thrips, and other soft-bodied insects as well as insect eggs. Most adults feed only on pollen and nectar.

Attract and Protect: Plant pollen and nectar flowers that attract adults, such as coriander, dill, daisies and other pollen flowers, and fennel; leave a few weeds, such as Queen-Anne's-lace or yarrow, to bloom near the garden.

Assassin Bugs

REDUVIIDAE

Adult

Adult actual size: ½ to 1 inch

Range: Many species throughout North America.

Description: Adults are oval, rather flattened, ½ to 1 inch (12.7 to 25.4 mm) long, with small narrow heads; most are dark brown, black, or reddish. They have a curved beak that extends outward when they're feeding and is held curved under when not in use; wings are crossed and folded flat on the abdomen. The abdomens of some species flare outward beneath their wings. Nymphs are shaped similar to adults, but without the wings. Some are brightly colored; others hide themselves by sticking small bits of debris to their bodies.

Life Cycle: Females of most species lay eggs in the soil, under stones or other protected sites; some lay eggs on leaves. Eggs hatch into nymphs that feed on small insects until fall. Assassin bugs overwinter as large nymphs and continue to develop in spring, reaching the adult stage by early summer. Most species have one generation per year.

Feeding Habits: Adults and nymphs are voracious predators that feed on both larvae and adult insects, including aphids, beetles, caterpillars, flies, and leafhoppers. They stalk or lie in wait for their prey, which they inject with venom to paralyze it. They can bite humans if aggravated.

Attract and Protect: Avoid use of pesticides.

Minute Pirate Bug, Insidious Flower Bug

Orius spp.

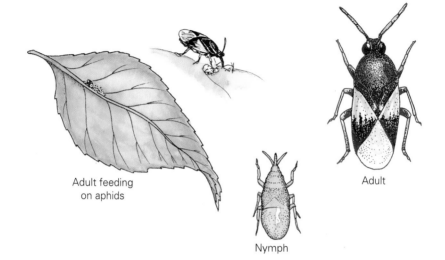

Adult feeding
on aphids

Nymph

Adult

Adult actual size: ¼ inch ▬

Range: Throughout North America; two species are sold commercially.

Description: Adults are ¼ inch (6.4 mm) long, with a black-and-white color pattern; their wings are folded flat on the abdomen. Nymphs are tiny, oval, wingless, and up to ⅕ inch (5.1 mm) long; early stages are yellowish, and their color darkens with each molt until they're shiny and dark brown.

Life Cycle: The adult females overwinter in protected crevices in weeds or leaf litter. In spring, they lay eggs, which are inserted directly into the leaves or stems of plants. The nymphs feed on insects and mites in flowers and on pollen for up to 4 weeks before molting to the adult stage. There are two to four generations per year.

Feeding Habits: Both adults and nymphs are voracious predators of mites, insect eggs, and small insects, such as leafhopper nymphs, small caterpillars, and thrips.

Attract and Protect: Grow flowers with a rich supply of pollen and nectar (especially clover, daisies, goldenrod, and yarrow); add a few sunflowers or corn plants to the garden if they aren't already present. To protect overwintering adults, don't disturb leaf litter or garden trash after mid-October. If thrips have become a serious problem in a greenhouse, release commercially reared *O. insidiosis* or *O. tristicolor*.

Stink Bugs
PENTATOMIDAE

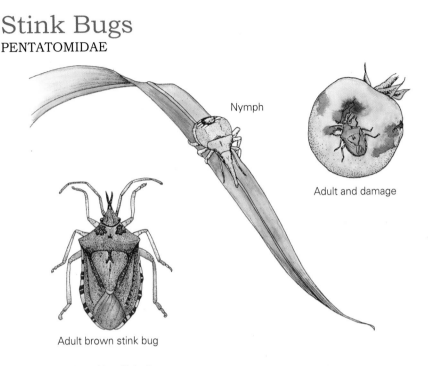

Nymph

Adult and damage

Adult brown stink bug

Adult actual size: ¼ to ⅝ inch

Range: Many species throughout North America.

Description: Adults are five-sided, shield-shaped, and ½ to ⅝ inch (12.7 to 15.9 mm) long, with wings folded flat on the abdomen. They give off an unpleasant odor when alarmed. Most are green, tan, brown, or gray. Nymphs are oval and similar to adults, only without wings; some are brightly patterned. Eggs are barrel-shaped and laid on end, in clusters or short rows, on undersides of leaves.

Life Cycle: Adults overwinter in weeds or garden debris and emerge in spring to lay eggs on plants. Nymphs feed for up to 5 weeks, then molt to the adult stage. Depending on the species and climate, there are two or more generations per year.

Host Plants: Most garden plants, especially beans, berries, corn, okra, peas, squash, tomatoes, and others; weeds.

Feeding Habits: Both adults and nymphs of plant-feeding stink bugs either suck sap from stems, buds, and leaves or puncture the skin of fruit to feed. Injured fruit has a cat-faced (puckered) or pitted appearance. Some stink bugs are predatory, such as the two-spotted stink bug (*Perillus bioculatus*) and the spined soldier bug (*Podisus maculiventris*), which are sold commercially for control of caterpillars and beetle larvae.

Prevention and Control: Knock pest species into containers of soapy water; check undersides of leaves for egg clusters to destroy. Control weeds in the garden, but maintain pollen and nectar plants among annual crops to attract beneficials. After harvest in fall, promptly shred and compost or till in crop residues. If necessary, spray canola oil.

Insect Predators: Parasitic wasps, tachinid flies (page 91).

Chinch Bugs
Blissus spp.

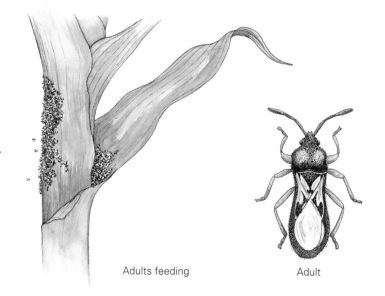

Adults feeding   Adult

Adult actual size: ⅙ inch ▬

Range: Throughout North America, including southern Canada; most destructive in central and eastern regions.

Description: Adults are black and ⅙ inch (4.2 mm) long, with white forewings that have a black, triangular spot near the outer edge; their legs are reddish brown. Young nymphs are red with a white stripe across their backs; later they turn black with white spots.

Life Cycle: Adults overwinter under leaf litter and in clumps of grass. They emerge in spring and lay eggs in the roots of grass or on the lower stems of grains. Nymphs chew on roots for up to 5 weeks, then molt to the adult stage. There are two or three generations per year.

Host Plants: Turf grasses, corn, and cereal crops.

Feeding Habits: Nymphs and adults suck sap from stems and roots, causing plants to wilt, and even die. Infested lawns may show patches of dying turf, whereas corn plants may wilt and dry up.

Prevention and Control: Organic lawn care encourages the insects and birds that eat chinch bugs. Remove excessive thatch (more than ¾ inch [19.1 mm] thick); aerate compacted soil. Where lawns are heavily attacked, overseed with endophytic turf grasses (don't plant these grasses where livestock graze). For light infestations in lawns, keep the turf very wet for a month as the soil warms to drive out the adults. For heavy infestations in lawns, apply the fungus *Beauvaria bassiana*, insecticidal soap, or as a last resort spray neem. Chinch bugs avoid shade; therefore, interplant corn and cereal crops with legumes to shade the root zone.

Insect Predators: Big-eyed bugs (*Geocoris* spp., also sold commercially), parasitic wasps (*Eumicrosoma* ssp.).

Harlequin Bug, Calico Back Bug

Murgantia histrionica

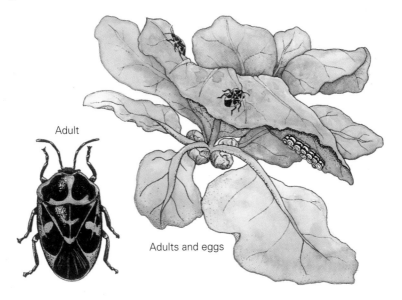

Adult

Adults and eggs

Adult actual size: ⅜ inch ▬▬▬

Range: Throughout eastern North America.

Description: Adults are ⅜ inch (9.5 mm) long, bright red and black, shiny, flattened, and shield-shaped. Nymphs are also red and black, oval in shape, and wingless. Eggs are white with black rings, barrel-shaped, and laid on end, in double rows on the undersides of leaves.

Life Cycle: Adults overwinter in crop debris in northern areas; in the South, they continue to reproduce year-around. In spring, adults feed on weeds, then lay eggs on crop plants. Nymphs feed on host plants for 1 to 2 months, then molt to the adult stage. There are three or four overlapping generations per year in the North; more in the South.

Host Plants: Brussels sprouts, cabbage, cauliflower, collards, kohlrabi, mustard, radishes, turnips; also other garden plants, fruit trees, and weeds.

Feeding Habits: Nymphs and adults suck sap from foliage, leaving white and yellow blotches; severely affected plants wilt, turn brown, and die. They're rarely damaging north of 40° latitude.

Prevention and Control: Plant varieties with tolerance to harlequin bug damage. In the morning, hand-pick or knock pests from plants into a pail of soapy water. Check undersides of leaves for eggs masses to destroy. If necessary, spray soap or canola oil. Remove nearby cabbage-family weeds, such as wild mustard and pigweed (*Amaranthus* spp.). Plant mustard or radishes as trap crops in early spring or late fall when main crop plants aren't present; spray trap plants when the bugs have congregated on them. Promptly shred and compost, or till in crop residues at the end of the harvest.

Insect Predators: Assassin bugs (page 93), predaceous stink bugs (page 95).

Squash Bug
Anasa tristis

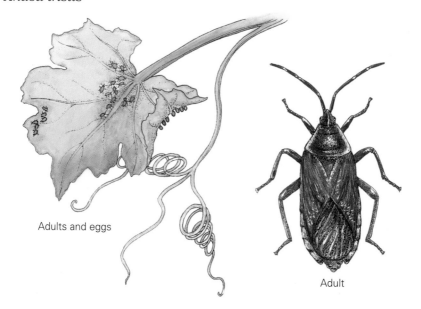

Adults and eggs

Adult

Adult actual size: ⅝ inch ▬▬▬

Range: Throughout North America.

Description: Adults are dark brown to black and ⅝ inch (15.9 mm) long, with a flattened body and a fine orange or brown edge around the abdomen. They give off an unpleasant odor when alarmed. Nymphs are light gray to pale green and wingless. Eggs are shiny and yellowish brown to dark red; they're laid on their sides, and evenly spaced apart in a group on leaves.

Life Cycle: Adults overwinter under garden debris and stones and in out-buildings and other protected sites. They emerge in spring, about the time cucurbit vines are starting to lengthen, and lay their eggs on the plants. Nymphs feed for up to 6 weeks, then molt to the adult stage. There are one to three generations per year.

Host Plants: Cucumbers, melons, pumpkins, and squash.

Feeding Habits: Adults and nymphs suck plant sap, causing leaves to wilt rapidly, turn black, dry out, and die. Small plants may be killed.

Prevention and Control: Plant a decoy crop—squash bugs seem to prefer summer squash over cucumbers, winter squash, and melons. Cover seedlings with floating row covers. Keep plant bases clear of debris, and don't use mulch, which provides hiding places during the day. Hand-pick adults, nymphs, and egg masses early in the day. Spray plants with canola oil. Dust diatomaceous earth around the base of plants. Lay boards along rows of squash seedlings, and check under them every morning to destroy hiding bugs. At the end of the season, pull all but one or two plants and allow bugs to collect on these for a couple of days, then shake the plants onto a sheet on the ground and destroy the bugs.

Insect Predator: Tachinid fly (*Trichopoda pennipes*) (page 91).

Tarnished Plant Bug

Lygus lineolaris

Adult

Adult actual size: ¼ inch ▬

Range: Throughout North America.

Description: Adults are quick-moving, oval, ¼ inch (6.4 mm) long, greenish yellow to brown, and mottled with darker markings; each forewing has a black-tipped yellow triangle on the side. Seen in profile, the wings have a sharply downward slant to the rear half. Nymphs are yellowish with five black dots on the body and are wingless. Eggs are inserted into the tissue of stems, buds, and leaves.

Life Cycle: Adults overwinter under garden debris and leaf litter and in hedgerows. They emerge in spring and feed on early buds and foliage before moving to garden plants or weeds to lay eggs. Nymphs feed for up to 4 weeks, then molt to the adult stage. There are three to five overlapping generations per year.

Host Plants: Most flowers, fruits, vegetables, and weeds.

Feeding Habits: Nymphs and adults suck plant sap, feeding mainly on stem tips, buds, and fruits. Their saliva is toxic, causing distorted and blackened buds and leaves as well as dwarfed, pitted, or cat-faced (puckered) fruit.

Prevention and Control: Grow plants to attract beneficials. Cover small plants with floating row covers before bugs emerge from overwintering sites. Where populations are high, remove weeds—particularly chickweed, clover, and dandelion—and clean up crop debris. Plant subterranean clover rather than other legumes as cover crops in orchards. To control adults and nymphs, spray *Beauveria bassiana*, canola oil, garlic oil, or kaolin. As a last resort, spray narrow-range oil (on plants that tolerate it).

Insect Predators: Big-eyed bugs, damsel bugs, minute pirate bugs (page 94), and parasitic wasps.

Aphids
APHIDIDAE

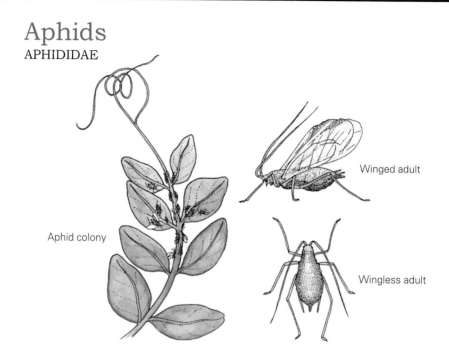

Aphid colony

Winged adult

Wingless adult

Adult actual size: 1/16 to 3/8 inch ▬▬▬▬

Range: Throughout North America.

Description: Both adults and nymphs are tiny, pear-shaped, sucking insects 1/16 to 3/8 inch (1.6 to 9.5 mm) long, usually found on undersides of leaves and new shoots. Some have wings, whereas others don't. Color, determined by species, includes pale green, pink, yellow, powdery gray, olive green, and black.

Life Cycle: For most of the season, females continuously give birth to live young. In fall, they lay eggs that over-winter on plants. These hatch in spring into females that don't need to mate to start producing offspring.

Host Plants: Most vegetables, fruits, and ornamentals fall prey to aphids.

Feeding Habits: Aphids suck plant sap, which distorts leaves, buds, and shoots, and may cause leaves and flowers to drop. Many species also ex-crete sweet, sticky honeydew. Some

aphid species can transmit plant viruses.

Prevention and Control: Aphids are usually sufficiently controlled by natural enemies, so before taking action, look for beneficials among the aphids. If necessary, spray a strong stream of water to knock aphids off plants, repeating once or twice. Spray narrow-range oil to control eggs overwintering on fruit trees; in fall, compost old vegetable plants. On growing plants, spray *Beauveria bassiana*, canola oil, garlic oil, or home-made garlic sprays, kaolin, or soap; as a last resort, spray cinnamon oil or narrow-range oil (on plants that tolerate oil sprays). For home orchards or in greenhouses where the cost is warranted, release purchased aphid midges (page 83).

Insect Predators: Aphid midges (page 83), braconid wasps (page 26) and other parasitic wasps, hoverflies (page 88), lacewings (page 92), and lady beetles (page 49).

Woolly Apple Aphid
Eriosoma lanigerum

Winged adult

Damage

Wingless adult

Adult actual size: 1/10 inch ▪

Range: Throughout North America.

Description: Adults are purplish brown, 1/10 inch (2.5 mm) long, and covered with white, cottony wax; nymphs are reddish brown with a bluish white coating.

Life Cycle: Females give birth to young "crawlers" throughout the growing season. The active crawlers move from tree to tree and from roots up to foliage or vice versa. In fall, the nymphs overwinter deep in the soil on apple roots.

Host Plants: Apple, hawthorn, mountain ash, pear, and quince.

Feeding Habits: Aphids feed on tree branches, covering them with cottony material and causing swollen galls on twigs. Feeding on roots causes nodules to develop. The aphids feeding on leaves produce honeydew, which leads to growth of sooty molds.

Prevention and Control: Root infestations do little damage to mature trees but can stunt or kill young trees. Where root-feeding colonies of this aphid have been a problem, plant resistant rootstock (MM series) and varieties, such as 'Northern Spy'. Prune out aphid colonies found on shoots in summer. Remove suckers at the base of trees and water sprouts on branches, and paint large pruning cuts to discourage aphids from colonizing these attractive sites. If necessary, spray trees thoroughly with canola oil, garlic oil, or insecticidal soap when crawlers are present in late spring to early summer; repeat if necessary in 2 weeks.

Insect Predators: Aphid midges (page 83), chalcid wasps (*Aphelinus mali*), hoverflies (page 88), lady beetles (page 49), lacewings (page 92).

Similar Insects: Mealybugs (page 106).

Beet Leafhopper
Circulifer tenellus

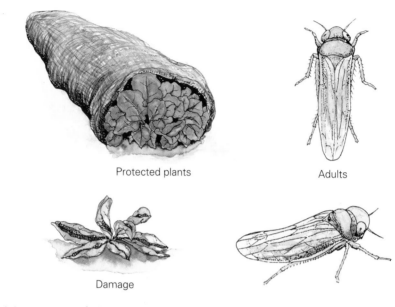

Protected plants

Adults

Damage

Adult actual size: ⅛ inch ▬

Range: Western North America, with similar species found elsewhere.

Description: Adults are wedge-shaped, pale green to brown, and ⅛ inch (3.2 mm) long, with dark, irregular markings. They hop and fly rapidly. Nymphs are pale green and look similar to adults without wings.

Life Cycle: Adults overwinter on host weeds. They move to crop plants in spring and lay eggs in the leaf veins and stems. The nymphs feed in the center of the host plants for up to 2 months. Starting in mid-May, the first generation of adults may fly long distances in large numbers to land on new host plants. There are one to three generations per year.

Host Plants: Beets and sugar beets, potatoes, tomatoes, and some weeds.

Feeding Habits: Adults and nymphs suck the sap of host plants. This alone doesn't usually cause serious damage; it's the transmission of the destructive, curly top virus in beets and yellows virus in tomatoes that does.

Prevention and Control: Plant early to avoid first-generation leafhoppers. Cover susceptible crops with floating row covers to prevent insects from reaching the plants. Remove nearby host weeds, such as greasewood, Russian thistle, salt bush, and wild mustard. Spray leafhoppers congregating on host weeds with *Beauveria bassiana*, canola oil, or soap. About 1 week before an infestation is expected, spray plants with kaolin to prevent leafhopper attack.

Insect Predators: Big-eyed bugs (*Geocoris* spp.) and other predator bugs, predatory flies.

Similar Insect: Potato leafhopper (opposite page).

Potato Leafhopper
Empoasca fabae

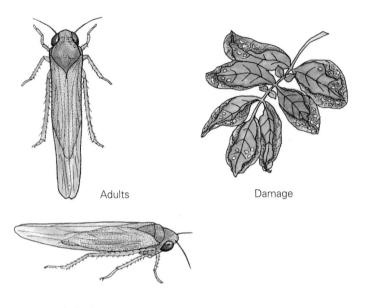

Adults

Damage

Adult actual size: ⅛ inch ■

Range: Eastern North America.

Description: Adults are wedge-shaped, green, and up to ⅛ inch (3.2 mm) long, with pale spots on their head and thorax. They hop and fly quickly. Nymphs are similar to adults but are paler and don't have wings.

Life Cycle: Adults survive over the winter on alfalfa and leguminous weeds in Florida and other Gulf states; they don't appear to overwinter in the North. The adults lay eggs in veins on the undersides of leaves. The nymphs feed for up to 2 weeks, mostly on the undersides of leaves. Adults migrate to northern areas during the growing season. There are two to four generations per year.

Host Plants: Apples, beans, celery, citrus, eggplant, peanuts, potatoes, and rhubarb.

Feeding Habits: Both adults and nymphs suck plant sap from leaf veins, causing brown spots in the leaves, distorted veins, and rolled edges ("hopperburn"). They also transmit viral diseases to host plants.

Prevention and Control: Cover plants with floating row covers to prevent leafhopper feeding. For serious infestations, spray *Beauveria bassiana*, canola oil, or soap; as a last resort, spray neem. About 1 week before an infestation is expected, spray plants with kaolin to prevent leafhopper attack.

Similar Insects: Beet leafhoppers (opposite page).

Spittlebugs, Froghoppers
CERCOPIDAE

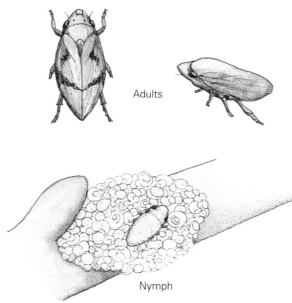

Adults

Nymph

Adult actual size: 1/8 to 1/4 inch ▬

Range: Various species throughout North America.

Description: Adults are brown or green, oval, and 1/8 to 1/4 inch (3.2 to 6.4 mm) long, with a blunt, froglike head. Some have yellow or red bands or spots on their wings. Nymphs are pale green and wingless and are surrounded by masses of frothy bubbles.

Life Cycle: Eggs overwinter in stems or crop stubble and hatch in spring. The newly hatched nymphs crawl onto new host plants and excrete a mass of bubbles. They feed inside the bubbles for up to 7 weeks, then molt to the adult stage. In August and September the adults lay overwintering eggs between the leaves and main stems of alfalfa, grasses, and weeds. There's one generation per year.

Host Plants: Corn, legumes and grain field crops, nursery plants, strawberries; many grasses and other weeds.

Feeding Habits: Both nymphs and adults suck plant sap. They usually aren't damaging, but in humid regions of the northeastern states and Pacific coast, they can be numerous enough to cause stunted or weakened plants.

Prevent and Control: Wash the masses of froth containing the nymphs off of plants with a strong spray of water; repeat if necessary.

Buffalo Treehopper
Stictocephala bisonia

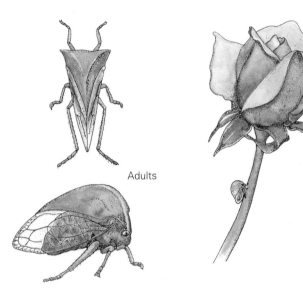

Adults

Adult actual size: ¼ inch ▬▬▬

Range: Throughout the United States and southern Canada.

Description: Adults are ¼ inch (6.4 mm) long and green, with a triangular wedge shape and a blunt head; they have a short projection on each "shoulder," giving them a shape like a buffalo. Nymphs are light green, similar to adults but with spines and without wings. Eggs are yellow and are laid in rows in C-shaped slits in bark.

Life Cycle: Eggs overwinter under tree bark and hatch in late spring. After hatching, the nymphs drop from the trees into the grass and weeds below to feed. They feed until August, then molt to the adult stage and move back into trees to lay eggs. There's one generation per year.

Host Plants: Eggs are laid in apple, cherry, peach, pear, and other fruit and ornamental trees; nymphs feed on corn, grasses, and many weeds.

Feeding Habits: Although treehopper feeding isn't damaging, the egg slits can seriously injure young fruit trees. Infested twigs are scaly and cracked, and grow poorly.

Prevention and Control: Prune out twigs with damaging eggs slits during winter pruning. Spray narrow-range oil on dormant deciduous trees to kill the overwintering eggs. Where local populations have built up to damaging levels, cultivate or apply mulches to control weeds under young fruit trees.

Mealybugs
PSEUDOCOCCIDAE

Female

Male

Colony

Adult actual size: 1/10 to 1/4 inch ▬▬

Range: Outdoors in the southern United States; throughout North America in greenhouses.

Description: Adult females are oval, segmented, 1/10 to 1/4 inch (2.5 to 6.4 mm) long, and pink or yellow; they're covered by white, cottony tufts. Long-tailed mealybugs (*Pseudococcus longispinus*) have long tail-like filaments. Males are minute, two-winged insects and are rarely seen. Nymphs are similar to females but smaller. Eggs are usually yellow ovals.

Life Cycle: Most species continue to develop over the winter in southern areas and in greenhouses. The females lay eggs inside protective white fluff, then the nymphs feed on host plants for 1 to 4 months. There are two to four generations per year.

Host Plants: Apples, avocados, citrus, grapes, and other fruit; potatoes, many ornamentals, and tropical foliage plants.

Feeding Habits: Both adult females and nymphs feed on plant sap and on the juice of leaves and fruit. They may cause leaves to turn yellow and fruit to drop prematurely. They also excrete sticky honeydew, which supports the growth of sooty molds.

Prevention and Control: Wash mealybugs and honeydew from plants with a strong spray of water or insecticidal soap. If necessary, spray canola oil, kaolin, or as a last resort, narrow-range oil (for plants that tolerate it) or neem. Release mealybug destroyers (page 53) in tropical greenhouses or on citrus or grapes.

Insect Predators: Mealybug destroyer (page 53), which is sold commercially, and parasitic wasps.

Similar Insects: Mealybug destroyer larvae (page 53), woolly apple aphids (page 101).

Brown Soft Scale
Coccus hesperidum

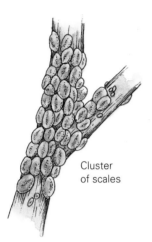

Cluster
of scales

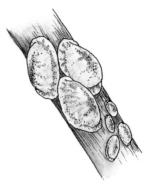

Female scales

Adult actual size: ⅕ inch ▬

Range: Southern United States; in greenhouses through North America.

Description: Adult females are smooth, oval, brown, flattened, and up to ⅕ inch (5.1 mm) long. Nymphs are similar but smaller and almost transparent. Both can be difficult to see on leaf veins and twigs. Adult males are tiny, two-winged insects.

Life Cycle: Scales remain on plants over winter months, reproducing very slowly. As weather warms, the females resume giving birth to a couple of nymphs each day. The nymphs move close by, then settle to feed. They mature into adults in about 2 months. There are two to six generations per year.

Host Plants: Citrus and other tropical and subtropical fruit; also a wide range of foliage plants and greenhouse ornamentals.

Feeding Habits: Scales suck plant sap from leaf veins, stems, and twigs. They excrete large amounts of honeydew, which supports the growth of sooty molds.

Prevention and Control: Grow pollen and nectar plants to attract beneficial insects. Spray plants with water to wash off honeydew, or spray with insecticidal soap, which also controls some nymphs (it has little effect on adults). Spray narrow-range oils on plants that tolerate oil sprays; on citrus, spray in fall or when developing fruit won't be affected. In summer, put affected houseplants outdoors, where native predators generally control the scale.

Insect Predators: Lady beetles (page 49) and parasitic wasps (*Microterys flavus* and *Metaphycus luteolus*).

California Red Scale
Aonidiella aurantii

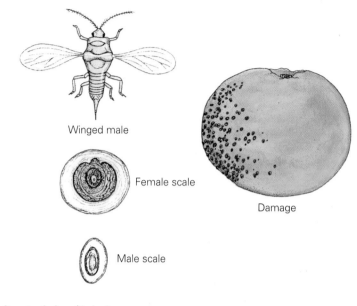

Winged male

Female scale

Male scale

Damage

Adult actual size: 1/12 inch ■

Range: Arizona, California, and Texas; similar species throughout citrus-growing regions.

Description: Adult females look like round, reddish brown bumps, 1/12 inch (2.1 mm) across, with a small dimple at the center. Adult males are tiny, two-winged insects that only live for a few hours. Nymphs are minute and brown, with a white, waxy covering.

Life Cycle: All stages spend winter on trees; reproduction never completely stops but becomes very slow in winter. In spring the females reproduce at a higher rate again, giving birth to several tiny "crawlers" each day. These move around for several hours until they find a suitable site, where they settle to feed. The females mature to adults in 2½ to 3½ months, while males mature to adults in 1 to 2 months. There are three to six generations per year.

Host Plants: Citrus; occasionally figs, grapes, walnuts, and other trees.

Feeding Habits: California red scale is a major pest of citrus. Adults and nymphs suck plant juices from all parts of trees, including fruit. Their saliva contains a toxic substance, which causes leaves and fruits to turn yellow or develop yellow spots. With serious infestations, branches die back, and trees may be seriously weakened.

Prevention and Control: Grow pollen and nectar plants to attract parasitic wasps. Where parasitic wasps aren't sufficiently controlling the scales, spray canola oil or narrow-range oil in fall or when developing citrus fruit won't be damaged.

Insect Predators: Various chalcid wasps (*Aphytis melinus, A. lingnanensis,* and *Prospaltella perniciosi*); *A. melinus* is sold commercially.

San Jose Scale
Quadraspidiotus perniciosus

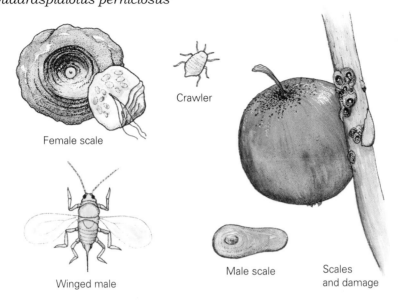

Female scale

Crawler

Winged male

Male scale

Scales
and damage

Adult actual size: 1/12 inch ▪

Range: United States and southern Canada.

Description: Adult females are round, gray to black bumps, 1/12 inch (2.1 mm) across, with a darker knob in the center; they have soft yellow bodies under the gray covering. Males are tiny, two-winged insects. Nymphs are tiny and yellowish. When born, they have legs and move around; they molt to an inactive stage that resembles a tiny yellow sac attached to bark or leaves.

Life Cycle: Partly grown nymphs overwinter on tree bark; at this stage the scale is sooty black. They resume feeding in spring when tree sap starts flowing. They mature about the time trees are in bloom. Females give birth to nymphs, which move around for a short time, then settle on bark or leaves to feed. Later generations also move onto fruit to feed. There are two to six generations per year.

Host Plants: Apples, cherries, peaches, pears, pecans, and quince.

Feeding Habits: Adults and nymphs attach themselves to bark on twigs and branches to suck plant sap; they also feed on fruit. When colonies are numerous, the bark looks like it's encrusted with a layer of gray ashes. Leaves and fruit have red spots and, if scale populations are allowed to reach high numbers, their feeding may kill the trees.

Prevention and Control: Grow pollen and nectar plants to attract beneficial insects. Prune out and destroy scale-encrusted branches during winter pruning. Spray canola oil or narrow-range oil in early spring, just before blossoms open.

Insect Predators: Lady beetles (page 49), and many parasitic wasps (*Aphytis proclia, Prospaltella aurantii,* and others).

Whiteflies
ALEYRODIDAE (Homoptera)

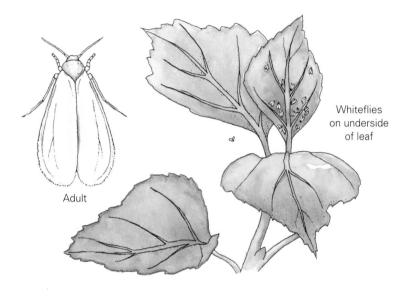

Adult

Whiteflies
on underside
of leaf

Adult actual size: 1/20 to 1/12 inch ■

Range: Outdoors in Southern and coastal United States; throughout North America in greenhouses.

Description: Adults are white and 1/20 to 1/12 inch (1.3 to 2.1 mm) long; their wings are covered with powdery white scales. Nymphs are translucent, flattened, legless scales, up to 1/30 inch (0.8 mm) long. Eggs are tiny gray or yellowish cones.

Life Cycle: Females lay eggs on the undersides of leaves. Tiny, mobile nymphs hatch in 3 to 4 days, and feed for 2 to 3 weeks before molting to the adult stage. There are many overlapping generations per year; reproduction continues year-round in greenhouses and warm regions.

Host Plants: Citrus, cucumbers, melons, squash, tomatoes; also other fruit and vegetables as well as ornamentals and some weeds.

Feeding Habits: Both adults and nymphs suck plant sap and can weaken or stunt plants. They excrete honeydew onto foliage below, which supports the growth of sooty molds. Whiteflies can also spread some viral diseases.

Prevention and Control: Hang yellow sticky traps near tops of plants to catch adult whiteflies. Vacuum adults from plants, using a handheld vacuum. To control nymphs, spray *Beauveria bassiana*, garlic oil, insecticidal soap, or jojoba oil; as a last resort, spray cinnamon oil or neem. Promptly shred and compost infested crop residue at the end of harvest, and remove host weeds.

Insect Predators: Parasitic wasps (*Encarsia* spp. and *Eretmocerus* spp.) and the lady beetle *Delphastus catalinae* are sold for use in greenhouses.

Pear Psylla
Cacopsylla pyricola

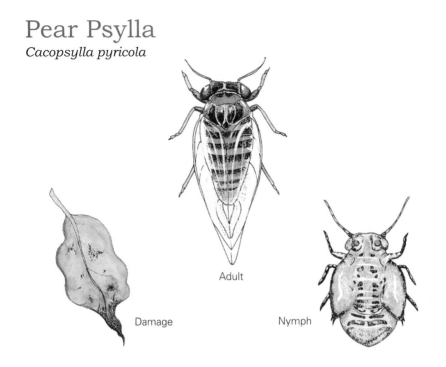

Adult

Damage

Nymph

Adult actual size: 1/10 inch ■

Range: Eastern United States and the Pacific Northwest; similar species distributed elsewhere.

Description: Adults are greenish or reddish brown and 1/10 inch (2.5 mm) long, with green or red markings and transparent wings. Young nymphs are yellow with red eyes; later stages are green. Eggs are white to yellow and pear-shaped.

Life Cycle: Adults overwinter under tree bark or other protected sites, emerging in early spring to lay eggs in bark and around buds. The eggs can take up to a month to hatch. Nymphs feed on stems and leaves for a month before molting to the adult stage. Eggs of later generations are laid on leaves. There are three to five generations per year.

Host Plants: Pears and quince.

Feeding Habits: Nymphs and adults suck sap from leaves and feed on fruit. They excrete large amounts of honeydew, which supports the growth of sooty molds. Infested leaves develop brown spots and may drop off of plants. Fruits are scarred and buds may fail to develop.

Prevention and Control: Attract earwigs, which are important predators, by stuffing crumpled newspaper or burlap in crotches of trees to provide shelters. Avoid vigorous growth caused by overfertilizing trees. Prune out water sprouts (suckers). Apply narrow-range oil in early spring just before buds break to kill adults and repel females from laying eggs. Spray water or use insecticidal soap sprays to reduce high numbers of nymphs and to wash off honeydew, or spray canola oil. Spray kaolin, starting at bud break.

Insect Predators: European earwigs (page 118); lacewings (page 92); parasitic wasps, including chalcid wasps (*Trechnites insidiosus*); predatory bugs (*Anthocoris* spp., *Deraeocoris brevis*).

Thrips
THRIPIDAE

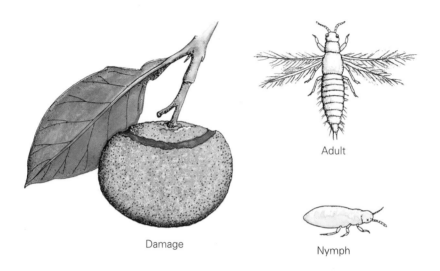

Damage

Adult

Nymph

Adult actual size: 1/50 to 1/25 inch ▪

Range: Many species throughout North America.

Description: Adults are yellow to brown, elongated insects that are 1/50 to 1/25 inch (0.6 to 1 mm) long, with fringed, straplike wings; they move very quickly and hide in crevices in foliage. Nymphs are lighter colored and lack wings. Eggs are inserted into plant tissue.

Life Cycle: Adults of most species overwinter in debris or cracks in bark. When they emerge, females lay eggs. Nymphs feed for up to 3 weeks, then molt to the adult stage. There are 5 to 15 generations per year; they reproduce year-round in greenhouses.

Host Plants: Cabbage, cucumbers, onions, and most garden plants and trees; citrus and other tree fruit.

Feeding Habits: Thrips suck juices, causing leaves to appear speckled or streaked with silver. Flowers are distorted and blotched or streaked with white or brown. Egg laying causes fruit blemishes. Some species spread tomato-spotted wilt virus.

Prevention and Control: Spray fruit trees with narrow-range oils on bark, or spray kaolin weekly before blossoms open. In greenhouses, use bright yellow or blue sticky traps to catch adults. On onions, spray kaolin, starting before an infestation is expected. On other plants, spray insecticidal soap, canola oil, garlic oil, or homemade garlic spray. As a last resort, spray *Beauveria bassiana*, cinnamon oil, or pyrethrins. Avoid mowing flowering plants in orchards during fruit bloom because this drives thrips up into trees.

Insect Predators: Lacewings (page 92), lady beetles (page 49), minute pirate bugs (page 94); predatory mites (*Amblyseius cucumeris* and others) are sold for use in greenhouses.

Periodical Cicada
Magicicada septendecim

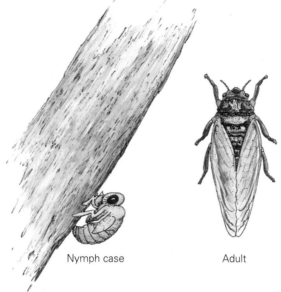

Nymph case   Adult

Adult actual size: 1½ inches ▬▬▬▬▬▬▬▬

Range: Eastern United States.

Description: Adults are brown to black, with wedge-shaped bodies, up to 1½ inches (3.8 cm) long; they have large heads, orange legs, and transparent wings. The males make a very loud, shrill, buzzing sound in the heat of the day. Nymphs resemble brown ants when young; later they're brown to black and stout-bodied. Eggs are inserted in slits in bark.

Life Cycle: Periodical cicadas spend most of their lives underground in the nymph stage, which lasts 13 to 17 years, depending on the species. Between May and July of the emergence year, the entire population of nymphs emerges from the soil, crawls up a nearby tree, and molts to the adult stage. The females lay eggs in slits in bark, and the eggs hatch in 6 weeks. The newly hatched nymphs drop to the soil and burrow down to the root zone, where they stay for many years.

Host Plants: Apple and many deciduous trees and shrubs.

Feeding Habits: Nymphs feed underground on tree roots, and adults suck sap from limbs and twigs, but neither activity causes noticeable damage. Instead, it's the process of slitting the bark and laying eggs in punctures in the wood that damages and even kills branch tips. In emergence years, when the entire population is in the adult stage and laying eggs from June to July, young trees can be seriously damaged.

Prevention and Control: In expected local emergence years, cover young or small trees with netting from May to mid-July to prevent egg laying. (Note that the last huge brood of 17-year cicadas in the northeastern United States was in1987; therefore expect another large brood in 2004.) Attract beneficial insects and birds, which all prey on cicadas.

Field Cricket

Gryllus assimilis

Adult

Adult actual size: ¾ to 1 inch ▬▬▬▬▬

Range: Throughout North America.

Description: Adults are brown or black and ¾ to 1 inch (19.1 to 25.4 mm) long, with large hind legs for jumping; they have long antennae and wings folded flat against their sides. Nymphs are similar, but smaller and without wings.

Life Cycle: In the warmest southern areas both adults and nymphs overwinter; elsewhere, the eggs overwinter in the soil and hatch from late May to June. Nymphs feed on plants until molting to the adult stage in late July. Females lay eggs in the soil from August to early September. There are one to three generations per year.

Host Plants: Beans, cucumbers, melons, peas, squash, strawberries, and tomatoes.

Feeding Habits: Adults and nymphs both chew on seedlings, foliage, seed-heads, and flowers of vegetable crops, and feed in the fruits of strawberry and tomato. They usually aren't numerous enough to be damaging, although sometimes large populations damage crops in the Gulf states.

Prevention and Control: Cover tomato and strawberry beds with floating row covers while fruit is ripening. If enough crickets were present to damage crops, cultivate the soil in the fall to kill eggs and expose them to predators. As a last resort, spray *Beauveria bassiana*.

Grasshoppers, Locusts
LOCUSTIDAE

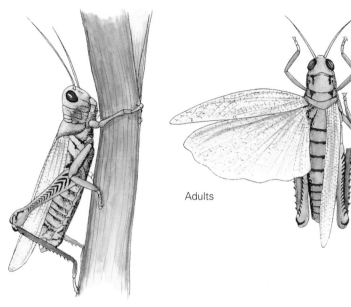

Adults

Adult actual size: 2 inches

Range: Hundreds of species throughout North America.

Description: Adults are brown, reddish yellow, or green and up to 2 inches (5.1 cm) long, with enlarged hind legs for jumping; forewings are dull colors, whereas hindwings may be brightly colored and are folded like fans. Nymphs are similar but smaller and without wings.

Life Cycle: Eggs of most species overwinter in the soil and hatch in spring; some species overwinter as nymphs. The nymphs feed on plants for 1 to 2 months before reaching the adult stage. The females of most species lay eggs in the soil from mid-August to September. There's one generation per year.

Host Plants: Various vegetable crops and weeds.

Feeding Habits: Grasshoppers feed during the day on leaves and stems. In most areas, they feed on weeds and don't noticeably damage garden crops. In local areas and in years where large numbers of locusts appear, they can defoliate corn and other plants.

Prevention and Control: In years when large populations are damaging, cover garden beds with floating row covers. A protozoan parasite of grasshoppers, *Nosema locustae,* and a fungal disease, *Beauveria bassiana*, are commercially available; these are most useful in a regional treatment program rather than for gardens. Cultivating soil in fall destroys eggs and exposes them to predators.

Insect Predators: Blister beetles (page 33), ground beetles (page 38), and parasitic flies.

Katydids

Microcentrum spp.

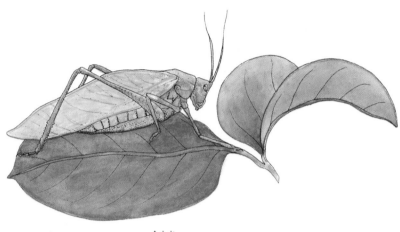

Adult

Adult actual size: 2 inches ▬▬▬▬▬▬▬▬▬▬▬▬

Range: Various species throughout North America.

Description: Adults are green, up to 2 inches (5.1 cm) long, with well-developed hind legs for jumping; they have large angular wings and very long antennae. Nymphs are similar but smaller and without wings. Eggs are grayish brown and flat, and are laid in double rows on twigs.

Life Cycle: Eggs overwinter on plants or in the soil. Nymphs feed on plants for 3 to 4 months before molting to the adult stage. There's one generation per year.

Host Plants: Citrus, willow, and other plants.

Feeding Habits: Both adults and nymphs feed on foliage, but they aren't present in large enough numbers to cause significant damage.

Praying Mantids
MANTIDAE

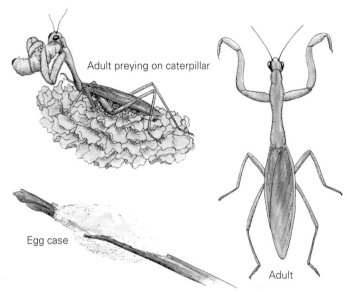

Adult preying on caterpillar

Egg case

Adult

Adult actual size: 2 to 3 inches

Range: Most of the United States and southern Canada.

Description: Adults of common species are elongated, green or brown, and up to 2 to 3 inches (5.1 to 7.6 cm) long. They have spiny front legs adapted for grasping and papery wings folded flat on the abdomen. Nymphs are similar, but smaller and without wings. Eggs are laid in large numbers inside light brown egg cases glued to stems or twigs.

Life Cycle: Eggs overwinter inside the protective cases. Nymphs hatch in spring and feed on other insects for most of the growing season before molting to the adult stage. There's one generation per year.

Feeding Habits: Newly hatched nymphs feed on small insects, whereas older nymphs and adults feed on larger insects, including bees, butterflies, caterpillars, flies, wasps, and each other. Because of their indiscriminate appetites, it isn't a good idea to buy eggs to release in gardens because the mantids prey on beneficial insects and butterflies as well as pests.

European Earwig
Forficula auricularia

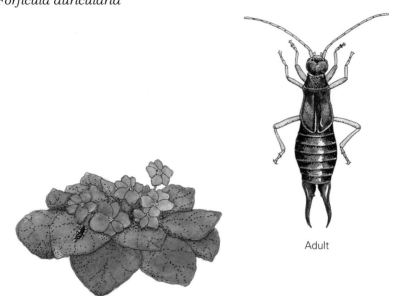

Adult

Adult actual size: ¾ inch ▬▬▬▬▬

Range: Throughout North America.

Description: Adults are elongated, ¾ inch (19.1 mm) long, and reddish brown, with short, leathery forewings; they have pincers on the tips of their abdomens. In males, the pincers are larger and curved; in females, they're short and straight. Nymphs look like adults, only they're smaller and paler. All stages hide during the day and are active at night. Eggs are white and round.

Life Cycle: Adults overwinter in nests in the soil, usually in pairs. Eggs are laid in the underground chambers in May and June. When the eggs hatch, the females tend the brood of nymphs, which return to the nest each night, until they can fend for themselves. They mature in August. There are one to three broods per year.

Host Plants: Many flowers, fruit trees, and garden plants.

Feeding Habits: Both adults and nymphs feed on decaying vegetable matter as well as flower petals, living leaves, pollen, and soft fruit. They also eat small insects such as aphids and pear psyllas. In damp and coastal regions, populations can be high enough to damage soft fruit and vegetables.

Prevention and Control: Earwigs are generally a nuisance because they fall out of hiding places in fruit and flowers. Where numbers are high and unacceptable damage is occurring, trap them by laying lengths of garden hose, hollow bamboo sticks, or rolls of corrugated cardboard in areas they frequent; in the morning, knock the earwigs out of the traps into a pail of soapy water. To attract them into fruit trees to eat aphids or pear psyllas, place crumpled newspaper or burlap in crotches of trees.

Insect Predator: Tachinid fly (*Triarthria septipennis*) (page 91).

Garden Symphylan

Scutigerella immaculata

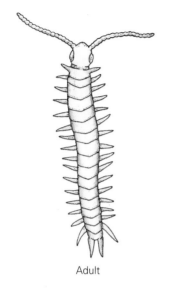

Adult

Adult actual size: ¼ inch ▬

Range: Throughout North America.

Description: Adults are slender, white, ¼ inch (6.4 mm) long, and flat; they have 12 pairs of legs and their antennae are one-third as long as their body. They move quickly. Immature stages are smaller and have fewer pairs of legs. Eggs are white and are laid in small clusters, up to a foot (30 cm) deep in the soil.

Life Cycle: Symphylans spend their lives in the soil. They overwinter deep in the soil and move up toward the surface in spring. They start laying eggs in spring and continue all summer. The eggs hatch in a month, and the nymphs feed on roots; they mature to adults in 45 to 60 days. They usually live in the top 6 to 12 inches (15 to 30 cm) of soil, but burrow deeper in hot weather. There are one to two generations per year.

Host Plants: Asparagus, beans, carrots, celery, cucumbers, lettuce, radishes, spinach, tomatoes, and other garden vegetables and ornamentals.

Feeding Habits: Adults and nymphs chew off fine roots and root hairs, leaving a blunt, scarred appearance. They gnaw small pits in larger roots and other underground parts of plants. When present in large enough numbers, their feeding can stunt plants and kill seedlings.

Prevention and Control: Where garden design allows it, flood the soil for 3 weeks in the summer to reduce symphylan numbers. Larger populations are found in soils with high levels of undecomposed crop debris; therefore clean up all crop debris and spread only well-aged compost on the soil. Soil solarization may be effective in suppressing symphylans in warm regions.

Insect Predator: Parasitic mite (*Pergamasus quisquiliarum*).

Millipedes DIPLOPODA
Centipedes CENTIPODA

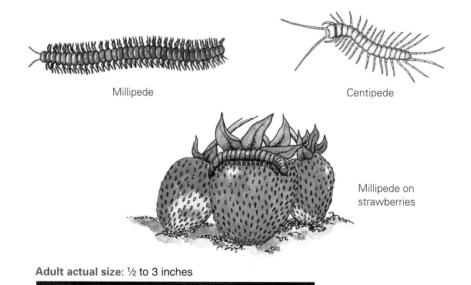

Millipede

Centipede

Millipede on strawberries

Adult actual size: ½ to 3 inches

Range: Throughout North America.

Description: Adults of both are slender, ½ to 3 inches (1.3 to 7.6 cm) long, with obvious segments; centipedes have one pair of legs per segment, and millipedes have two pairs of very short legs per segment. Centipedes move quickly when annoyed, and larger ones may even inflict a poisonous bite; millipedes coil up when disturbed. Younger stages of both are similar to adults but smaller. Eggs of both are laid in the soil.

Life Cycle: Both overwinter in the soil and live their lives on the surface of the soil or just below it. In spring, they start laying eggs; a few species of centipedes give birth to live young. As they grow, immature centipedes and millipedes add a segment with each molt until they reach maturity. Development can take 2 to 5 years for millipedes. There is one generation per year. Centipedes are long-lived, with some living up to 6 years.

Host Plants: Vegetables, strawberries (millipedes).

Feeding Habits: Millipedes feed mainly on decaying vegetable matter and occasionally on plant roots, seedlings, and soft fruit resting on the ground (such as strawberries or tomatoes). They usually aren't a serious problem. Centipedes are beneficial predators of slugs, fly pupae, and other soil-dwelling insects; they occasionally eat earthworms.

Prevention and Control: Where millipedes are damaging, take measures to dry out the soil, rake back decomposing mulches, stake up tomatoes, and remove hiding places around the garden, such as boards and garden debris. As a last resort, dust diatomaceous earth or wood ashes around affected plants or seedlings.

Similar Insects: Wireworms (page 48).

Rust Mites
ERIOPHYIDAE

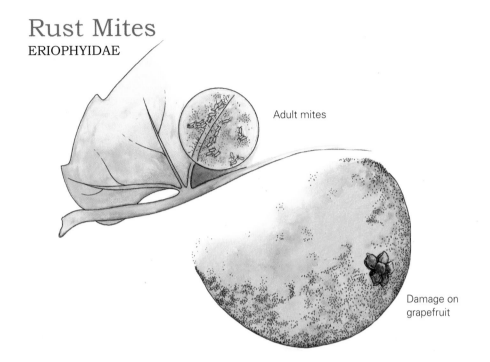

Adult mites

Damage on grapefruit

Adult actual size: 1/100 inch ı

Range: Throughout North America.

Description: Most rust mites are less than 1/100 inch (0.25 mm) long and can be seen only under magnification. They're straw-colored or tan and elongated, with two pairs of legs at the head end; nymphs are similar to adults but even smaller.

Life Cycle: Rust mites overwinter in cracks in bark or at the base of buds. In spring they move back onto flowers and leaves to feed and reproduce. One generation may take 7 to 10 days; there are many overlapping generations per year.

Host Plants: Apples, citrus, grapes, and other fruit; tomatoes and many other vegetables; ornamentals.

Feeding Habits: Rust mites feed on leaves, flowers, and the skin of fruits. Leaves may be silvery or streaked and may wilt or drop. Attacked fruit may be russeted, bronzed, or roughened, and rinds of citrus may crack. Some plants react to rust mite feeding by producing blisters or galls on leaves. In apple and other tree fruit, rust mites are beneficial because they provide an early alternate diet for the predatory mites that keep spider mite numbers in check.

Prevention and Control: Under organic management, rust mites are rarely a problem. If control is necessary, spray soap, kaolin, canola oil, or any sprays or dusts containing sulfur. Sulfur is very effective but also harms native predatory mites found on fruit trees; it's best used indoors for tomato russet mite on greenhouse tomatoes. Apply narrow-range oil with lime sulfur on dormant deciduous trees, after leaves drop in the fall or just before bud break.

Insect Predators: Predatory mites (*Typhlodromus* spp., *Zetzellia mali*).

Spider Mites
TETRANYCHIDAE

Adult

Mites and damage

Adult actual size: ⅟₇₅ to ⅟₅₀ inch ▮

Range: Throughout North America.

Description: Adults are barely visible, ⅟₇₅ to ⅟₅₀ inch (0.3 to 0.5 mm) long; they have eight legs and fine hairs on their bodies. Two-spotted spider mite (*Tetranychus urticae*) is pale green with a dark patch on each side; its overwintering form is brick red. Other common species are dark red. Nymphs look like adults but paler and with fewer pairs of legs. Eggs are minute, transparent ovals.

Life Cycle: Eggs or adult mites overwinter under bark or debris; feeding begins in early spring. There are many overlapping generations per year; reproduction continues year-round on greenhouse and indoor plants.

Host Plants: Apples, citrus, and other fruits; beans, cucumbers, eggplant, melons, tomatoes, and other vegetables; also houseplants and ornamentals.

Feeding Habits: Adults and nymphs pierce leaf cells and feed on the juices, usually from the underside of the leaves. Affected leaves are speckled with yellow, eventually becoming bronzed or silvery; leaves may turn yellow or brown and drop. Fine webbing may be present (not all species produce webbing).

Prevention and Control: Wash plants with water to remove mites. Mist plants daily to raise humidity, which suppresses mite reproduction. As a last resort, spray soap, garlic oil, kaolin, thyme oil, cinnamon oil, or canola oil on growing plants. On dormant fruit trees, apply narrow-range oil to control overwintering mites and eggs.

Insect Predators: Lady beetles (page 49), lacewings (page 92), minute pirate bugs (page 94), native predatory mites (*Typhlodromus* spp., *Zetzellia mali*), predator midges (*Feltiella* spp.); *T. occidentalis* is sold commercially.

Slugs and Snails
MOLLUSCA

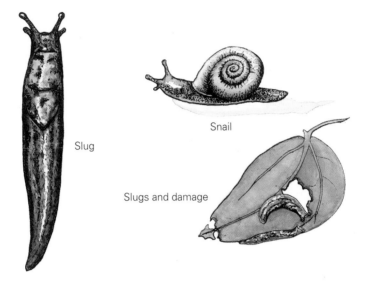

Slug

Snail

Slugs and damage

Adult actual size: ⅛ to 1 inch ▬▬▬▬▬▬

Range: Various species throughout North America.

Description: Adults are tan, gray, black, or brown mollusks with soft, slime-covered bodies; they move on a muscular foot beneath the body. Sizes range from ⅛ to 1 inch (3.2 to 25.4 mm) for common garden slugs and snails, and 4 to 6 inches (10 to 15 cm) for banana slugs. Snails have a coiled shell on their back. Eggs are clear and round, and are laid in jellylike masses.

Life Cycle: Adults lay eggs in soil or under rocks or debris. The eggs hatch in 2 to 4 weeks. Slugs take 5 months to 2 years to reach maturity; most snails take 2 years to mature. Both overwinter in the soil and under garden debris.

Host Plants: Most tender plants and shrubs.

Feeding Habits: Both slugs and snails feed mainly on decaying organic matter, but they'll also feed on new shoots, seedlings, and other tender plant parts. They feed at night, scraping ragged holes in leaves and leaving a trail of slime. They hide during the day under boards or garden debris.

Prevention and Control: Water gardens in the morning rather than evening. Hand-pick slugs and snails at night or in wet weather. Lay boards, grapefruit rinds, or other covers on soil; lift during the day and destroy hiding slugs. Protect young seedlings by spreading a band of wood ashes, diatomaceous earth, or sharp sand beside rows. Wrap copper or zinc strips around tree or shrub trunks; metal strips can also be used around greenhouse benches or growing beds. Attract and drown slugs in containers set level with the soil surface and filled with beer or a mixture of yeast, sugar, and water.

Insect Predators: Ground beetles (page 38), rove beetles (page 44).

Sowbugs and Pillbugs
ISOPODA

Pillbugs

Sowbug

Adult actual size: ¼ to ⅝ inch ▬▬▬▬

Range: Throughout North America.

Description: Adults are gray or brown, oval, somewhat flattened, and ¼ to ⅝ inch (6.4 to 15.9 mm) long; they have many overlapping segments and seven pairs of short legs, which are barely visible under their armored body. They avoid dry conditions and are active at night. Pillbugs can curl into a tight ball when disturbed. Nymphs look like adults but are smaller and paler.

Life Cycle: Both adults and immature stages overwinter in protected, damp sites, under rocks and debris. They become active in spring. The female lays eggs in a brood pouch under her body. She protects the eggs and young nymphs for 3 months or more until they can take care of themselves. There are one to two generations per year. Individuals can live up to 3 years.

Host Plants: Any tender seedlings or plants.

Feeding Habits: Both sowbugs and pillbugs feed on decaying and damaged plant matter in damp conditions. They also feed on emerging seedlings and tender roots and in soft fruit lying on the ground—especially if damaged by birds or insects. Sowbugs and pillbugs found in homes get there by accident, usually because they've wandered in under doors or through other openings.

Prevention and Control: Drain wet areas. Remove piles of debris or boards from around garden areas and buildings. Delay applying mulches around crops until plants are well established. Water gardens in the morning to allow soil surfaces to dry before evening. Don't overwater seedlings. Where populations are damaging, dust diatomaceous earth, silica gel, or boric acid along rows of seedlings. Make traps by spreading sticky glue on pieces of paper folded in half; set them out like pup tents, with the sticky side down.

Diseases

An Overview

Plant diseases can be hard to diagnose compared to insect problems. After all, potato beetles are quite visible, but it takes a microscope to see a virus or most fungi and bacteria. Diagnosing a disease is also difficult because symptoms can look like those that excessive cold or heat, sun scald, high salt levels, nutrient deficiencies, waterlogged soils, low light levels, and other problems can cause.

If you maintain well-drained fertile soil, enriched with compost, and take sensible precautions, such as cleaning up crop debris after harvest, you won't see many diseases in the garden. If, however, a disease problem recurs year after year or is especially damaging, you would be wise to learn what it is, how it spreads, and how to manage it and prevent it in the future.

As with any type of plant problem, it's essential to correctly identify the problem. The table "Common Diseases of Garden Vegetables" on pages 138–141 should help you with this identification and get you started.

Learning about the host plants and life cycle of the organisms causing the disease is the next step. Below are descriptions of the main types of disease-causing organisms in plants—these are called plant *pathogens.*

Bacteria

Bacteria are microscopic, single-celled organisms. Each bacteria cell reproduces by dividing in two. The bacteria that attack plants produce toxic compounds that kill the plant cells; the bacteria then use the contents of the plant cells for their own growth. Plants react to such attacks by triggering the death of cells around the bacterial infection, which isolates the bacteria colony from the rest of the plant and causes the characteristic spots, or shothole appearance, in leaves as the dead tissue drops out.

Bacteria enter plants through openings such as pores and wounds. Some cause wilting, as the multiplying bacteria kill the cells in the vascular system or plug it with masses of bacteria. Others cause spots, rots, and blights, which are all symptoms of dying plant tissue. Some bacteria cause plant tissue to grow abnormally into galls.

Fungi

Fungi cause the majority of plant diseases. As a group, these microscopic organisms are distinguished by their lack of chlorophyll, which means that they can't make food for themselves and so must rely on getting their nutrients from other organisms or organic matter. Some fungi, called *saprophytes,* live only on dead organic matter. They break down organic material in compost piles and soils into forms that other organisms can use. Most pathogenic (disease-causing) fungi parasitize living plant tissue, but some can live off of both living and dead plant material. Many live all summer in plants, then they overwinter on dead crop debris.

Fungi have cells made up of branching filaments, or minute tubes, called *hyphae.* A group of hyphae form a *mycelium,* which typically looks like a velvety spot or coating on a leaf. Some fungi reproduce asexually from sections of hyphae called *sclerotia,* whereas others make reproductive units, called *spores.* Sclerotia are generally quite easy to see, whereas spores are usually microscopic.

Most fungi can make different types of spores to guarantee their survival in almost any situation. In general, asexual spores are produced in the best growing conditions. They are released from a special structure, generally called a "fruiting body." They're carried by wind, rain, animals, and sometimes people to new sites, where they germinate if temperature and humidity are right. Furthermore, pathogenic fungi that spend most of their life cycle on roots and debris underground commonly produce swimming spores, or *zoospores.* Fungi that attack plant parts above ground may also produce swimming spores that navigate through dew and rain on the leaves.

> Some pathogenic fungi are also capable of forcing their way into plant cells by exuding enzymes that kill the cells.

Spores that can remain dormant until they encounter good germinating conditions and an appropriate host are called *resting spores.* Fungi typically produce them in fall in preparation for winter. Some dormant spores can remain viable, or capable of germination, for years.

When spores germinate, they send out a tube, or *hypha.* This usually enters the plant through a wound or natural opening. Some pathogenic fungi are also capable of forcing their way into plant cells by exuding enzymes that kill the cells or by using a strong hypha tip that can bore into plant tissue.

Fungi cause wilting when mycelium plugs the plant's vascular system or destroys the cell walls. They also cause rots and blights as they release toxins that break down cells in seeds, roots, and fruits. Infected plants can appear *chlorotic* (yellowed) or have other discolorations caused as the plant cells die and as photosynthesis and other metabolic activity is restricted. Some fungi cause *galls* and *smuts,* which are abnormal growths of plant tissue.

Nematodes

Nematodes are actually a group of unsegmented roundworms. They range in size from microscopically small to several inches long. Some species break down organic matter, some attack insects, and others attack plants. The plant-feeding species are usually discussed with plant diseases because their mode of action and ways to control them are similar. Like fungi, some species of nematodes have a dormant state that can remain in the soil for many years.

The mouthparts of nematodes pierce plant tissue. Some species excrete a digestive juice that rots cells before they feed. Others exude substances that stimulate nearby plant cells to enlarge or multiply abnormally. They also carry many viral diseases. But even when they don't carry disease, the small holes they make allow other diseases to enter the plant.

Although they can move, nematodes are so tiny that they rarely travel more than a foot (30 cm) through the soil. They're usually introduced to a piece of land by infected planting stock, infested soil, or running water.

Viruses

Viruses are minute parasitic bits of genetic material (DNA or RNA) with a protein casing. Their genetic material causes host cells to make more viruses. Viruses can multiply only in a living host. Some viruses can remain inactive but viable for as long as 50 years in dead plant material.

Many viruses are carried by insects, which are then called *vectors*. Seeds may carry viruses, and infected propagating stock is certain to produce infected plants. Viruses can also be spread from one plant to the next on knives, equipment, and tools.

Three symptoms of viral infection are yellowing or other discoloration, stunting, and malformations. Mosaic patterns, ring spots, and a uniform pale color are all symptoms of infection. Stunting can affect a whole plant or one part, such as a leaf, branch, ear, or other part. Malformations include leaf rolls, puckering, and "shoestring" leaves (extremely narrow, twisted leaves).

Common Disorders of Vegetable Crops

CONDITION	CROP	SYMPTOMS	CAUSE
Black heart	Beet, turnip	Darkening in center, sometimes hollow	Boron deficiency; sometimes potassium or phosphorus deficiency
	Potato	Same	Lack of oxygen
	Celery	Same	Fluctuating soil moisture; calcium deficiency
Blasting	All flowers	Buds or flowers drop prematurely	Soil too wet or dry
	Onion	Leaf tips bleach, brown, and wither	Bright light after cloudy, wet conditions
Blossom-end rot	Tomato, pepper, cucurbits	Dark, sunken area at blossom end of fruit	Dry conditions after wet; calcium deficiency
Cracked stem	Celery	Stem cracks	Boron deficiency
Hollow heart	Crucifers	Hollow stem	Boron deficiency
Sunscald	Tomato, pepper	White area appears, blisters before secondary rotting occurs	Excessive loss of foliage; heavy pruning or trellising of tomatoes
Tipburn	Lettuce, potato	Leaf tips brown	Bright light after cloudy, wet conditions; potassium deficiency; calcium imbalance

Using the Entries

Diseases listed in this chapter are the most common in the United States and southern Canada. They are categorized by the type of organisms (bacteria, fungi, nematodes, or viruses) that causes them, and alphabetized by common name(s) within each category. The scientific names are also given for each organism.

Some diseases affect so many plants that a full list of possible hosts would fill the page; therefore, the most commonly affected plants or plant families are given. This information is important not only for identifying the disease but also for planning crop rotations.

Descriptions of both symptoms and signs of diseases are included. Symptoms are effects of the pathogen, such as wilting, yellowing, or stunted growth. A sign is the visible presence of the organism that caused the disease, such as the large galls of corn smut.

Diagnosing the cause of a plant disease is difficult because symptoms vary with type, age, and health of the host plant; the stage of the disease; and environmental conditions. Spots caused by the same organism can look large and distinct on some plants, but small and vaguely defined in others. If you have trouble diagnosing a disease that's causing serious damage, contact your local extension office or diagnostic laboratory for assistance.

The Spread of Disease

Plant pathogens spread in various ways. Spores and bacteria may be blown on the wind or carried on splashes of water. Many pathogens can be moved from plant to plant mechanically, meaning that animals, tools, equipment, and even gardeners that have come into contact with infected plant material can spread the pathogens. Insects can also spread some diseases by carrying the pathogens in their saliva from one plant to the next. As they feed on the sap, they release the pathogens into the new host. For any disease, knowing the life cycle of the pathogen and the way it spreads can help you avoid bringing it into your garden and spreading it further.

Disease Resistance

Plants are immune to many diseases because the pathogen simply can't attack a particular host. For example, potatoes are immune to attack from corn smut fungi and corn is immune to late blight. In contrast, *resistance* means that the plant may have some degree of susceptibility to the pathogen, but it's able to fight against it. Many varieties of garden vegetables have been bred for resistance to certain common diseases.

Resistance can be *genetic,* meaning it's an inherited characteristic of the plant, or *induced,* meaning that the plant's immune system has been activated to fight off infection. Plants that have been bred for resistance may have physical characteristics, such as a thicker leaf cuticle (the exterior surface of the leaf) or woodier stems, which repel the action of germinating spores.

Plants can also be selected for their strong immune response that helps them tolerate diseases well enough to produce a useful crop. Some plants can quickly mobilize a cell response that neutralizes invading pathogens. This response causes the cells around an infected area to die. The layer of dead cells isolates the infection from the rest of the plant and causes the corky spots or holes in leaves that are characteristic symptoms of some diseases. Other plant responses to infection are uncannily like our own immune system because exposure to a pathogen activates genes that cause the plant to become resistant to later attacks.

The environmental conditions a particular plant is growing in also helps determine whether or not it can resist infection. For example, a variety with cuticles thick enough to repel germinating spores when it's growing in good conditions might still be infected in low-light conditions when the leaf growth is weaker and the cuticle thinner. Plant nutrition, watering, light levels, and other conditions also contribute to disease resistance.

Prevention and Control

Before any disease can occur, the three elements of the "disease triangle" must be present: a susceptible plant, the disease-causing agent (pathogen), and favorable environmental conditions for growth of the pathogen. A disease can't develop if even one of these elements is absent. Most prevention and control measures for managing plant diseases are based on removing one or more of these elements.

For example, susceptible plants can be removed from the equation by planting resistant or immune crops. Pathogens can be removed from the equation by removing infected plants from the garden. Although gardeners can't control the weather, they can make environmental conditions unfavorable for pathogens by avoiding overhead watering, pruning to promote good air circulation, and taking other precautions.

Prevention

Healthy plants. Start with certified disease-free seeds, tubers, and plants where possible, and give them the best care. Of course, fertile soil, fed with compost and enriched with high levels of organic matter, is the key to growing healthy plants that resist infection. It's important to correct any problems with soil drainage. Reduce the length of time plant leaves are wet by installing drip irrigation, watering only at the base of the plant, or using sprinklers only in the morning so that leaves have a chance to dry before evening. Pruning and spacing plants to increase air circulation between plants also allows leaves to dry faster and thwarts the spread of many fungi. Plant the right plant in the right spot—for instance, a shade-loving plant won't do well in full sun and in such a weakened state will be more susceptible to attack.

Resistant varieties. Whenever possible, choose disease resistant or tolerant varieties when buying seeds, tubers, transplants, and nursery stock. Read descriptions in seed catalogs to find varieties that have disease-fighting characteristics. Tomato varieties are commonly labeled with V, F, or N (sometimes all three): The "V" means verticillium-resistant, "F" means fusarium wilt–resistant, and "N" means root-knot nematode–resistant. For other types of plants, look for descriptions such as "resistant to powdery mildew," "tolerant of anthracnose," or "scab-resistant."

Preserve natural enemies. Finished compost is a rich source of beneficial soil fungi, bacteria, and other organisms that help protect plants from disease. These naturally occurring microorganisms are invisible, but they're vital in protecting plants. Some suppress pathogens in the soil by producing compounds that inhibit their growth. Others actively attack pathogens and some colonize plant roots, which keeps pathogens out. Airborne fungi, yeasts, and other microorganisms also live on the surface of leaves and protect them from attack. Because sprays aimed at controlling pathogens can also kill these beneficial microorganisms, it may be good to avoid using such sprays unless they're absolutely necessary.

Cultural Controls

Remove alternate hosts. For example, some rusts can't complete a life cycle without a specific, alternate host plant, such as cedar for cedar-apple rust or juniper for pear-trellis rust. If there are a few of the alternate host plants in the area, removing them can reduce or eliminate the disease locally. If there are many alternate hosts in the area, then it may be hard to have an effect.

Crop rotation. A way to reduce the spread of soil-borne pathogens is to avoid planting susceptible plants in infected soil until infective spores die off. Because some pathogens can live in the soil for a couple of years, it's necessary to grow nonsusceptible plants in those soils during that time. Crop rotation is also a preventive measure to ensure that pathogens that might be present at low levels don't have a chance to build up to damaging levels.

With that in mind, though, crop rotation in a home garden is less effective than in a larger area because it's hard to rotate the susceptible crop a great distance from the initial site of infection. It helps to use permanent raised beds, especially if coupled with careful sanitation measures. Where the whole garden is plowed or tilled at one time, infected soil is spread around.

To rotate crops effectively, it's important to know which plant belongs in each family so that you don't mistakenly plant related crops one after the other. For example, tomatoes, potatoes, eggplant, and peppers are all in the same family (Solanaceae), and cabbage, cauliflower, broccoli, mustard, radishes, turnips, Chinese cabbages, and brussels sprouts are all related (Cruciferae).

When planting herbs and annual flowers in the garden, they should also be considered in the crop rotation because many belong to the same families as garden vegetables. For example, sweet alyssum is a member of the cabbage family (Cruciferae), and dill and coriander are in the same family as carrots and celery (Umbelliferae).

Physical Controls

Sanitation. The sources of disease infection (*inoculum*) around the garden can be reduced or eliminated by cleaning up crop debris and pulling out infected plants. Where allowing infected plants to remain could jeopardize the whole crop, it's advisable to pull the whole plant, including roots and sometimes the surrounding soil, and remove it from the garden. Whether or not infected plant material can be composted depends on what the organism is and how hot the composting process is likely to be. In some cases it's advisable to burn, bury deeply, or discard infected plants in the garbage rather than compost them.

Cleaning tools and implements, as well as shoes and hands, is an especially important sanitation measure when moving from infected plants or soils to uninfected areas. Also, avoid moving from plant to plant when humidity is high enough to leave a film of moisture on leaves, as diseases can be spread quickly this way.

Removing weeds in the garden and from nearby areas can help manage some diseases if the weeds are likely to harbor diseases affecting crop plants. This is most effective if there are very few such disease host plants in the area. Some plant diseases are spread so widely on the wind that host plant removal doesn't contribute to control.

Barriers. If a disease is spread by sucking insects, such as aphids or leafhoppers, screening out the insect carrier can exclude the disease. Sprays of kaolin clay (discussed in more detail on page 17) can be used to coat leaves and fruit with a fine barrier of clay, which foils the leafhoppers and other insects and prevents some pathogenic fungi from attacking.

Hot-water treatments. Hot-water treatments can be used to kill some pathogens carried in certain types of seeds. Some commercial seeds are already heat treated; gardeners can also use hot water to treat their own seeds. Follow recommendations given under the disease entries for exact temperatures and timing.

Solarization. Solarization involves covering soil with clear plastic during the summer months to heat it 6 to 8 inches deep to temperatures that kill pathogens. Solarization has been shown to keep soil-borne pathogens—such as verticillium, fusarium, southern blight, and nematodes—in check for 2 to 3 years. First, remove all vegetation, rake the soil smooth, soak it well with water, then cover with clear plastic stretched tight over the surface. A clear plastic tarp or 4-mil-thick plastic sheeting can be used. Bury the edges of the plastic 6 inches deep to achieve a good seal. Leave in place for 6 to 14 weeks in the hottest part of the summer. This works best in the warmest regions. In northern regions, use two layers of plastic with a thin air space between them to increase the heating effect, and leave the soil covered for the maximum length of time.

Biological Controls

Fermented compost tea. The many beneficial microorganisms found in compost can be used effectively as a disease treatment by steeping compost in water to make a tea. It has been found that the tea is more effective as a disease control when it's allowed to ferment. Use finished compost and steep 1 part compost to 5 to 8 parts water for 3 to 7 days (2-week fermentations may be more effective cn some diseases). Strain the liquid and filter it through a fine screen before putting it in the sprayer. Apply the tea to the lower part of the plant stem and around the roots for soil-borne diseases or onto leaves for powdery mildews.

Commercial products. Various naturally occurring fungi (e.g., *Ampelomyces quisqualis*) and bacteria (e.g., *Bacillus subtilis, Pseudomonas* spp.) are becoming increasingly available to buy. Depending on the product, they're applied to leaves, roots, or branches to suppress plant diseases. However, these products are probably more useful for commercial growers than home gardeners, who may find them too expensive for use on the few plants that might benefit.

Fungicides

As with any type of treatment, it's important to make sure that the problem is correctly identified and that treatment is really necessary before using sprays or dusts. Unfortunately, these must be applied before pathogens infect plants to provide a protective barrier—once plants have been infected, they can't be cured by such treatments (though healthy plants can fight some types of infections). Most sprays and dusts can also harm beneficial microorganisms that help protect plants from pathogens. Fermented compost tea sprays are an exception because they actually add beneficial microorganisms.

Water. In the case of powdery mildew, the presence of water on the leaf stops spores from germinating. Spraying leaves thoroughly on both sides with plain water in midday several times a week can provide satisfactory control. This isn't a useful method where plants are also susceptible to other diseases that would develop in wet conditions.

Milk. Fresh milk sprays made from 1 part milk and 9 parts water and sprayed twice a week have been shown to suppress powdery mildew of cucumber and zucchini. It's thought that the milk may work by preventing the fungus from invading, or it may boost the plant's immune system by providing nutrients.

Oils. Narrow-range oils are mainly insecticidal, but they can be used to control plant diseases such as powdery mildew. Mix according to product instructions for use on plants during the growing season.

Botanical extracts. Garlic sprays and essential oils from some plants have some disease-suppressing properties. These are becoming increasingly available in commercial products.

Baking soda. Homemade baking soda sprays are typically recommended to control powdery mildew. A common recipe calls for mixing 1 teaspoon of baking soda, 1 drop of liquid soap, and 2 quarts of water. A spray of baking soda and oil can also be used to control powdery mildew: Mix 1 tablespoon baking soda, 1 tablespoon narrow-range oil, 1 drop of detergent, and 1 gallon of water. Commercial baking soda sprays are also available.

Sulfur. Both sprays and dusts containing sulfur are available to control plant diseases caused by fungi. Sulfur binds with the spores to prevent them from germinating. To be effective, the sulfur must be present on all susceptible leaves before the fungi invade; therefore, it must be used at 7- to 14-day intervals during damp weather to protect new foliage. Sulfur harms the beneficial mites that live on leaves of fruit trees and other plants; therefore, it should be used with caution. It also shouldn't be used when temperatures are over 80°F (27°C) because it can damage leaves. Because some plants can't tolerate sulfur, always check labels before using it.

Copper. Sprays containing copper (fixed copper, Bordeaux mixture) are sold to control bacterial diseases and some fungal diseases. Copper sprays can damage leaves and must be used according to instructions on the package. Copper is also a heavy metal and can build up in the soil if used continually. Where frequent spraying with copper is required to control a disease, it would be better to concentrate on finding ways to prevent the problem in future.

A Word of Encouragement

In your garden, you probably won't have the chance to get to know more than a few diseases that are common problems in your region. Organic gardeners know that diseases aren't very common. Healthy plants growing in a healthful environment are resistant or tolerant to most pathogens. They have a lot of unseen help from beneficial fungi and bacteria, in the air and in the soil, that suppress the pathogens. A balanced, organic garden is your best insurance against disease problems.

Common Diseases of Garden Vegetables

The most common diseases are listed here, with a brief description of the most obvious symptoms. Several diseases have similar symptoms; this table is meant as a guide to help you narrow down the possibilities. You will need to read the detailed descriptions given in the disease entries to make a final diagnosis.

DISEASE	DESCRIPTION	PAGE NUMBER
MOST VEGETABLES		
Botrytis	Wet, rotted tissue with fuzzy, gray, moldy growth.	160
Damping-off	Seedlings collapse at soil line; seeds do not germinate.	165
Fusarium wilt	Leaves and branches wilt; dark lesions present on lower stems.	169
Mosaic viruses	Leaves with yellow or white, mottled, streaked, or ringed patterns.	183
Powdery mildew	Whitish patches on leaves, starting with the oldest.	172
Root-knot nematodes	Plants stunted, with scabby lesions or galls on roots.	180
Root rot	Plants stunted or dying; roots dark and rotted.	174
Rust	Bright orange, reddish, or yellow spots or patches on leaves or other plant parts.	175
Southern blight	Plants wilt; stems have dark lesions at soil line.	177
Tobacco ring spot	Plants stunted, distorted, and bushy, with small dark rings on leaves or fruit.	185
White mold	Soft, wet spots with white, cottony, moldy growth.	179
ALLIUMS (GARLIC, LEEKS, ONIONS)		
Downy mildew	Blue-gray, sunken spots on leaves.	166
Onion smut	Black masses of spores show under the skin of the bulb.	176
BEANS, LIMA		
Downy mildew	Whitish or light gray patches on pods.	166
BEAN, SNAP		
Anthracnose	Brown to purple lesions with raised edges on leaves and stems.	155
Ascochyta blight	Dark spots with concentric rings on leaves and stems.	157
Powdery mildew	Powdery white patches on all parts of plant.	172
Verticillium wilt	Part or all of the plant wilts; leaves drop.	178

DISEASE	DESCRIPTION	PAGE NUMBER
BEETS		
Beet curly top	Dwarfed, crinkled, upward-curled leaves.	182
Downy mildew	Leaves are stunted and grow in a rosette pattern.	166
Scab	Brown, sunken spots on roots.	142
CABBAGE FAMILY (Broccoli, Brussels Sprouts, Cabbage, Cauliflower, Turnips)		
Black rot	Yellow, V-shaped lesions on leaf edges; veins turn black.	150
Cabbage yellows	Lower leaves turn yellow and drop; plants taste bitter.	162
Clubroot	Plants wilt and look stunted; roots have swollen, spindle-shaped galls.	163
Peppery leaf spot	Small brown or purplish spots on outer leaves.	153
CARROTS		
Alternaria blight	Dark brown lesions with yellow borders on leaf edges.	154
Aster yellows	Leaves turn yellow to purple; plants have short, bushy growth.	181
Scab	Brown, sunken spots on roots.	142
Soft rot	Water-soaked spots on leaves or roots.	146
CELERY		
Aster yellows	Stalks twisted and stunted, turning brown in the center.	181
Early blight	Round yellow spots on leaves; long gray lesions on stalks.	168
CORN		
Corn leaf blight	Long, narrow lesions on leaves, starting on lower leaves.	164
Corn smut	Spongy white galls found mainly on ears.	176
CUCURBITS (Cucumbers, Pumpkins, Squash)		
Alternaria blight	Small spots with green halos on upper side of lower leaves.	154
Angular leaf spot	Small, water-soaked spots between veins on leaves.	143
Anthracnose	Dark lesions on leaves; dark, sunken lesions on fruit.	155
Bacterial wilt	Dull, wilted patches on leaves; branches wilt.	149
Downy mildew	Oldest leaves have white to gray patches on undersides.	166

(continued)

Common Diseases of Garden Vegetables—Continued

DISEASE	DESCRIPTION	PAGE NUMBER
Powdery mildew	Oldest leaves or other plant parts have white patches.	172
Tobacco ring spot	Tiny brown spots on leaves; small bumps or ring spots on fruit.	185
Verticillium wilt	Part or all of the plant wilts.	178

LETTUCE

Aster yellows	Center leaves bleached and pale; plants stunted.	181
Botrytis	Brown lesions on stems or lower leaves with gray, fluffy, moldy growth.	160

PEAS

Ascochyta blight	Small, round, tan spots with dark borders on all parts of the plant.	157

PEPPERS

Bacterial spot	Small, water-soaked spots with yellow halos on leaves.	148
Late blight	Dark, water-soaked spots on leaves; plants collapse and rot quickly.	170

POTATOES

Anthracnose	Dark lesions with small black dots on all parts of plant.	155
Blackleg	Base of stem inky black and rotted.	147
Early blight	Round dark spots with target pattern on leaves.	167
Late blight	Dark, water-soaked spots on leaves; plants collapse and rot quickly.	170
Potato leaf roll	Pale or reddish leaves with leaf edges rolled upward.	184
Ring rot	Leaves or branches wilt; stored tubers have dark rings inside.	145
Scab	Small, corky scabs on skin of tubers.	142
Soft rot	Spreading, water-soaked spots on tubers.	146
Tobacco ring spot	Leaf stems abnormally short and grow in a rosette.	185
Verticillium wilt	Part or all of the plant wilts; oldest leaves turn yellow.	178

SPINACH

Downy mildew	Leaves are purplish and stunted.	166
Tobacco ring spot	Large, irregular, yellow areas on leaves.	185

DISEASE	DESCRIPTION	PAGE NUMBER
TOMATOES		
Anthracnose	Dark, sunken spots with concentric rings on fruit.	155
Ascochyta blight	Dark spots with concentric rings on leaves and stems.	157
Bacterial canker	Leaf margins turn brown; raised white spots on fruit.	144
Bacterial spot	Small, water-soaked spots with yellow halos on leaves.	148
Early blight	Round, dark spots with target pattern on leaves; dark rotten areas inside fruit.	167
Fusarium wilt	Oldest leaves curl downward; plant wilts.	169
Late blight	Dark, water-soaked spots on leaves; plants collapse and rot quickly.	170
Tomato ring spot	Plants stunted, leaves small or distorted; raised brown or yellowish rings on leaves.	185
Verticillium wilt	Part or all of the plant wilts; oldest leaves turn yellow.	178

Common Diseases of Garden Fruit

MOST FRUIT		
Crown gall	Irregular soft tumors on roots or stems near soil line.	151
APPLES, CRABAPPLES, PEARS, QUINCE		
Apple scab	Gray to olive green spots on leaves and fruit.	156
Fire blight	Shoots wither and blacken and are curved in crook shape.	152
STONE FRUIT (PEACHES, CHERRIES, PLUMS, APRICOTS)		
Black knot	Knotty black swellings on branches of cherries and plums.	158
Brown rot	Velvety, light brown mold on flowers, stems, and fruit.	161
Peach leaf curl	Leaves of peaches and nectarines puckered, distorted, and reddish.	171
BRAMBLE BERRIES		
Botrytis	Fruit rotting with fuzzy gray layer of mold.	160
Rust	Bright orange patches on leaves.	175

Scab of Root Vegetables

Streptomyces scabies

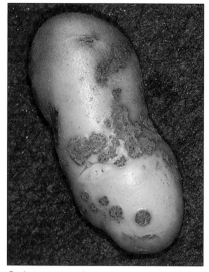

Scab on potato tuber

Range: Throughout the United States and southern Canada.

Description: Rounded, warty, or corky scabs, less than ½ inch (12.7 mm) across, appear on potato tubers. Other root crops may show brown, sunken depressions on the skin of the root. Disease severity ranges from a few scabs on a tuber to complete coverage of the surface. The infection doesn't penetrate far into the root, nor does it affect flavor. Scab-infected roots don't store well, and secondary rot organisms can enter through the scab lesions.

Life Cycle: *Streptomyces* is a bacteria-like organism that grows as a mycelium and produces spores. It can survive indefinitely in the soil, living on decaying plant residue, manure, and plant roots. *Streptomyces* infects potatoes early in their development by entering through natural openings in the skin. It colonizes the first few layers of cells, which die, forming the corky lesions. Rain, wind-blown soil, and infected roots all play a role in spreading the spores.

Host Plants: Potatoes, beets, carrots, parsnips, radishes, rutabagas, and turnips.

Transmission: Soil, rain, wind, tubers, manure.

Prevention and Control: Plant resistant varieties ('Nooksack' is highly resistant; 'Cherokee', 'Huron', 'Norgold Russet', 'Seneca', 'Superior', and others are resistant; 'Russet Burbank', 'Netted Gem', 'Norgold', 'Russet Sebago', and others have some resistance). Maintain a soil pH below 5.2; don't apply alkaline materials such as lime or wood ashes to soil before planting root crops. Maintain good soil moisture levels, especially after tubers set. Because *Streptomyces* passes unharmed through animal digestive systems, always compost manure before using it. Practice crop rotation of several years between susceptible crops; if the problem is severe, rotate with green-manure crops such as grasses and legumes.

Notes: Infections are more common when the soil is allowed to dry out because the naturally occurring soil bacteria that prevent scab from invading the roots disappear. Compost-enriched soils have many fungi and bacteria that suppress scab organisms.

Angular Leaf Spot of Cucurbits

Pseudomonas syringae pv. *lachrymans*

Angular leaf spot on zucchini

Range: Throughout the United States and southern Canada.

Description: The first symptoms are small, water-soaked spots on leaves and stems. Because the spots spread no farther than the veins surrounding them, they're irregularly angular. They turn yellow to tan or brown and may give off a brown ooze on the underside of the leaf; when the ooze dries, it leaves a white residue behind. The spots may drop out after they dry, leaving ragged holes and areas in affected leaves. Spots on fruit are small, round, and white; it's common for the tissue under the spots to rot deep into the fruit.

Life Cycle: The bacteria overwinter on infected plant roots and on seeds. They enter plants through leaf pores or wounds in stems, leaves, or fruit that comes in contact with the soil, and they multiply quickly in the plant tissue. People, equipment, and insects moving among plants spread the bacteria from one plant to the next.

Host Plants: Cucumbers, muskmelons, summer squash, and other cucurbits.

Transmission: Seed, soil, rain, mechanical.

Prevention and Control: Plant resistant varieties of cucumbers, and use disease-free seed. Avoid planting in wet, poorly drained sites. Use at least a 2-year rotation for cucurbits. Don't work with cucurbits before the dew has dried or in rainy weather. If infection is slight, prune off and burn affected leaves or whole plants, preferably before the bacterial ooze has formed on the underside of the leaf. Remove diseased plants and compost or burn them; at the end of the season, promptly dig under or compost all crop debris.

Notes: This disease grows most abundantly in warm, moist weather and is also spread by rain and dripping dew.

Bacterial Canker (Blight) of Tomato

Clavibacter michiganensis subsp. *michiganensis*

Bacterial canker on tomato

Range: Throughout the United States and southern Canada.

Description: Seed-borne infections cause stunted seedlings. When bacterial blight attacks older plants, the leaf margins turn brown to black, with a lighter band between the dying tissue and the rest of the leaf. The damage shows up first on one side of a leaf; later, the entire leaf may turn brown and die. The disease generally proceeds up one side of the plant before affecting the other side. Small, raised, white spots show on fruit, and later the centers of the spots turn brown with a white halo around them. Fruits may also be stunted or malformed.

Life Cycle: The bacteria persist on un-decomposed plant residues in soil and in seeds for up to 5 years. They enter plants through wounds or natural openings, then they multiply and move throughout the plant.

Host Plants: Tomatoes.

Transmission: Soil, seed, rain.

Prevention and Control: Plant disease-free seed, or heat-treat saved seed in 122°F (50°C) water for 25 minutes. Maintain healthy plants; avoid excessive nitrogen fertilization, and make sure calcium levels in the soil are optimum. Use at least a 3-year rotation between tomato crops. Pull infected plants during the season, taking as much of the surrounding soil as possible. Burn them or dispose of them in the garbage.

Notes: Bacterial blight is infective at any temperature that's tolerable to tomato plants. The disease spreads quickly in wet weather.

Bacterial Ring Rot of Potato

Clavibacter sepedonicus

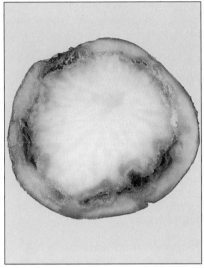

Bacterial ring rot on potato

Range: Throughout the United States and Canada.

Description: The first symptom of ring rot is usually wilted foliage late in the season. In many cases, only a few branches of the plant wilt. Lower leaves on wilted stems turn yellow between veins, and the leaf edges may curl upward. When the stems are cut, a cream-colored ooze can be squeezed out. Mature tubers in storage may have ragged cracks in the skin. Under cool growing conditions, plants may have no obvious symptoms, but the infection is still present in tubers; tubers may not appear damaged until they've been stored for a few weeks or months. When tubers are cut, the darkened vascular system may be visible; the ooze appears in later stages of the disease. Secondary rot organisms commonly infect damaged tubers.

Life Cycle: Ring rot bacteria enter plants through wounds or are spread to seed pieces on cutting knives. Once inside the plant, they multiply within the vascular system. Ring rot overwinters inside tubers left in the soil, but it can remain viable in dry bacterial slime on walls, bags, and bins for several months at freezing temperatures. The bacteria quickly lose their viability in warm, moist soil when host plants are absent.

Host Plants: Potatoes.

Transmission: Seed (tubers), insects, mechanical.

Prevention and Control: Sanitation and inspection regulations in potato-growing regions control this very serious potato disease. Plant only certified disease-free potato seed, and preferably plant whole, uncut seed potatoes to prevent spreading the disease. If you must cut seed pieces, inspect each potato as you cut for dark flesh and dispose of any that are darkened. Sterilize knives when cutting seed pieces: Have a container of clean water and another container with three or four knives soaking in a 10-percent bleach solution (the container should be narrow enough so the knives can soak in the bleach with their handles sticking out). Use a knife to cut up one potato, then stand it in the bleach so the blade is disinfecting while you grab another knife, swish it in the clean water, and cut up the next tuber. Follow a 2- to 3-year rotation between potato crops, and remove any potato plants that sprout from tubers that were missed during last year's harvest and left in the garden. Control Colorado potato beetles and aphids, which may help spread the bacteria. Thoroughly wash and sanitize all storage bins as they're emptied. Watch for signs of disease in the field, removing the roots, tubers, and tops of infected plants.

Notes: Ring rot lives well under all the conditions that its host plant tolerates.

Bacterial Soft Rot

Erwinia carotovora subsp. *carotovora*

Bacterial soft rot on potato

Range: Throughout the United States and southern Canada.

Description: Infections start as small, water-soaked spots on roots or leaves of growing or stored crops. The spots quickly enlarge; while the surface of the affected tissue darkens and remains intact, the underlying tissue becomes soft, watery, and mushy. The lesions become slimy, and the liquefied tissue may ooze from cracks in the roots. Secondary rot organisms also invade, in many cases causing a foul odor.

Life Cycle: Soft rot bacteria can survive in the soil for several months. They're spread by irrigation water in the field and from infected roots to healthy roots in storage. The bacteria enter roots or leaves through mechanical injuries or wounds caused by freezing, insect attack, or infection by other organisms. In lettuce, soft rot commonly invades old leaves or leaves with tipburn damage. The bacteria multiply in the plant tissue, exuding enzymes and toxins that destroy the plant cells.

Host Plants: Carrots, potatoes, and other vegetables; also irises and other ornamentals.

Transmission: Soil, mechanical.

Prevention and Control: Grow crops in well-drained soil. Rotate susceptible crops with corn, clover, beets, beans, or small grains to reduce inoculum in the soil. Handle roots carefully when harvesting, and check all stored vegetables for signs of decay. Store vegetables at the lowest recommended temperature (e.g., store carrots as close to 32°F (0°C) and 95 percent humidity as possible). After harvest, allow the soil on root crops to dry before placing them in storage. Don't wash vegetables before placing them in storage. Where soft rot has been a problem, wash and sanitize storage bins before reuse.

Notes: Warm temperatures and wet conditions favor the spread of soft rot bacteria.

Bacterial Soft Rot of Potato (Blackleg)

Erwinia carotovora subsp. *atroseptica*

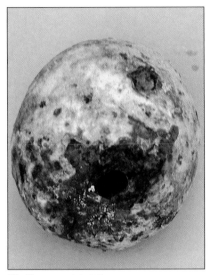

Blackleg on potato tuber

Range: Throughout the United States and southern Canada.

Description: One or more stems of potato plants have inky black, decayed lesions near, or several inches above, the soil line. As the base rots, the whole stem may fall over. Lower leaves on infected stems turn yellow and curl upward at the edges; later, they turn brown and drop. Plant growth is abnormally erect and less spreading than usual. Dark slime sometimes appears on the outside of infected stems. Infected tubers may show some internal discoloration, or they may rot completely. On tomatoes, the rot is first noticeable as water-soaked or dark spots on fruit, followed by rapid decay.

Life Cycle: Bacterial soft rot persists in soil on roots of cereal grains, black nightshade, lamb's-quarters, pigweed, purslane, and mallow; without a host, the bacteria may not survive for more than a year in soil. The bacteria readily enter the plant through natural openings or small wounds, such as from insect damage, near or below the soil line. The bacteria multiply in the stems and gradually move both upward to the foliage and downward to the roots. Slightly infected tubers may not be noticed and can become the source of an infection that's spread from knives used during seed cutting.

Host Plants: Potatoes; rarely tomatoes.

Transmission: Soil, rain, seed, mechanical.

Prevention and Control: Use only certified disease-free seed potatoes. Ideally, plant small, whole-seed potatoes; otherwise, disinfect cutting knives as described for prevention of potato ring rot (page 145). Grow 'Russet Burbank' potatoes, which are tolerant of bacterial soft rot. Plant when soil temperatures are 50°F (10°C) or higher, in well-drained soil; avoid excessive watering. Allow at least 2 to 3 years rotation between potato and tomato crops, and make sure that weeds in the same family as tomatoes and potatoes (such as black nightshade) are removed. Remove infected plants and surrounding soil, and burn or compost them at 160°F (71°C) for a minimum of 3 to 4 days (don't use this compost on future potato crops). Compost all crop debris, and cull potatoes after harvest.

Notes: Bacterial soft rot develops quickly in cool, wet, poorly drained soil conditions.

Bacterial Spot of Pepper
Xanthomonas campestris pv. *vesicatoria*

Bacterial spot on pepper leaf

Bacterial spot on pepper

Range: Throughout the United States and Canada.

Description: The first symptoms on leaves are small, dark, water-soaked spots with a yellow halo. The spots may be slightly raised on the undersides of leaves. The spots darken and look greasy as the disease progresses, and dark, sunken streaks appear on stems. Spots on immature fruit begin as small, translucent areas, then they become slightly raised above the surface as they increase in size and darken. Later the spots become scabby or corky with gray or brown centers. Many organisms that cause rot invade through the spots.

Life Cycle: The bacteria survive in the soil in undecomposed crop debris and on seeds from infected plants. They enter plants through natural openings and wounds and multiply rapidly. They're spread between plants by splashing rain, by equipment, and by people working in the garden.

Host Plants: Tomatoes and sweet peppers.

Transmission: Seed, rain, wind, mechanical.

Prevention and Control: Plant disease-free seed, or heat-treat seed in 132°F (56°C) water for 30 minutes. Use at least a 3-year crop rotation between susceptible plants. Space, prune, and stake plants to ensure good air circulation around foliage. At the first sign of disease, pull the plant, and burn it or dispose of it in the garbage. Copper fungicides can be used, but they must be applied at intervals of 4 days or less to be effective.

Notes: Warm (75° to 86°F [24° to 30°C]), wet weather favors the spread of this disease.

Bacterial Wilt of Cucurbits
Erwinia tracheiphila

Bacterial wilt on cucumber

Range: North central and eastern United States, southern Canada; rare in the South and the Far West.

Description: The disease first appears on individual leaves as large, dull, irregular patches. The affected section of the leaf wilts, followed by the rest of the leaf. As the disease develops, whole branches wilt, and the plant may die. More-resistant plants wilt slightly during the heat of the day, and growth may be stunted. When an infected stem is cut and squeezed, a milky ooze can be seen; when the cut ends are touched together, the ooze forms a sticky strand up to ½ inch (12.7 mm) long.

Life Cycle: Bacteria overwinter in the gut of both spotted and striped cucumber beetles. In spring, the beetles emerge and transmit the bacteria to plants while they're feeding. They may also transmit bacteria when their excrement drops on leaves. The bacteria enter the plant through leaf pores or small wounds, then multiply in the plant. Cucumber beetles then pick up the disease as they feed on the sap.

Host Plants: Cucumbers; occasionally other cucurbits.

Transmission: Cucumber beetles.

Prevention and Control: Control cucumber beetles (pages 46 and 47). Plant bacterial-wilt–resistant cucumber varieties ('County Fair'). Cover young plants with screening or floating row covers to prevent cucumber beetles from landing on them; if parthenocarpic cucumbers are grown (they don't need to be pollinated by bees), the covers can be used to protect the crop for the whole season. Rotate crops to prevent overwintering cucumber beetles from emerging underneath the row covers. Grow the next planting of cucumbers as far away as possible from the site of the previous crop.

Notes: The disease develops most quickly in dry weather because this is when the beetles are likely to be most active. Temperatures over 86°F (30°C) slow the course of the disease.

Black Rot

Xanthomonas campestris pv. *campestris*

Black rot on cabbage

Range: Throughout the United States and southern Canada, but less common in the West.

Description: The first symptoms on leaves are yellow, V-shaped lesions, with the tip of the V at the edge of the leaf and the base of the triangle along a vein. Later, the veins turn black. As the bacteria multiply, the plant's vascular system darkens (this can be seen when the stem is cut). Leaves may dry up and drop, leaving a bare stem. On infected seedlings, the edges of the seed leaves turn black, and the plants usually die. A yellowish ooze can be squeezed from cut stems. It's common for secondary rot organisms to infect tissue damaged by black rot.

Life Cycle: Black rot bacteria overwinter in infected crop debris and in seeds; they can survive for up to 2 years on undecomposed crop debris, but they survive for only 40 to 60 days in soil. The bacteria enter plants through pores in the leaves or small wounds, then they move through the vascular system. As they multiply, they plug the vascular system with bacteria and slime.

Host Plants: Broccoli, cabbage, cauliflower, and other brassicas.

Transmission: Seed, soil, rain, mechanical.

Prevention and Control: Rotate crops, leaving at least 3 years before growing brassicas in the same soil; also, remove related weeds (for example, shepherd's purse, wild mustard, and peppergrass) from garden beds. Buy certified disease-free seed, or treat seed in a 122°F (50°C) hot-water bath for 15 minutes (for cauliflower, kohlrabi, kale, turnips, and rutabagas) or 25 minutes (for cabbage, broccoli, and brussels sprouts). Choose varieties that are tolerant of or resistant to black rot (many are now available). Plow down or compost crop residues immediately after harvest. Pull infected plants and compost them; compost made from infected plant material shouldn't be spread on beds used for brassica crops, but it can be used for other crops.

Notes: Black rot develops most quickly in warm (75° to 86°F [24° to 30°C]), moist weather.

Crown Gall
Agrobacterium tumefaciens

Crown gall on rose

Crown gall on cherry

Range: Throughout the United States and southern Canada.

Description: Pea-size or larger, irregularly shaped soft tumors appear on roots or stems near the soil line. On some plants (grapes, bramble fruit), galls may also appear on leaves and stems above ground. When small, the galls are pale and spongy; later, they become dark and woody. Plants may wither and grow poorly as the galls interfere with transport of nutrients. Secondary rot organisms commonly attack galls.

Life Cycle: Crown gall bacteria overwinter in galls and infected crop debris and can survive in the soil for at least 2 years. The bacteria enter plants through wounds on the lower stem and roots. As they multiply, they produce compounds that promote abnormal cell division and cause tumors. As the galls grow, they interrupt the transport of water and nutrients within the plant. The bacteria are shed from the surface layer of the galls into surrounding soil, where they can infect new hosts.

Host Plants: Many plants; most destructive on apples, pears, stone fruit, brambles, and grapes; rhubarb, carrots and other vegetables, and roses and other ornamentals may also be affected.

Transmission: Soil, water.

Prevention and Control: Crown gall is most commonly brought into new sites on infected planting stock— therefore, check the roots of all imported stock carefully, and discard those that show galls. Dig up infected plants with all roots and surrounding soil, and burn them; don't replace the plant with another plant that's susceptible to crown gall. Take care not to wound plants during cultivation. For vegetables, practice long crop rotations with immune crops such as onions, corn, and oats. A nonpathogenic strain of *A. tumefaciens* is available for inoculating stone fruit, roses, and other plants against crown gall before planting out. Solarize soil during the summer months in warm regions to reduce bacteria in the soil.

Notes: Because crown gall enters plants through wounds, nematodes and soil insects that attack roots can spread it.

Fire Blight
Erwinia amylovora

Fire blight on Asian pear

Range: Throughout the United States and southern Canada.

Description: Flowers and twigs become water-soaked, then wilt and turn black. Infected shoots curve into a characteristic shepherd's-crook shape and look scorched. On branches and trunks, a black or brown ooze seeps from cankers that are 1 to 8 inches (2.5 to 20.3 cm) long or more, appearing somewhat sunken, with irregular cracked or smooth edges. Trees with root infections wilt and die. The crowns turn dark, and reddish streaks may appear under the bark.

Life Cycle: Fire blight overwinters in the cankers formed on branches during the previous season. In spring, the bacteria are spread by wind, rain, birds, and insects to flowers, developing shoots, and fruit. Under wet, warm conditions of 75° to 85°F (24° to 29°C), the infection can quickly spread internally. Fire blight bacteria can infect trees through wounds caused by hail, insects, frost, or severe weather. Tree roots can also be infected (usually those of newly planted trees), through mechanical injury or insect damage to the roots.

Host Plants: Apples, crabapples, pears, quince; also related ornamentals, including cotoneasters, firethorns, and hawthorns.

Transmission: Wind, rain, insects, birds, mechanical.

Prevention and Control: Plant resistant varieties, such as 'Delicious', 'Winesap', 'Liberty', 'Enterprise', and 'Freedom' apples or 'Harrow Delight' pear; some pear ('Old Home') and apple ('M.7') rootstocks are also resistant. Look for infected wood during winter pruning, and promptly remove. Cut at least 12 inches (30.5 cm) below the infection, preferably cutting back into 2-year old wood, where fire blight bacteria are less likely to be growing. Remove whole trees, if necessary, to prevent spread to other trees. During the growing season, check for infections at 2- to 4-day intervals, and prune out infected shoots. Prune trees only in dry weather in summer, and disinfect tools with a 10 percent bleach solution after each tree. Burn prunings. Avoid overhead irrigation, and don't stimulate succulent growth with excessive fertilizer. Where severe infections jeopardize trees, a product containing naturally occurring *Pseudomonas* bacteria ("Blightban") may be sprayed on trees at bloom to prevent fire blight. Copper or Bordeaux mixture may also be sprayed, starting at bloom, but it must be repeated to ensure protection; copper sprays damage fruit, so they're best used on young trees.

Notes: Fire blight spreads rapidly where susceptible plants, warm, wet conditions, and an infection source are present.

Peppery Leaf Spot
Pseudomonas syringae pv. *maculicola*

Peppery leaf spot on mulberry

Range: Northeastern and Mid-Atlantic United States.

Description: The first symptoms are small, brown or purplish spots on outer leaves. The spots eventually grow together, and the tissue becomes tan and dry. The leaves turn yellow and may drop. Leaves may also look puckered. Plant growth is stunted, and small gray or brown spots may appear on cauliflower heads during cool, wet weather.

Life Cycle: The bacteria survive on seed and overwinter in infected plant debris and roots. They can remain viable in the soil for 2 to 3 years. Bacteria enter the plant through wounds or natural openings, then multiply rapidly. Symptoms may not be apparent for 3 to 6 days. The bacteria are spread to new plants by rain splashing or people working among the plants.

Host Plants: Mainly cauliflower; also broccoli, brussels sprouts, and other brassicas.

Transmission: Seed, soil, rain, mechanical; possibly by insects.

Prevention and Control: Plant disease-free seed, or use seed that has been treated with hot water. Use a 3-year crop rotation when planting brassicas. Start seedlings in sterile soil mix. Dig under noninfected crop residues, or compost them promptly after harvest. If spots appear on any growing plants, remove them immediately, and destroy them by burning them or disposing of them in the garbage.

Notes: Young plants in wet weather are most susceptible to these bacteria; the disease develops quickly at 75°F (24°C) but may disappear at temperatures over 88°F (31°C).

Alternaria Blight
Alternaria Blight of Carrot *Alternaria dauci*
Alternaria Blight of Cucurbits *Alternaria cucumerina*

Alternaria blight on carrots

Alternaria blight on watermelon

Range: Throughout the United States and southern Canada.

Description: In carrots, infections appear on leaf edges as dark brown spots with a yellow border. The spots enlarge and grow together, and the leaves turn brown and die. In cucurbits, small, circular brown spots with concentric light green halos appear on the upper surfaces of older leaves; leaves curl and may die. Infected fruit has sunken spots. In damp, cool conditions, a velvety layer of dark brown to black mycelium and spores may be seen on the lesions. Infected seedlings suffer from damping-off.

Life Cycle: Alternaria fungi overwinter on plant debris and host weeds; they also survive in infected seed. The spores germinate over a wide temperature range, depending on the species, but most are favored by temperatures of 68° to 86°F (20° to 30°C). Spores need mois-

ture from dew or rain to germinate and are spread by wind, rain splashes, and people working among plants.

Host Plants: Carrots, parsley, cucurbits, beans, onions, ginseng, and many ornamentals.

Transmission: Seed, wind, mechanical.

Prevention and Control: Plant disease-free seed, and choose varieties that are tolerant of or resistant to alternaria. Use a 2- to 3-year rotation between susceptible crops. Avoid overhead irrigation. Prune off and destroy affected plant parts before spores form. Remove diseased plant debris from the garden, or turn it under immediately after harvest. Enrich soil with finished compost to increase populations of beneficial soil microorganisms.

Notes: Warm, damp weather favors the spread of the disease.

Anthracnose

Colletotrichum spp., *Gloeosporium* spp.

Anthracnose on lima bean seedling

Range: Eastern and central United States and southeastern Canada.

Description: Symptoms and severity of anthracnose infections vary widely with the species and variety of host plant. Most infections start as yellow, brown, or purplish spots with slightly raised edges on stems, leaves, or fruit; the spots expand and darken as the infection progresses. When fruiting bodies form in lesions, the spores are a distinctive pinkish color. On bean plants, lesions on stems are round and dark, whereas on leaves they're elongated and angular and may follow the veins; on pods, spots are dark brown with a lighter border. On melon leaves, lesions are light brown, turning reddish brown (muskmelons) or black (watermelons).

Fruit of cucurbits have dark, sunken lesions. Tomato fruit shows dark, depressed spots with concentric rings, sometimes with pinkish orange spores visible in the centers. On potatoes, anthracnose is called black dot because of the very small black sclerotia that show on the skin of tubers and lesions on stems.

Life Cycle: The fungus overwinters on seeds and on crop and weed debris. In the spring, the fungus produces spores, which are splashed by rain or blown onto new host plants. The spores germinate on the leaves in wet conditions and either penetrate the surface or enter through wounds.

Host Plants: Beans, bramble fruit, cucumbers, melons, mustard, peas, peppers, strawberries, tomatoes, turnips, and other garden plants; also many weeds.

Transmission: Soil, wind, rain, seed.

Prevention and Control: Crop rotation is the primary control for most crops. Plant disease-free seed. Pull infected plants and till under or compost plant residues immediately after harvest. Avoid overhead irrigation. Handle plants or work in the garden only when leaves are dry.

Notes: Spores need water to germinate, so moist or rainy weather favors the growth and spread of anthracnose. The disease grows well over a wide temperature range (59° to 77°F [15° to 25°C]).

Apple Scab
Venturia inaequalis

Apple scab on apples

Range: Throughout North America.

Description: Light gray spots appear initially on the undersides of the first leaves. The spots later turn olive green and velvety, then chocolate brown, and eventually metallic black. Developing fruit shows rough olive patches that later become corky and cracked. In light infections, a few spots show up on the fruit skin; severely infected fruit, however, can be russetted, cracked, or deformed.

Life Cycle: The fungus overwinters on infected leaves that are under the tree or still attached to branches. In spring, spores are produced about the time blossom petals fall. The spores are readily spread by rain and wind to new leaves and fruit, where they germinate during wet weather and infect the plant tissue. At 32° to 40°F (0° to 4°C), it takes 48 hours of continuously wet conditions for spores to germinate; at 58° to 76°F (14° to 24°C), it takes 9 hours. The fungus passes through several life cycles each season. Most spores are produced in the first few weeks, when lesions are in the "velvety" stage.

Host Plants: Apples, crabapples, pears; also ornamentals, such as hawthorns.

Transmission: Rain, wind.

Prevention and Control: Plant scab-resistant varieties, which are now widely available (e.g., 'Freedom', 'Liberty', 'Jonafree', 'Prima', 'Redfree', 'Sweet 16', and 'William's Pride' apples; 'Prairifire' crabapple). Rake up all fallen leaves and compost them in a hot pile (don't use this compost around susceptible trees), or shred the leaves, and till them into the soil to hasten decomposition. Prune trees to ensure good air circulation. As a last resort, spray sulfur products at 7- to 10-day intervals starting at bud formation; continue until leaves have stopped expanding or until a dry weather pattern is established.

Notes: Resistant varieties are so immune to scab that it's well worth it to replace susceptible trees in regions where scab is a serious problem every year because of wet, spring weather.

Ascochyta Blight

Ascochyta spp., *Mycosphaerella pinodes*

Ascochyta blight on pea pods

Ascochyta blight on pea leaves

Range: Throughout the United States and southern Canada; but most prevalent in eastern areas.

Description: Three related species of fungi cause a complex of leaf, pod, and root blight diseases. On peas, small, circular, tan spots with distinct dark borders appear on leaves, stems, and pods. The spots enlarge, run together, and darken; the spots on pods are generally sunken, and the pods may wither. Elongated lesions may also appear on stems near the soil line and extend up the stem for 6 inches (15.2 cm) or more. On okra, beans, and tomato-family (Solanaceous) crops, dark spots with concentric rings appear on leaves and stems.

Life Cycle: All three species of fungi overwinter on infected seed; two species can also colonize crop debris on or below the soil surface. Spores are carried to new hosts through wind or through rain splashes. A new crop of spores can be produced in less than 2 weeks.

Host Plants: Solanaceous crops, okra, and peas; alfalfa, clover, vetch, and other legumes; also many ornamentals.

Transmission: Seed, wind, rain.

Prevention and Control: Plant disease-free seed. Practice a 4- to 5-year crop rotation between legumes and other susceptible crops. Clean up and compost all crop residues, or plow down immediately after harvest. Don't plant early and late varieties of peas or beans beside each other or in succession in the garden.

Notes: High humidity and rainfall favor the spread of the disease.

Black Knot of Cherry and Plum

Dibotryon morbosum

Black knot on cherry tree

Range: Throughout North America; mainly a problem in the Eastern United States and Canada, and in the coastal regions.

Description: In dormant trees, large, black, knotty swellings are easy to see on twigs and branches. Knots usually girdle smaller branches and twigs, but they may also run lengthwise on larger branches. In the spring, the knots have an olive green, velvety appearance as spores develop. Later in the season, the knots harden and turn a flat, tarlike black. Severely infected trees are stunted, with large black swellings distorting and killing branches.

Life Cycle: In late winter, the fungus produces spores from the knots. Spores are spread through the wind and by birds moving from tree to tree. This first generation of spores infects trees just before they're in full bloom. There's also a summer generation of spores. Infections start as small knots on twigs; the knots continue to expand every year as the infection grows.

Host Plants: Cherries, plums, wild cherries.

Transmission: Wind, birds.

Prevention and Control: In regions where black knot is prevalent, plant resistant or less-susceptible varieties (e.g., 'President', 'Shiro', 'Santa Rosa' plums). In late winter, inspect branches carefully for knots. Prune infected branches and twigs at least 6 to 12 inches (15.2 to 30.5 cm) below the knots. Burn prunings. In regions where wild cherry and plum are commonly infected, remove them from around orchards to reduce the amount of disease inoculum present.

Notes: Careful inspection and regular removal of infected twigs can provide good control.

Black Spot of Rose

Diplocarpon rosae

Black spot on rose foliage

Range: Throughout North America.

Description: Small to large, rounded black spots appear on the leaves of roses. The spots have characteristic fringed or feathery-looking margins, and the leaf turns yellow around the spots. As the infection advances, the spots run together, and the entire leaf turns yellow and drops prematurely. In severe infections, plants may be entirely defoliated by mid-season. Occasionally spots appear on petals, hips, and canes.

Life Cycle: The fungus overwinters on infected leaves left on the ground, and in infected canes. In spring, the fungus produces spores, which are splashed by rain onto leaves and stems. In wet conditions, it can take as little as 1 day for spores to infect plants (at 70°F [21°C], it can take as little as 7 hours). Another generation of spores can be produced from the infected leaves within 10 to 14 days.

Host Plants: Roses.

Transmission: Rain, wind.

Prevention and Control: Plant black spot–resistant varieties, choosing from those known locally to be resistant. Variations in local races of black spot can mean that a variety that's resistant in one region may be more susceptible in another, so consult local extension office publications and rose growers for rose ratings. Plant roses in sunny areas, and allow plenty of space around plants to promote good air circulation, to hasten drying of leaves after rainfall. Avoid overhead irrigation, or water only in the morning to give leaves time to dry quickly during the day. Remove infected and fallen leaves throughout the season and destroy them; they can be composted, but don't use the compost on roses. In fall, carefully clean up leaves, and prune out infected canes. Mix 1 tablespoon (15 ml) baking soda, 1 tablespoon (15 ml) narrow-range oil, 1 drop of detergent, and 1 gallon (3.8 l) of water, and spray as a preventive measure. As a last resort, apply sulfur fungicides weekly during wet weather, ensuring thorough coverage.

Notes: Use of fungicides will have little effect unless sanitation and preventive practices are also used.

Botrytis, Gray Mold
Botrytis spp.

Botrytis spores

Gray mold on raspberries

Range: Throughout the United States and southern Canada.

Description: First symptoms are pale, water-soaked spots on flowers, leaves, and stems. These grow a soft, fuzzy gray layer of mold within a day or two. By the time the gray mold appears, affected parts underneath are rotting. Seedlings, lettuce, and berries are the typical targets. In consistently warm, damp, and cloudy weather, seedlings may succumb to botrytis before or just after emergence. Lettuce plants grown too close together show brown lesions on the stem or on leaves that touch the soil. Tomatoes show small brown spots of dead tissue on fruit, surrounded by a pale halo. Berries are attacked near the stem or where they touch the ground. Botrytis causes many postharvest rots, particularly in berries.

Life Cycle: Botrytis fungi overwinter on dead organic matter. In spring, spores form and spread to dying, wounded, or very soft plant tissues. It's common for botrytis infections to move in after an infection from a different organism. The fluffy gray mold is made up of spores ready to drift to new infection sites.

Host Plants: Many garden plants, especially beans, greenhouse cucumbers, lettuce, tomatoes, and fruits such as apples, strawberries, grapes, and bramble berries; also many flowers.

Transmission: Wind, rain.

Prevention and Control: Space plants properly, and prune and stake them to ensure good air circulation. Pick off old flower petals. Maintain good soil drainage. Avoid injuring plants. Prune off leaves close to the soil. Remove infected leaves or plants; burn plants, dispose of them in the garbage, or bury them deeply. Apply compost mulches to increase the number of naturally occurring microorganisms that suppress botrytis fungi. Spray foliage with compost tea that has fermented for 2 to 3 weeks. The beneficial soil fungus *Trichoderma harzianum* is sold for use on food crops grown in greenhouses to control botrytis; thyme oil sprays also show promise.

Notes: Botrytis is common in greenhouses because of warm temperatures, high humidity, and low air circulation. Succulent growth and careless handling of plants increase chances of infection.

Brown Rot of Stone Fruit
Monilinia fructicola

Brown rot on nectarine

Range: Throughout North America.

Description: Infections first appear as small brown spots on flower petals, which quickly spread to entire flowers and stems. Infected tissue is covered with a velvety, light brown mold. Sunken, brown cankers appear on infected twigs and commonly girdle the twig as they grow. Fruit have small, round, brown spots, which spread rapidly over the ripening fruit, typically in concentric circles; the spots grow into velvety tufts. The fruit eventually shrivels and becomes mummified; it may drop or stay on the tree over the winter.

Life Cycle: The fungus overwinters on mummified fruit, both on the tree and on the ground, and in infected twigs and cankers. In spring, spores are produced in warm, wet weather. They're carried by rain and wind to open flowers; bees and other insects can also carry the spores between flowers. The spores germinate and infect the plant tissue; infection is made easier where fruit has been wounded by insect feeding or other damage. Spores are produced all season, and infections continue as long as rainy, warm conditions are present. Fruit becomes increasingly susceptible as it ripens, and infections continue to spread on fruit in storage.

Host Plants: Almonds, apricots, cherries, nectarines, peaches, plums, and quince; occasionally apples and pears.

Transmission: Rain, wind.

Prevention and Control: Plant resistant varieties (e.g., 'Hardired' and 'Mericrest' nectarines; 'Reliance' peach). Prune to ensure good air circulation at all times. Avoid overfertilizing with nitrogen, because succulent shoots are most susceptible to infections. Avoid injuring twigs, flowers, and developing fruit. Collect and destroy all mummified fruit in the fall or early winter, both from the ground and in the tree, before spores begin to form. Rake up and compost fallen leaves and twigs. Look for overwintering cankers on twigs (the twigs appear to have sunken or varnished patches), and remove them during winter pruning. As a last resort, spray sulfur products when blossoms are showing pink, before petals fall and again before harvesting soft fruit. To avoid storage losses, handle ripe fruit carefully, making sure only perfect, dry fruit is stored; refrigerate it immediately. Wash storage bins and containers between uses.

Notes: Brown rot spreads quickly in wet years, and losses may be very high in such conditions.

Cabbage Yellows

Fusarium oxysporum f. sp. *conglutinans*

Cabbage yellows on cabbage

produces resting spores that are viable in the soil for more than 10 years. The fungus invades host plants through roots and wounds near the soil line. Spores are produced in dying tissue and released into the surrounding soil, where they're carried on water to new hosts. Fusarium develops rapidly at 80° to 85°F (27° to 29°C).

Host Plants: All cabbage-family plants.

Transmission: Soil, water, wind, seed, mechanical.

Prevention and Control: Plant yellows-resistant or tolerant cabbage, broccoli, radishes, brussels sprouts, and cauliflower (many varieties are available). Inspect imported transplants carefully before setting them out in the garden. Keep soil moisture high, and maintain good nutrient balances. Mulch with compost, or apply compost tea to roots to boost the populations of naturally occurring soil fungi and bacteria that suppress fusarium fungi in the soil. Products containing beneficial bacteria are also available commercially.

Notes: In hot, dry seasons, even some resistant varieties of broccoli, brussels sprouts, cabbage, and cauliflower may become more susceptible.

Range: Throughout the United States and southern Canada.

Description: Leaves turn dull green, then yellow, starting with lower leaves first and spreading upward throughout the plant. The affected leaves turn brown and drop from the stem. Inside the stem, the vascular system is a dark, discolored, yellowish brown. Plants have a bitter taste.

Life Cycle: Fusarium overwinters on crop debris in the field, but it also

Clubroot of Cabbage
Plasmodiophora brassicae

FUNGUS

Clubroot on cabbage

Range: Throughout the United States and southern Canada.

Description: Early symptoms are weak or slightly yellowing plants that wilt in the midday sun. Severely infected plants are stunted and may die before heading or flowering. The roots have swollen, somewhat spindle-shaped galls. With plants that are severely infected, all main roots may be swollen into a mass of large, distorted galls.

Life Cycle: Clubroot overwinters as resting spores in decomposing roots and in the soil, where they can remain dormant for more than 18 years. They germinate in spring into mobile spores that swim in the water found in the soil around susceptible roots. Once inside the root, the growing fungus stimulates the root cells to grow abnormally. Spores remain viable for 10 years. Clubroot does best in acidic soils with poor drainage. The optimum temperature range is 68° to 72°F (20° to 22°C), but germination can occur at soil temperatures as low as 48°F (9°C).

Host Plants: Cabbage-family crops and related weeds; also dock, bentgrass, orchardgrass, and ryegrass.

Transmission: Soil, water, mechanical.

Prevention and Control: Avoid importing clubroot by growing your own seedlings in clean soil. Once clubroot is present, the key to controlling it is maintaining a soil pH over 7.0, with adequate levels of calcium and magnesium. Maintain good drainage and fertilize with well-aged compost to increase populations of beneficial soil microorganisms that suppress clubroot. Use long rotations of 7 years or more between cabbage-family crops, and remove related weeds from planting beds. Dig up stunted plants to check roots; if clubroot is present, dig out and burn as much root as possible. A few resistant or tolerant varieties are available (e.g., 'Richelain' cabbage, 'Kingston' and 'York' rutabagas, and 'Yuki' Chinese cabbage).

Notes: Attack of the cabbage maggot (page 85) can cause some distortion of roots and can also cause plants to wilt. Carefully inspect the roots to determine whether maggots are present.

Corn Leaf Blight

Northern *Exserohilum turcicum (Setosphaeria turcica)*
Southern *Bipolaris maydis (Cochliobolus heterostrophus)*

Northern corn leaf blight

Southern corn leaf blight

Range: Southern corn leaf blight occurs in the southern United States and in the North through the corn belt. Northern corn leaf blight is widespread from the eastern part of the corn belt to the Atlantic coast.

Description: Southern corn leaf blight usually appears first as small, light-colored spots on lower leaves. These grow quickly to become long, narrow, straw-colored lesions with brown borders, up to 8 inches (20 cm) long. Eventually, the entire leaf area, ears, husks, and stalks become tan and dry. Stalks may rot. During warm and humid weather, black spores appear on the kernels and lesions on other parts of the plant.

Northern corn leaf blight shows up first as long, narrow, gray-green lesions on lower leaves. These progress up the plant, becoming tan and dry as they age. Lesions can be up to 6 inches (15 cm) long. They can appear on the husks, but they don't infect the ears. Plants look like they've been injured by frost or drought. During humid weather, velvety, dark green to black spores form in the centers of lesions.

Life Cycle: Southern corn leaf blight produces microscopic spores that emerge from infected leaves and are windblown to new plants. The fungus reproduces quickly in warm (70° to 85°F [21° to 29°C]), wet weather. It overwinters in plant debris. Dormant spores remain viable for at least two growing seasons. Northern corn leaf blight follows a similar life cycle, overwintering in crop debris and producing windborne spores in spring and throughout the season.

Host Plants: Corn, sorghum, and other grasses.

Transmission: Wind; seed (Southern corn leaf blight).

Prevention and Control: Plant corn varieties resistant to leaf blight (abbreviated as SCLB and NCLB in seed catalogs). Use at least a 2-year crop rotation between susceptible crops; because spores are carried by the wind, this measure is only partially effective in corn-belt areas. Plow under all crop debris at the end of the season or compost in a hot pile.

Damping-Off

Pythium spp., *Rhizoctonia* spp., and other species

Damping-off on cabbage seedling

Range: Throughout North America.

Description: Seedlings are damaged at the soil line and rapidly collapse. Some pathogens attack before seedlings emerge from the soil. Such preemergent damping-off is difficult to verify but should be suspected when seedlings fail to emerge or rows have many gaps. Postemergent damping-off appears as a water-soaked or rotting lesion on the stem, close to the soil line; roots may be small and rotted. Older seedlings may survive attack, but lesions on stems may stunt their growth.

Life Cycle: Most damping-off fungi can live indefinitely on dead and decomposing organic matter in the soil. Their life cycles vary, but they're all able to attack the soft tissue of seedlings. They reproduce most quickly in cool, wet soil. Fortunately, many naturally occurring fungi, bacteria, and other microorganisms suppress damping-off fungi in the soil.

Host Plants: Most plants.

Transmission: Soil, water.

Prevention and Control: Cold, wet conditions favor damping-off organisms; therefore, wait until soil is warm to plants seeds (particularly heat-loving crops). Make sure soil is well drained, and don't overwater seedbeds. Keep flats of seeds at the optimum temperature for germination. Sow seeds thinly to avoid the need to thin seedlings, which damages roots and promotes infection. Water seedling flats from below, and don't overwater (wait until the surface is dry before watering). Maintain good air circulation in greenhouses and coldframes. Make seed-starting mixes from clean soil, fertilized with finished compost, which inoculates the mixture with beneficial fungi that suppress damping-off. Cover seeds in flats with a layer of perlite, sand, or milled sphagnum moss (not peat moss) to keep the surface dry. A tea made from horsetail (*Equisetum* spp.) may slow the progress of damping-off; several products containing beneficial soil fungi that suppress damping-off are also available commercially.

Downy Mildew

Bremia lactucae, Peronospora spp., *Phytophthora phaseoli,*
Pseudopheronospora cubensis

Downy mildew on broccoli leaf

Downy mildew on onion

Range: Throughout the United States and southern Canada.

Description: Upper leaf surfaces are pale green or yellowish, and lower surfaces are covered with a white, light gray, or slightly purple, downy-looking mildew, starting with the oldest leaves. Affected leaves wither, turn brown, and die. The fruit of cucurbits are stunted and flavorless. On limas and soybeans, mildew usually attacks the pods. Beet leaves may grow in a rosette pattern. Spinach leaves look purple. Onions display a blue-gray mildew on the leaves and don't store well.

Life Cycle: Downy mildew overwinters in seeds and in crop residue in the soil. Resting spores can survive for up to 15 years in the soil. Infective spores are released in spring and are spread through wind and rain. Infections spread rapidly. Most downy mildews favor cool, wet conditions and can germinate at temperatures as low as 45°F (7°C).

Host Plants: Beets, carrots, cabbage-family crops, cucurbits, lettuce, lima beans, tomato-family crops, onions, peas, soybeans, spinach, and strawberries.

Transmission: Seed, wind, rain, soil.

Prevention and Control: Plant resistant or tolerant varieties. Plant disease-free seed. Treat seed with hot water (25 minutes at 122°F [50°C] for spinach). Follow a 2- to 3-year crop rotation with non-host plants, such as corn and grains. Avoid planting fall spinach or cabbage-family plants next to areas where infected spring crops were grown. Remove and burn affected plant parts. Don't work in the garden when plants are wet. Avoid overhead irrigation. Space, prune, and stake plants for good air circulation. Remove weeds that act as alternate hosts (e.g., shepherd's purse, wild mustard, and peppergrass are alternate hosts for downy mildew of cabbage-family crops). Spray foliage with fermented compost tea. Mulch with compost. Products containing beneficial bacteria (e.g., *Bacillus subtilis, B. laterosporus*) that suppress downy mildew are available.

Notes: The species of downy mildew that attacks one family of plants doesn't necessarily attack others.

Early Blight of Potato and Tomato
Alternaria solani

Early blight on tomato leaf

Early blight on potato foliage

Range: United States and Canada; especially problematic in the central and Atlantic states.

Description: Leaves have circular, dark brown spots with a target pattern of concentric rings. Spots enlarge and run together. The leaves eventually turn yellow and may drop. Infected tomato seedlings have dark, sunken lesions at the soil line (known as "collar rot"). On tomato fruit, the disease starts at the stem end and develops into a dark rot inside. Leaves of potato plants are usually affected about the time of blossoming. The tubers have small, dark spots. Disease spores are dark and velvety.

Life Cycle: The fungus overwinters on infected crop debris and on tomato seeds. Infective spores develop when the weather warms in spring and are windblown to host plants. The fungus enters plants through cracks and wounds. There are several generations of spores during the summer.

Host Plants: Mainly tomato and potato; also related plants.

Transmission: Wind, rain, seed.

Prevention and Control: Plant resistant varieties (e.g., 'Mountain Supreme' tomato); late-maturing varieties of potatoes are generally more resistant than early maturing. Space, prune, and stake plants, taking care not to wound them when transplanting or cultivating. Avoid overhead irrigation, and wait until leaves are dry to work among plants. Apply mulches of compost or clean straw to prevent spores from splashing. Pull infected plants, and burn or compost them in a hot compost pile; don't use this compost on future tomato crops. Use a 3-year rotation on all tomato-family crops, and control related weeds (e.g., hairy nightshade, black nightshade, and bittersweet). Allow potato tubers to mature fully before harvest, handle them carefully, and avoid harvesting in wet soil. Spray leaves with fermented compost tea to slow the spread of the disease. Apply homemade or commercial baking soda sprays. Products containing beneficial bacteria (e.g., *Bacillus subtilis*) that suppress early blight are available.

Notes: Temperatures above 80°F (27°C), wind, heavy dew, and frequent rain encourage early blight.

Early Blight of Celery
Cercospora apii

Early blight on celery leaf

Range: Throughout the United States and southern Canada, but most severe in warm regions.

Description: The disease first shows up as small, round, yellow spots on foliage of young plants. They appear first on outside leaves, then spread inward and upward. The spots enlarge to ½ inch (12.7 mm) or more across and turn brownish gray and brittle. Elongated, brown lesions appear on stems later in the season. Plant vigor and yields are greatly diminished.

Life Cycle: The fungi overwinter on seeds and on crop debris in the soil. Resting spores remain viable in the soil for up to 2 years. Infective spores are produced in the spring and are blown or splashed onto new host plants. The fungus spreads within the plant and infective spores are produced on lesions in 5 to 14 days. Temperatures of 60° to 86°F (16° to 30°C) with high humidity favor development of the disease.

Host Plants: Celery and celeriac.

Transmission: Seed, wind, rain, soil.

Prevention and Control: Where the disease has been a problem, plant tolerant varieties (e.g., 'Emerson Pascal', 'June-Belle', and 'Earlibelle' celery). Plant disease-free seed, or heat-treat seed in 120°F (49°C) water for 30 minutes. Practice 3-year crop rotations between susceptible crops. Avoid crowding plants, and immediately pull and destroy diseased plants. Apply compost mulches to increase the population of beneficial soil microorganisms.

Notes: Warm, moist weather hastens the spread of the disease, whereas temperatures below 40°F (4°C) slow its development.

Fusarium Wilt

Fusarium spp.

Fusarium wilt on 'Green Zebra' tomato

Range: Throughout North America and southern Canada.

Description: Older leaves generally wilt first, followed by the leaves and stems on one side of the plant or throughout the whole plant. Yellowish patches may appear on the leaves, which later turn brown and die. Plants may be infected at the seedling stage or anytime later. In tomato seedlings, the first symptom is a downward curling of the oldest leaves. On beets and chard, younger leaves may curl inward, and the outer leaves may wilt. Plants with fusarium wilt usually have brown or black lesions on the lower stem and upper roots. The interior of stems is also discolored, and when stems are cut lengthwise, brown to black lengthwise streaks are usually visible.

Life Cycle: Fusarium overwinters on crop debris in the soil. Resting spores develop in the rotting debris and can remain viable in the soil for more than 10 years. Plants are initially infected through the roots, and from there the fungus spreads through the plant. Fusarium favors warm soil and warm air temperatures, so development may be inhibited at temperatures below 60°F (16°C).

Host Plants: Beets, cabbage-family crops, cucurbits, tomato-family crops, onions, spinach, Swiss chard; also other vegetables and many ornamentals.

Transmission: Soil, water, wind.

Prevention and Control: Many species and races of fusarium exist; they're crop-specific, and they don't spread to unrelated plants. This helps in planning crop rotations; however, rotations must be as long as possible (at least 4 years). Plant resistant and tolerant varieties (many are available). Maintain healthy, vigorous plants, which are less susceptible to attack, and take care not to wound plants during transplanting and cultivating. Mulch to keep the soil cool in the summer, using compost mulches to boost the populations of beneficial fungi and other soil microorganisms that suppress fusarium in the soil. Spray leaves with fermented compost tea to reduce the spread of the disease. Where infections are a continuing problem, solarize the soil during the summer.

Late Blight of Potato and Tomato
Phytophthora infestans

Late blight on cherry tomatoes

Range: All humid areas of the United States and southern Canada.

Description: Small, pale green to dark, water-soaked spots appear on leaves, later turning dark brown and papery. Shoots turn black. Large numbers of plants may collapse suddenly, giving off a foul odor from the rotting tissue. In humid conditions, a ring of white spores may be visible in the morning around the edges of the lesions, on the undersides of leaves. Infected potato tubers have shrunken, brown or purplish spots on their skin. Beneath the spots, a reddish brown dry rot develops in cool, dry storage conditions, or a wet rot covered with white fuzz develops in warm, damp conditions. The upper halves of tomato fruit are usually affected with grayish green, water-soaked spots that enlarge and darken.

Life Cycle: Late blight overwinters in tubers or living plant tissue, producing spores in spring that infect new plants.

The fungus invades plants through leaf pores or the cuticle and produces new spores about a week after infection.

Host Plants: Potatoes, tomatoes, and peppers.

Transmission: Wind, rain, soil, seed.

Prevention and Control: Plant only certified disease-free seed potatoes. Choose potato varieties tolerant or resistant to late blight (e.g., 'Elba', 'Allegheny', 'Fundy', 'Kennebec', 'Brador', 'Nooksack', 'Sebago'). Pull infected plants at the first sign of late blight, and destroy (don't compost them). Keep plants well hilled to prevent spores from washing through the soil to the tubers. Remove and burn all above-ground parts of infected potatoes at least 2 weeks before harvesting to prevent spread of spores during digging. Dig tubers only in dry weather, and inspect carefully for spots; the disease can spread in storage. Spraying foliage with compost tea that's been fermented for at least 1 week may slow the progress of the disease on potatoes with some resistance. Plant resistant tomato varieties; a few are now available. Where late blight has devastated crops, tomatoes can be grown successfully by keeping all rain, dew, and irrigation water off plant leaves (rig simple plastic shelters above plants, leaving sides wide open for maximum ventilation to prevent condensation). Plants can also be grown against buildings where overhanging eaves keep off rain. As a last resort, apply protective sprays of fixed copper every 5 to 10 days during wet weather, being sure to cover the plant thoroughly.

Notes: Watch for the disease when cool, moist nights are followed by warm, muggy days or when a week of cool, rainy days is followed by warming and high humidity.

Peach Leaf Curl
Taphrina deformans

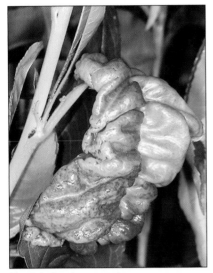

Peach leaf curl on nectarine

Range: Throughout North America.

Description: In early spring, parts of developing leaves or whole leaves become puckered, thickened, and distorted, curling down and inward. The distorted areas turn reddish or purple, then grayish or with a white coating as new spores form. Later, infected leaves turn yellow or brown. They may drop or stay attached to the tree. With severe infections, blossoms, new shoots, and developing fruit may be affected. The disease is worst in areas with wet spring weather.

Life Cycle: The fungus overwinters in the bud scales on trees, where it can remain dormant for several years until the right conditions occur. The spores germinate in wet weather and infect buds early in the year, well before the first leaves appear. The infection develops in the leaves as they expand over the next 2 to 4 weeks. Eventually spores are formed on the surface of the leaves and blow through the wind or splash in the rain to other branches and trees. These spores will cause infections the following spring. The severity of the infections depends on how long wet conditions are present in early spring, when leaf buds are most susceptible.

Host Plants: Peaches and nectarines; a similar disease affects plums.

Transmission: Wind, rain.

Prevention and Control: Where leaf curl is a common problem, choose resistant or tolerant varieties (e.g., 'Red Haven' peach). If foliage can be kept dry in late winter and very early spring, even susceptible trees may suffer little or no infection; espalier trees against the south side of buildings where the overhang of eaves keeps off the rain, or protect trees with a temporary canopy of plastic during the infection period. Where possible, pick off infected leaves as soon as they appear, and burn them, compost them, or dispose of them in the garbage to reduce next year's inoculum. Control the overwintering spores by applying dormant sprays of lime-sulfur, fixed copper, or Bordeaux mixture in fall, after leaves have dropped, and again in early spring just before buds begin to swell; be sure to cover all plant parts thoroughly with the spray.

Notes: Rain is necessary for infection; infection spreads quickly at temperatures of 50° to 70°F (10° to 21°C), and slowly below 45°F (7°C).

Powdery Mildew
Erysiphe spp.

Powdery mildew on monarda

Range: Throughout North America.

Description: Small, round, powdery white or gray spots, usually appearing on oldest leaves first, are characteristic of powdery mildew. The spots spread quickly and run together in large patches, and the white growth finally covers both sides of leaves as well as shoots, flowers, and pods. Leaves turn yellow, then brown, and then shrivel. Cucurbit fruits ripen prematurely, with poor texture and flavor.

Life Cycle: The fungus overwinters on plant debris or in the living plants, such as ornamentals and weeds. Infective spores are blown through the wind to crop plants, where they germinate and penetrate the plant cells. The fungus grows in leaves for several days before producing spores. Powdery mildew can spread in dry conditions because it doesn't need water to germinate. Spore production is rapid at moderate temperatures, and the disease develops quickly in late summer and fall, when day and night temperatures are significantly different.

Host Plants: Beans, cucumbers, squash, cabbage-family crops, apples, strawberries, and many other garden plants; also ornamentals, including delphinium, hollyhocks, phlox, roses, and zinnias.

Transmission: Wind, seed (pea, bean).

Prevention and Control: Plant resistant varieties of beans, grapes, peas, squash, roses, and other plants as available. Avoid overfertilizing with nitrogen and overwatering, which produces soft, succulent growth that's susceptible to mildew attack. Space, prune, and stake plants to promote good air circulation, and reduce shade on leaves. Pull and destroy infected plants, and clean up plant debris in fall to remove overwintering sites. Powdery mildew spores die in water; therefore, thoroughly washing both sides of leaves with water in midmorning, every 2 to 3 days, stops spores from germinating (this is advisable only for plants that aren't at risk for infection from other fungi that germinate in wet conditions). Spray fermented compost tea on leaves, or apply homemade or commercial baking soda sprays. Fresh milk sprays (1 part milk and 9 parts water) twice a week have been shown to suppress powdery mildew of cucumber and zucchini (*Spaerotheca fuliginea*). Various other products are available to help control powdery mildew, including jojoba oil, canola oil, cinnamon oil, and kaolin, as well as several species of naturally occurring fungi (e.g., *Ampelomyces quisqualis*) and bacteria (e.g., *Bacillus subtilis*).

Notes: Powdery mildews don't need moisture to germinate; even relative humidity levels as low as 20 percent are sufficient to promote germination.

Red Stele

Phytophthora fragariae

Red stele on strawberry roots

Range: Throughout the United States and southern Canada; particularly important north of 40° latitude.

Description: In spring, strawberry plants start to wilt, especially in areas with poor drainage. Plants are stunted, and leaves lose their green color; young leaves may take on a gray or purplish cast; older leaves turn yellow or red, and yields are greatly diminished. When roots are sliced lengthwise, the central vascular system (stele) looks red and rotted.

Life Cycle: Red stele infects root tips of small feeder roots first, then grows up into other parts of the plant. Swimming spores are released from the surface of infected roots into the soil solution, where they move in soil water to new roots. Resting spores form inside infected roots as they rot and die; these carry the fungus through the months when the soil is too warm for the disease to thrive. Resting spores can remain viable in the soil for 10 years or more. The optimum temperature for growth is 57°F (14°C); the fungus is inactive below 40°F (4°C) and above 86°F (30°C).

Host Plants: Strawberries; occasionally loganberries and potentilla.

Transmission: Soil, mechanical, water.

Prevention and Control: Plant only certified red stele–free stock. Ensure rapid drainage, which is a key control method to prevent the disease from spreading (most movement of the swimming spores occurs only in saturated soils). Strawberry beds should be located on well-drained soil that warms early in the season. Choose strawberry varieties with resistance to local strains of red stele (follow local extension office recommendations for varieties suited to the region), especially where inadequate drainage or previous infection makes the risk of infection high. If red stele invades, destroy the crop, and replant certified stock elsewhere; don't grow strawberries in the infected soil for at least 10 years. This disease spreads quickly and is nearly impossible to eradicate.

Notes: Cool, wet, poorly drained soils encourage the spread of this fungus.

Root Rot

Pythium spp., *Rhizoctonia* spp., and other species

Root rot on cyclamen

Range: Throughout the United States and southern Canada.

Description: The first symptoms of root rot are leaves that turn yellow or become discolored and plants that grow slower than normal. If plants are infected while young, they generally die. Feeder roots are affected first; they rot off as the disease progresses to the main roots or taproots. Dark, damaged lesions may be visible on crowns. Seedlings may rot and die quickly, whereas older plants may survive in a stunted form.

Life Cycle: Many species of fungi cause similar, root-rot diseases. Most can survive on decomposing organic matter, and therefore can remain viable in the soil indefinitely. Some species also produce hardy resting spores. Most root rot pathogens travel in soil water and grow most quickly under cool, wet conditions.

Host Plants: Most plants.

Transmission: Soil.

Prevention and Control: The best approach is to provide good soil aeration and drainage and to fertilize with mature compost, which is a rich source of the naturally occurring soil microorganisms that suppress root rot fungi. In wet regions, using raised beds for garden plants improves drainage and allows soils to warm quickly in spring. Avoid overwatering seed flats and beds. Don't cultivate too close to plants, which can injure roots and promote infection. Sow seed and set out plants (especially heat-loving plants) when soil is warm enough for good growth. Incorporate finished compost in soil or drench soil with fermented compost tea to boost populations of beneficial microorganisms that suppress root rot. Some beneficial soil fungi and bacteria are available commercially for use in soil drenches. Where infections are a continuing problem, solarize soil during the summer to reduce root rot fungi.

Notes: Cool, wet soils favor these organisms. Generally, infections are the worst in spring before the soil warms and in fall during wet weather.

Rust

MELAMPSORACEAE, PUCCININACEAE

Rust on rose foliage

Cedar-apple rust gall on red cedar

Range: Throughout the United States and southern Canada.

Description: Bright rusty red, reddish brown, or yellow spots or patches appear on leaves and stems, and sometimes on flowers and fruit. Seriously affected plants are stunted and may die. Many species of rust exist, each adapted to different host plants. They range in appearance from small orange spots and cavities on asparagus stems to bright orange spores covering the entire underside of the leaves of blackberries or roses. Some rusts produce galls or swellings. The spores produced at the end of season are typically black.

Life Cycle: Rusts have complicated life cycles. Some species produce five types of spores in one life cycle. Some rusts complete a life cycle on only one host, whereas others, such as cedar-apple rust and pear-trellis rust, must alternate between hosts to complete a cycle. Spores generally overwinter on plant debris or on alternate host plants. They germinate in spring, infect new plants, and produce the next cycle of spores. Rust spores can be spread many miles on the wind, and infections develop quickly in humid weather.

Host Plants: Apples, pears, asparagus, beans, beets, bramble fruits (except red raspberries), carrots, corn, currants, eggplants, lettuce, okra, onions, peas, peanuts, salsify, spinach, and sweet potatoes; also many ornamentals.

Transmission: Wind.

Prevention and Control: Keep plants spaced, pruned, and trellised to promote good air circulation. Plant disease-free nursery stock and choose varieties of asparagus, beans, blackberries, corn, and other plants that are tolerant of or resistant to rust. Avoid overhead watering. Don't work among wet plants in the garden. Pick off and destroy infected leaves, and pull infected plants, including weeds. Remove and compost garden debris in fall to remove overwintering sites. Remove nearby alternate host plants. As a last resort, spray or dust with products containing sulfur (this measure isn't effective on all rusts).

Notes: Rusts are specific to one or a few host plants. For example, rust spores from roses or bramble fruit can't infect beans, corn, or other plants.

Corn Smut *Ustilago maydis*
Onion Smut *Urocystis cepulae*

Corn smut galls

Smut on onions

Range: Throughout the United States and southern Canada. Corn smut is most destructive in the South; onion smut is a problem primarily in the North.

Description: Spongy white galls form mainly on corn ears, but the galls also appear on leaves, stems, and other parts of the plant. The galls range in size from very small tumors on leaves to ones that are several inches long in the ears. Galls have a white surface at first, with a greenish white interior, but as the fungus grows, the white covering bursts to release masses of black spores. Symptoms of onion smut appear on young plants as blisters under the skin on the first leaves and near the surface of bulbs and roots. As galls mature, a mass of dark spores is visible through the skin.

Life Cycle: Corn smut overwinters in infected seeds, on crop debris, and as resting spores in the soil, where they can remain viable for up to 7 years. Infective spores produced in spring are blown onto plants. Galls form on plants at the sites of infections. Spores develop in mature galls and are blown onto new plants. Onion smut attacks seedlings from the day after germination to the time when the first leaf is mature; the fungus can penetrate

only young roots and seed leaves. The fungus grows through the plant until it reaches the leaves, where it forms blisters just under the skin. Spores are produced inside these galls and are released into the soil, where they infect new plants or lie dormant for many years.

Host Plants: Corn (*Ustilago maydis*), onions (*Urocystis cepulae*).

Transmission: Wind (corn smut); soil and mechanical (onion smut).

Prevention and Control: Plant corn varieties with resistance or tolerance to smut (most sweet corn is susceptible, but some resistant or partially resistant varieties are available). Provide plants with an even supply of water. Where infections form, pick galls off of plants and ears (the undamaged part of the ear is edible, as is the gall itself), and burn them before spores form; don't compost infected plants. Use 5- to 7-year rotations between corn plantings. Check onion seedlings for smut pustules, and destroy infected plants.

Notes: Optimum temperatures for corn smut infection are 80° to 90°F (27° to 32°C). Onion smut doesn't develop in temperatures above 80°F (27°C).

Southern Blight
Sclerotium rolfsii

Southern blight on soybeans

Range: Southern United States.

Description: The first symptom of infection is usually wilting, yellowing leaves. The fungus attacks plants first at the soil line, producing a brown, water-soaked lesion and causing plants to wilt. The fungus may girdle the stem or continue to grow up and out from the initial point of infection. Within a few days, a thick, white, mycelial growth covers infected areas and may even spread on the surface of the soil around the plant; sclerotia form within the growth. Their initial light color makes them difficult to see, but they later darken to yellow, then to a reddish or dark brown color as they mature, finally resembling mustard seeds. Infections also cause soft rot on carrots, melons, and tomatoes.

Life Cycle: Southern blight can infect many different kinds of plants and feeds on living as well as dead plant tissue. The fungus overwinters within plant debris left in the garden, and germinates in the warm, wet conditions of spring. It grows on organic debris in the top 2 to 3 inches (5.1 to 7.6 cm) of soil before it infects living plants. Southern blight can survive in the soil for many years, but it's reduced significantly after 2 to 3 years if host plants haven't been grown.

Host Plants: Beans, cantaloupes, carrots, peas, peanuts, peppers, potatoes, sweet potatoes, tomatoes; also a wide variety of other plants, except grasses.

Transmission: Soil, mechanical, sometimes seed.

Prevention and Control: Rotating susceptible crops with corn or grasses is an effective means of reducing the level of Southern blight in the soil. Use finished compost to feed the soil and encourage populations of fungi and bacteria that help suppress southern blight. The fungus needs a supply of oxygen to grow, so deep-plow debris from susceptible crops so it's well covered with 3 to 5 inches (7.6 to 12.7 cm) of soil. Take care not to throw soil containing plant debris against plant stems during cultivation, and keep all leaves and organic debris away from stems of susceptible plants. Pull infected plants, and carefully scrape up the top inch (2.5 cm) of soil for a diameter of about 8 inches (20.3 cm) around the plant, taking care not to drop any southern blight sclerotia. Where infections are a continuing problem, solarize soil during the summer months to reduce the inoculum.

Notes: The disease develops most rapidly at temperatures over 85°F (27°C).

Verticillium Wilt
Verticillium albo-atrum

Verticillium wilt on tomato foliage

Range: Throughout the United States and southern Canada.

Description: The first symptom of verticillium infection is wilting during the heat of the day. Plants become less vigorous, and leaves and stems wilt on one or more branches. Edges of leaves may curl, then leaves turn yellow and drop. On tomatoes, the oldest leaves become yellow, with dying tissue in a V-shaped pattern between the veins. The branches may die one by one, or the whole plant may collapse. Fruit is generally small. Like all wilts, verticillium travels through the vascular system, plugging it and giving it a characteristic dark look when a cross-section of the stem is viewed.

Life Cycle: Verticillium overwinters in crop debris, and spores can remain infective on organic matter in the soil for 10 years or more. The fungus enters through roots and wounds near the soil line and infects the vascular system.

Host Plants: Tomatoes, potatoes, eggplant, cucurbits, and beans; many other vegetables, ornamentals, and trees.

Transmission: Soil, water, mechanical.

Prevention and Control: Plant resistant varieties of tomatoes, peppers, potatoes, eggplant, and other crops; plant certified disease-free potato sets. Make sure plants aren't drought-stressed or lacking in nutrients. Mulch with mature compost, or drench soil around roots with fermented compost tea to increase beneficial fungi in the soil. Crop rotations of 3 to 4 years between susceptible crops can help reduce the amount of inoculum present, but this won't prevent all infection because of the wide host range and long-term persistence of verticillium. Pull infected plants, and remove all infected crop debris at the end of the year; burn it, dispose of it in the garbage, or bury it deeply. Solarize infected soil during the summer to reduce inoculum.

Notes: Verticillium favors somewhat cooler temperatures than fusarium; thus it's more common in the North or during cool periods. The optimum temperature for infection is 70°F (21°C).

White Mold, Sclerotinia Wilt
Sclerotinia sclerotiorum

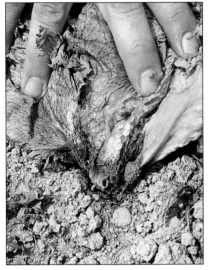

White mold on lettuce

Range: Throughout the United States and southern Canada.

Description: White mold fungi can attack both growing and stored crops. Although this rot looks like many other diseases in the early stages, it's identified by the characteristic pure white, cottony mycelium with large, black sclerotia embedded in it. Lower leaves and stems of a plant are usually attacked first. Plants develop a soft, watery rot, and affected leaves turn brown and drop to the ground. Stems may be girdled, and flowers and buds are commonly attacked by a wet rot. The white mycelium and black sclerotia may not be visible until the affected part of the plant is lying on the ground. Depending on the species, the tough, black sclerotia range from $\frac{1}{10}$ to $\frac{3}{4}$ inch (2.5 to

19.1 mm) long; sclerotia of some species stick together in larger clumps. Look for them inside the stems of woody ornamentals and on the rotted tissue of herbaceous plants.

Life Cycle: The fungus produces sclerotia or resting bodies that overwinter in crop debris or in the soil, where they can remain dormant for 5 to 10 years. In cool, wet conditions in the spring, cup-shaped fruiting bodies on long stalks grow from the sclerotia. These cups are usually easy to see, being relatively large (up to $\frac{1}{4}$ inch [6.4 mm] in diameter on stalks up to 1 inch [25.4 mm] high). Spores are discharged into the air from the cups and are carried on the wind to other plants. The disease develops most rapidly between 68° and 78°F (20° and 26°C). Sclerotia are formed in infected tissue and may fall to the ground with the crop debris or remain in pods, fruit, and roots in storage.

Host Plants: Most garden plants and ornamentals.

Transmission: Wind, water, mechanical.

Prevention and Control: Crop rotation is of limited value because so many hosts exist, but it's worth using nonsusceptible plants such as corn and other grasses for 3 to 4 years. Plant resistant varieties where available. Make sure the soil is well drained. Space, prune, and stake plants to increase air circulation and rapid drying of leaf surfaces. Remove and destroy all infected plant debris, being careful not to scatter the sclerotia.

Root-Knot Nematodes

Meloidogyne spp.

Root-knot nematode galls on carrots

Range: Throughout the United States, though more common in the South.

Description: The first symptom of root-knot nematode attack is usually a stunted plant. Plants typically wilt, the leaves turn yellow, and the plant may die. Roots or tubers of infected plants have galls, swellings of various sizes, or scabby lesions on the roots. There may be secondary infections by fusarium and other pathogens.

Life Cycle: Newly hatched nematode larvae move through the upper layer of soil on a film of water to reach plant roots. They penetrate the root and once inside become sedentary. Glandular secretions injected by the nematode into the root cause surrounding cells to enlarge and form a gall, or root knot, on which the nematode feeds. Adult females are pear shaped and whitish; males are threadlike. The female deposits 300 to 3,000 eggs in a yellow-brown gelatinous mass. Larvae escape into the soil when the infected root cracks or decays. A life cycle usually takes 3 to 4 weeks. Nematodes overwinter in the soil.

Host Plants: Corn, lettuce, peppers, potatoes, tomatoes; also many garden and greenhouse crops, ornamentals, and fruit trees (grains and grasses aren't attacked).

Transmission: Soil, infected roots.

Prevention and Control: Some root-knot species are more host-specific than others; if nematodes are causing crop losses, an expert (e.g., from the local extension office) may need to identify the species. Plant nematode-resistant varieties (e.g., carrot and tomato varieties are available); in seed catalog descriptions, nematode-resistant tomatoes are designated with "N" after the variety name. For most root-knot nematodes, interplanting with marigolds (*Tagetes patula* or *Tagetes erecta*) helps suppress nematodes; where infections have been severe, grow marigolds as a cover crop, chopping the plants into the soil after 2 months. Rotate crops with a year of cereals (e.g., rye, wheat, or barley), which don't host root-knot nematodes. Solarize infested soil during the summer to reduce nematode populations. Till in green manure crops to increase the populations of naturally occurring fungi that prey on nematodes. Applying compost also increases the number of beneficial microorganisms that attack nematodes.

Notes: Don't mistake the galls caused by root-knot nematodes for the beneficial root nodules that form on legumes. Legume nodules are small, often pinkish inside, and the plants look healthy, whereas roots with nematode galls are distorted, many of which end in abnormally branching roots.

Aster Yellows
Aster Yellows Phytoplasma

Aster yellows on carrot

Range: Throughout the United States and southern Canada.

Description: Once thought to be a virus, aster yellows is caused by a microscopic single-celled organism. Symptoms vary with the strain of pathogen, the type of plant, and other factors. Affected carrots are stunted, and the roots are thin, with an abnormally large number of feeder roots; they usually taste bitter. Carrot leaves are yellow, turning to red or purple, and distorted with a dense, bushy appearance. In lettuce, the disease is known as white heart because the interior of heads is unnaturally pale. Potatoes and tomatoes display leaf rolling and stem distortion when infected. Celery stalks are twisted and stunted, particularly toward the center, which later turns brown and rots. Soft rot organisms typically infect the plant crowns late in the season.

Life Cycle: Aster yellows is transmitted when an infected leafhopper feeds on a susceptible plant. The phytoplasma multiplies rapidly in the plant and is picked up by leafhoppers when they feed. It must live within the leafhopper for 2 to 3 weeks before it can infect a new plant. Many crops and common weeds (plantain, chicory, knotweed, pineappleweed, stinkweed, wild asters, lamb's-quarters, ragweed, wild carrot, quackgrass, and Kentucky bluegrass) can harbor the phytoplasma from one season to the next.

Host Plants: Carrots, celery, lettuce; also many other garden crops, ornamentals, and weeds.

Transmission: Insect—aster leafhoppers (*Macrosteles* spp.).

Prevention and Control: Plant resistant or tolerant varieties (e.g., 'Six Pak', 'Royal Chantenay', 'Scarlet Nantes', 'Impak', 'Hi Color', 'Gold King', and 'Charger' carrots). Where aster yellows is a recurring problem, cover plants from seeding to harvest with screens or floating row covers to keep out leafhoppers. Pull host weeds around the garden and destroy them.

Beet Curly Top

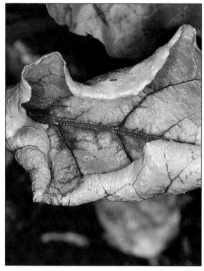

Beet curly top on beet leaf

Range: Western United States and southern Canada.

Description: Symptoms vary according to the crop. On beets, the leaves are dwarfed and crinkled and curl upward; on the undersides of leaves, the veins appear swollen and clear. Leaves eventually turn yellow, wilt, and die. There may also be an abnormally large number of roots growing from the main root.

Life Cycle: The virus is spread by beet leafhopper (page 102) as it feeds on plants. The virus travels to the phloem tissues of the plant, causing distortion of new tissues, an off-color, and general stunting. The leafhopper overwinters on many annual and perennial weeds, then spreads to garden plants when they're available.

Host Plants: Beans, beets, cabbage-family crops, cucurbits, New Zealand spinach, Swiss chard, tomatoes, and many ornamentals.

Transmission: Insect—beet leafhopper (page 102).

Prevention and Control: Grow resistant varieties where available (some beet and sugarbeet varieties). Where beet curly top is a recurring problem, cover plants in beds from seeding to harvest with screen or floating row covers to keep leafhoppers from feeding on plants. Pull and destroy infected plants.

Notes: This disease is most severe in warm, dry, and bright conditions, which is when leafhoppers are most active.

Mosaics (Bean, Cucumber, Tobacco)

Mosaic virus on bean leaf

Mosaic virus on crookneck squash foliage

Range: Throughout the United States and southern Canada.

Description: Many different viruses cause mosaic diseases in plants. Symptoms and severity depend on how old the plant is when it's infected. Common leaf symptoms are white or yellow mottled areas or streaks on a green background; the lighter mottling may be in ring patterns, lines, or banded along veins. Leaf margins commonly roll downward, and there may be a general blistering or puckering along the veins, or the veins may be clear. Some viruses cause "shoestring," a condition in which leaves are extremely narrow and twisted. Plants are stunted, with abnormally shortened stems between leaves. Fruit and pods may also be streaked or stunted.

Life Cycle: Mosaic viruses can be spread by insects (e.g., aphids and cucumber beetles); borne on infected plant parts, such as seed potatoes; or spread mechanically, through pruning and cutting seed potatoes. Because of their small size, viruses readily enter plants through small wounds. Once within the host, viruses multiply rapidly. Most overwinter in crop debris or in living weeds, and most can remain viable without a host for many years.

Host Plants: *Bean mosaic:* beans, clovers, peas, gladiolus, freesia. *Cucumber mosaic:* celery, cucurbits, tomato-family crops, spinach, geraniums, delphiniums, petunias. *Tobacco mosaic virus:* all tomato-family crops, nicotiana; also beets, spinach, some cabbage-family crops, and other plants.

Transmission: Insect, seed, mechanical.

Prevention and Control: Plant certified virus-free potatoes and other stock. Choose resistant varieties where available. Pull and burn any plants that display signs of mosaic. Collect and compost all crop debris after harvest. People can spread tobacco mosaic virus when they touch an uninfected plant after handling cigarettes or a diseased plant. Always wash hands and tools after handling infected plants; milk inactivates tobacco mosaic virus and can be used to disinfect hands and tools between plants.

Note: Mosaic diseases are more severe at high temperatures.

Potato Leaf Roll

Potato leaf roll on potato

Range: Throughout the United States and Canada.

Description: Plants infected during the growing season display an upward rolling of the leaf edges, usually toward the top of the plant. New leaves may be pale yellow or have a pink or reddish cast. Plants grown from infected tubers are more seriously affected. They're stunted and abnormally upright, with leaves rolled upward. The leaves are purplish or reddish on the undersides and are very thick and leathery; potato production is greatly reduced. When infected tubers are sliced in half, a pattern of dark brown or black netting may appear where the virus has killed the vascular tissue (the disease is also known as net necrosis). Symptoms on plants grown from infected seed stock don't usually show up until plants are a month old.

Life Cycle: The virus overwinters either in infected tubers or on perennial weeds and crops. It's spread by aphids (particularly the green peach aphid, *Myzus persicae*). The aphids feed on infected plants, then move to new host plants. By the time symptoms appear on plants grown from infected seed stock, aphids may have already spread it to other plants. The virus reproduces rapidly in the plant.

Host Plants: Potatoes, tomatoes, and other tomato-family weeds and crops.

Transmission: Insects; seed (potato).

Prevention and Control: Plant only certified disease-free seed potatoes. Pull all infected plants, and burn them. Control aphids (page 100). Pull and destroy nearby tomato-family weeds with leaf-roll symptoms.

Tobacco Ring Spot
Tomato Ring Spot

Ring spot virus on currant

Range: Throughout the United States.

Description: Symptoms vary with the type of plant. Generally, small dark circles or raised brown or yellowish rings appear on leaves or fruit. Plants are stunted, typically with abnormally shortened stems and small or distorted leaves; trees gradually decline over time. On spinach, large, irregular areas turn yellow. On cucurbits, tiny brown dots appear on leaves; small bumps or pimples as well as ring spots appear on fruit. The disease is known as bouquet disease in potatoes because plants have shortened leaf stems, giving them a rosette appearance. On soybeans, the disease is known as bud blight because the shoots are crooked and plants are stunted and bushy. Tomato ring spot causes similar symptoms in berries, tree fruit, and other woody plants.

Life Cycle: Tobacco ring spot is spread by dagger nematodes (*Xiphinema* spp.), which feed on the outer surface of plant roots. Once in the plant, the virus multiplies, affecting the production of chlorophyll and the formation of plant tissues. It overwinters in susceptible weeds and perennial crops and on petunia seed. Tomato ring spot is also transmitted by dagger nematodes and possibly by thrips and aphids.

Host Plants: Beets, blueberries, celery, cucurbits, grapes, tomato-family crops, soybeans, spinach, and many other garden plants, fruit trees, and weeds.

Transmission: Dagger nematode, insect, seed (petunia, some weeds).

Prevention and Control: Pull and destroy infected plants. Control weeds (particularly chickweed, dandelion, plantain, and pigweed) in and around garden areas. Reduce populations of nematodes by solarizing soil during the summer (see page 135) or by leaving the soil fallow for a season (keep weeds pulled, and mulch with compost).

Weeds

An Overview

What makes a weed a weed? For some people, it's a plant out of place or a plant that competes with crops. Some weeds are poisonous or may cause allergies in livestock or people, while others may harbor insect pests and plant diseases.

But weeds can also be beneficial. Many weeds are excellent food sources for butterflies, bees, and the many beneficial insects that control pests. Handled correctly, they can make good green-manure crops. Some break up heavy soil and otherwise improve soil texture, and others bring up nutrients from the subsoil. Many birds and other wildlife depend on weedy areas for food and shelter. Some weeds are beautiful, some protect soils from erosion, some stabilize steep banks, and some are good food in their own right. As indicator plants, weeds can also tell you about your soil and growing conditions. (See the table, "Weeds as Indicator Plants," on pages 188–189.)

Weeds as Indicator Plants

SOIL CONDITION	WEED	PAGE NUMBER
Hardpan or crust; compacted	Mustards	229, 232
	Horse nettle	256
	Morning glory	217
	Plantain	238–39
	Quackgrass	273
Compacted, but with good nutrition	Chickweed	203
	Lamb's-quarters	213
Often come with cultivation	Carpetweed	201
	Dandelion	248
	Mallow	205
	Pigweed	222, 224
	Plantain	238–39
	Prickly lettuce	219
	Prostrate knotweed	221
	Stinging nettle	260
	Thistle	240
Rich soils	Burdock	230
	Ground ivy	252
	Lamb's-quarters	213
	Pigweed	222, 224
	Purslane	223
Saline soils	Shepherd's purse	225
Dry soils with low humus	Mustards	229, 232

SOIL CONDITION	WEED	PAGE NUMBER
Sandy soils with low humus	Pinks	207, 208, 237
	Ragweed	206, 211
	Multiflora rose	266
	White cockle	237
	Wild garlic	262
	Mustards	229, 232
	Prickly lettuce	219
Acid soils	Chickweed	203
	Dock	247
	Plantain	238–39
	Sorrel	259
	Sow thistle	199
	Yarrow	245
Alkaline soils	Lamb's-quarters	213
	Mustards	229, 232
Poorly drained soils	Beggar-ticks	209
	Goldenrods	251
	Curly dock	247
	Hedge bindweed	254
	Purple loosestrife	257
	Sheep sorrel	259
	Smartweed	214, 218

Weed Seeds

Soils contain millions of weed seeds. Researchers in England once sifted through the top few inches of soil on a hectare (2.47 acres) of land. They counted 1.33 million prostrate knotweed seeds, 1.73 million shepherd's purse seeds, 3.21 million chickweed seeds, and 16.6 million annual bluegrass seeds. This isn't surprising when you consider the number of seeds a single weed plant can produce. For example, curly dock sets an average of 29,500 seeds per plant, purslane sets 52,300, and redroot pigweed sets 117,400.

Not all seeds survive, of course, and many are eaten by birds and other animals. The ones that do survive don't germinate all at once. In many cases, environmental conditions inhibit sprouting and growth. The seed may be buried so deeply that the level of oxygen in surrounding soil is too low or the level of carbon dioxide too high to allow them to germinate. Temperature, light, day length, or moisture levels may not be right. Seeds can remain dormant for many years, waiting until conditions become right for germination (for example, being brought up to the surface when the soil is disturbed). Some seeds are "innately" dormant. They must go through the alternate freezing and thawing cycles of winter or some other process to break their dormancy.

Annual, Biennial, or Perennial?

Annual weeds live only one season. They usually germinate in spring, grow to maturity, produce seed in summer, and die in fall. They guarantee their survival by producing a significant number of seeds. Most weeds in your garden are annuals. They generally sprout quickly and grow rapidly. Common annuals include chickweed, knotweed, lamb's-quarters, pigweed, purslane, ragweed, and smartweed.

Winter annuals act almost like biennials (see below). They usually germinate in late summer and grow into a small *rosette* of leaves on the soil surface during their first year. The leaves may die back with heavy frosts, but they grow again in spring of the following year along with the flowering stalks. Flowering and seed production occur in spring or early summer, then the plant dies. Shepherd's purse is an example of a winter annual.

Perennials have
lifespans of
3 years or more

Biennials live for two seasons, producing leaves the first year—typically in the form of a low-lying rosette of leaves—and flowering and setting seed in the second year. Common biennials are burdock, mullein, Queen-Anne's-lace, and teasel.

Perennials have lifespans of 3 years or more. They produce seeds, and they also spread by their roots or bulbs. Many grow long, tenacious *taproots* that make them almost impossible to pull out. Some have long *runners* or underground roots that can send up new plants yards away from the parent plant. Common perennial weeds are bindweed, chicory, dandelion, goldenrod, and plantain.

Some of the most invasive and troublesome weeds are *woody perennials*. These include Japanese honeysuckle, kudzu, multiflora rose, and poison ivy. Birds enjoy the nutrient-rich seeds of woody perennials and are one of the main ways these noxious weeds spread— they ingest the seeds and deposit them elsewhere in their droppings. The stems of some of these plants can root wherever they touch the soil, so they multiply rapidly.

Grasses may seem like the worst weeds because they produce so many seeds and the plants are hard to uproot. Some perennial grasses, such as quackgrass, can produce new plants from underground stems yards away from the original plant. Most perennial grasses reproduce from *rhizomes* (creeping underground roots) as well as from seeds. Even some annual grasses, such as crabgrass, can send up new plants from stem joints that contact the soil.

Visual Glossary of Plant Parts

FLOWER TYPES

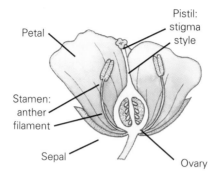

Petal

Pistil:
stigma
style

Stamen:
anther
filament

Sepal

Ovary

Simple Flower

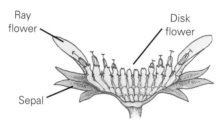

Ray
flower

Disk
flower

Sepal

Compound Flower

LEAF SHAPES

Simple, Entire

Simple, Lobed

Compound, Entire

LEAF ARRANGEMENTS

Alternate

Opposite

Rosette

Whorled

ROOT TYPES

Fibrous

Taproot

CREEPING STEMS

Runner
(aboveground)

Rhizome
(underground)

Using This Guide

Weeds in this section are listed alphabetically by common name within groups divided according to their growth habits. There are chapters for annuals, biennials, perennials, woody perennials, and grasses. Scientific names are also given.

Prevention and Control

Weeds must be controlled in gardens because they compete for light, water, and food with desired plants. It's most important to keep weeds down when crop plants are small. Later, however, when crops are well established, an understory of low-growing weeds usually doesn't harm the crops. Crops may even benefit if the weeds attract beneficial insects or make it harder for pests to find their foods plants.

Whether or not you should try to control weeds in nearby areas around the garden depends on the situation. Weeds that produce windblown seeds and those that are spread by birds feeding on the fruit have the potential to spread the farthest. This means that preventing them from going to seed in nearby areas could help reduce the number of weeds falling on your garden. For common weed species, however, there are usually so many growing in the area that it would be impractical to try to control them. Also, because many weeds are important food plants for bees, butterflies, and other beneficial insects as well as birds and other wildlife, it might be more important to leave the weedy hedgerows and ditches undisturbed. Where a new, invasive species is showing up, controlling the weed as it appears can be an effective way to slow its spread.

Learning about the life cycles of weeds can help you manage them effectively and can stop you from unintentionally making a weed problem worse. For example, tilling up quackgrass only makes it multiply faster. In general, annuals are managed by preventing them from setting seeds, whereas managing perennials means you also need to remove or kill the roots. It may take 3 years or more to completely eradicate some woody perennials.

Because many garden weeds are most simply dealt with by hoeing or pulling them as early as possible before they flower, the hardest part can be to tell weed seedlings from crop seedlings. With experience you'll be able to recognize younger weeds. At first, however, you may want to sow seeds in rows (rather than broadcast them randomly over a bed) so that you can safely pull plants that grow between the rows. A trick that helps is sowing a few radish seeds in each row—these germinate quickly, marking the row before the intentionally planted crop and weeds come up.

Prevention

Soil conditions. Although many weeds seem to be able to grow anywhere, some thrive only in certain conditions. By altering the conditions, you can make it harder for the weeds to grow, while at the same time improving conditions for garden plants. Examples include remedying poor drainage, which would inhibit the growth of weeds that like wet conditions, or adding lime to correct a low soil pH, which would discourage weeds that like acidic soils. In heavy soils, weeds are difficult to pull; but if you add compost and turn in organic matter, the soil becomes lighter, and weeds are easier to pull when they do sprout up.

Cultural Controls

Smother crops. Growing green-manure crops can be used to smother some types of weeds while also benefiting the soil. Sow the smother crop thickly, and turn it under before any weeds that might have sprouted have a chance to set seed. When using green manure to control weeds, it's better to turn under two or three crops in quick succession during the season than to leave the cover crop to grow longer.

Closely seeded garden crops, such as leaf lettuce and other leafy greens, can also smother weeds or prevent their germination by shading the soil. Interplanting tall crops, such as corn, with crops that run over the ground, such as squash, can also reduce the amount of light reaching the weeds.

Biological Controls

Research into biological controls for weeds has resulted in economical, long-term control of various introduced weeds. Most such weed control programs involve finding insects that fed on the weeds in the region they originally came from. The insects are extensively tested to make sure that they don't eat any desirable plants, and then they're released to attack the target weed.

Biological control insects have been released in North America for purple loosestrife, tansy ragwort, spurges, St.-John's-wort, various thistles, and others. Some plant disease fungi have also been developed as biological controls. Government agencies usually release these controls to benefit a whole region; they aren't something a home gardener would buy. An exception to this would be several fungi that are being developed to control dandelions in lawns.

Physical Controls

Simply hoeing and pulling weeds are tried-and-true weed-control methods that most gardeners use. Many well-designed weeding tools are available to help make this task easier and more efficient. Most annual weeds, if pulled before they flower, can be left in the garden to mulch the soil or can be composted. Annuals that readily sprout roots from stem joints and most perennial weeds should be removed from the garden and allowed to dry thoroughly before being composted. Here are a few more ideas for physical controls:

Cultivation. Repeated cultivation can greatly reduce the number of weed seeds in the soil. Allow the weeds to germinate, then destroy them by tilling or cultivating the soil. Allow the weeds to germinate for another 2 weeks, then cultivate again. If you have time to allow several cycles of germination and cultivation before sowing garden plants, you can considerably reduce the number of weeds that come up later in the crop.

Mulches. With respect to managing weeds, mulches have several advantages. First, the soil under mulches stays moist and loose, so it's easier to pull any weeds that grow. The thicker the mulch is, the more it will shade the soil and smother germinating weed seedlings. A 2- to 4-inch layer is usually enough to control most annual weeds if applied early in the season. Make sure the mulch is free from weed seeds, however, so that it doesn't cause more weed problems. Shredded leaves, clean straw, compost, and other organic materials help suppress weeds as well as provide other benefits to garden plants.

Extremely dense, light-excluding materials—such as black plastic, landscape fabric, or thick layers of newspaper or cardboard—can be used to smother all vegetation under them. These are commonly used to kill sod or smother established patches of weeds so that the soil can be used for a garden the following season. The heavy mulches may be needed for several years to control extremely vigorous woody perennials.

Mowing. For annual weeds, periodically mowing or cutting off the tops so they can't set seed will eradicate them in 1 year because the roots die in fall. For perennials, close cutting or mowing at 2- to 4-week intervals can also eventually kill the plants, because the roots become exhausted from sending up shoots.

Applying heat. There are several ways to apply heat to weeds to kill them—but heat is more useful for weeds on driveways, patios, and sidewalks than in gardens because the heat can also kill the garden plants. Pouring boiling water on weeds is an effective control for seedlings growing in crevices in bricks and pavement. Soil solarization (described on page 135) can heat the soil enough to kill weed seeds in the top layer of soil. Handheld flamers and infrared weeders can also be used to control weeds.

Herbicides

Although home recipes using salt, vinegar, or other household substances can be used to kill weeds, they're also very harmful to other plants and organisms in the soil. Salt, for example, is highly soluble and moves through the soil, damaging roots of trees and other desirable plants. In the garden setting, there's little use for herbicidal products because of the risk of harming desirable plants. Two organic herbicides that have some limited uses are as follows:

Fatty acids. A commercial nontoxic herbicide (Safer's) is made from fatty acids, which are naturally occurring ingredients used in making soap. It kills the leaves of plants but not the roots; therefore, it's most effective on annual weeds and on seedlings of perennials. Because a fatty-acid spray can also kill garden seedlings, it's best used in hard-surfaced areas or in garden areas before seeds are sown. There's no residual effect, so seeds can be planted immediately after using the fatty acids.

Corn gluten meal. A substance in corn gluten meal (a byproduct of animal feed) has been found to suppress germination of seeds without affecting growing plants. Several products are available for use on lawns, where they can both prevent weed seeds from germinating and provide some nutrients such as nitrogen. Corn gluten meal can also be used in garden areas where transplants, not seeds, are being planted.

Annual Sow Thistle

Sonchus oleraceus

COMPOSITAE

Seed

Range: Throughout the United States and southern Canada; particularly troublesome in coastal regions.

Description: Plants grow 1 to 6 feet (30.5 to 183 cm) tall. Stems are erect and branched and ooze a milky sap when cut. Leaves are alternate on the stem and more numerous toward the base of the plant. The largest leaves are deeply cut into irregular lobes on each side, with an arrow-shaped tip and toothed, spiny leaf margins. Flower heads are pale yellow and rounded and resemble dandelions. Seeds have tufts of long hairs that allow them to be carried on the wind. Blooms June to October.

Life Cycle: Annual, reproducing by seeds.

Prevention and Control: Hoe or pull plants or apply a thick mulch to prevent germination and to smother seedlings. Watch waste places for blooming sow thistles, and mow them before seedheads begin to form.

Notes: Sow thistles are common in both cultivated and uncultivated areas with good light exposure. Perennial sow thistle, a troublesome weed in northern areas, looks like annual sow thistle, but the leaf is less prickly, and the flower is a more vivid yellow. The perennial species spreads from both the rootstock and the seeds and must be dug up to be eradicated. Both sow thistles are a source of food for hoverflies and other beneficial insects.

Black Nightshade
Solanum nigrum

SOLANACEAE

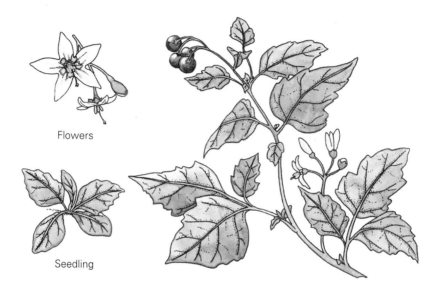

Flowers

Seedling

Range: Eastern half of the United States and southeastern Canada.

Description: Plants grow 1 to 2 feet (30.5 to 61 cm) tall. Plants are low and spreading and branch prolifically. Leaves are alternate on the stem and are wide at the base of the leaf and narrow at the tip, with wavy edges. The star-shaped, five-petaled flowers are white and grow in clusters. Small green berries turn black upon maturity and contain numerous seeds. Seeds are wrinkled, flattened, and a dull yellow to brown color. Blooms from July to September.

Life Cycle: Annual, reproducing by seeds.

Prevention and Control: Nightshade is rarely present in large numbers, so it's effective to pull or hoe any plants that take root in the garden. Prompt removal is advisable because nightshade can host pests that attack other tomato-family crops, such as Colorado potato beetle (page 34), and the bacteria that cause blackleg of potato (page 147), which survives on nightshade roots.

Notes: Nightshade is especially common in disturbed soils.

Carpetweed
Mollugo verticillata   AIZOACEAE

Flowers

Seedling

Range: Throughout the United States (except north-central areas) and southern Canada.

Description: Stems grow to 1 foot (30.5 cm) long. Plants are bright green and prostrate and spread outward from a central taproot. They branch profusely at the base, making a flat, carpetlike mat. Leaves are smooth and narrow and taper to a point. They grow in clusters of five or six leaves in whorls from stem joints. Two to five small, white, five-petaled flowers also grow from stem joints. Seed capsules are tiny and three-lobed and hold numerous orange-red, ridged seeds. Blooms from June to September.

Life Cycle: Annual, reproducing by seeds.

Prevention and Control: Pull carpetweed immediately because it grows, flowers, and sets seeds rapidly. Hoeing it off just below the soil line is effective. Apply dense mulches to smother seedlings.

Notes: Carpetweed tolerates a wide range of soil conditions.

Catchweed Bedstraw, Cleavers

Galium aparine   RUBIACEAE

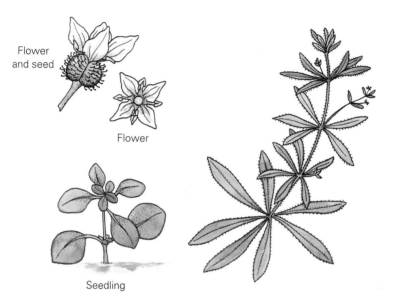

Flower and seed

Flower

Seedling

Range: Throughout the United States and southern Canada.

Description: Stems grow from 8 to 60 inches (20.3 to 152 cm) long. They lie on the ground or over other plants and are jointed, slender, and tough, with four lengthwise ridges. Short, downward-pointing bristles grow along the ridges. Leaves are lance-shaped, with a central vein and sharp bristles on the top surface and edges; they grow in clusters of six to eight leaves in a whorl at each stem joint. Flowers are small and white with four lobes joined into a tube; they grow in groups of one to three, on stalks that arise from leaf axils. Seedpods are round and bristly and are divided into two chambers. Blooms from May to July.

Life Cycle: Annual, reproducing by bristly seeds that stick to passing animals and people.

Prevention and Control: Hoeing and pulling will eradicate bedstraw from the garden. When removing the weed, dig down to get all roots because it readily sprouts again. Apply dense mulches to smother seedlings. Remove seeds from shoes and socks after working in infested areas, such as along edges of fields and pastures.

Notes: Catchweed bedstraw prefers moist, rich soils with moderately good drainage. It's commonly found in soils that once formed creek or river beds, on the edges of woodlands, and in slightly shaded areas formed by hedgerows and fences. Flowering occurs fairly early in the season, so remove plants as soon as you notice them.

Common Chickweed
Stellaria media   CARYOPHYLLACEAE

Flower

Seedling

Range: Throughout the United States and southern Canada.

Description: Stems usually grow 4 to 12 inches (10.2 to 30.5 cm) long, but they can reach up to 18 inches (45.7 cm) long. Plants are bright green and grow in a loose mat on the soil surface. Stems branch profusely from the central crown, which grows from a fibrous, shallow root system. Leaves are small and oval, are pointed at the tip, and are opposite each other on the stem. Flowers are white, with five split petals, giving the appearance of ten petals. Sepals are green and hairy and extend beyond the petals. Seed capsules are oval and hold many red-brown, ridged seeds. Blooms from early spring to early winter.

Life Cycle: Annual or winter annual, reproducing both by seeds and by rooting along stems. Typically sets seed in fall and can grow vigorously during winter in mild climates.

Prevention and Control: Pull or hoe plants before they set seed. Because stems root easily, remove plants from the garden, and allow them to dry in the sun before composting them. Use dense mulches to smother seedlings.

Notes: Though this plant likes rich soil, it tolerates high acidity. It makes the most vigorous growth during cool weather when soil moisture is high and can serve as a protective groundcover over garden soils in areas with mild winters. Edible.

Common Cocklebur
Xanthium strumarium

COMPOSITAE

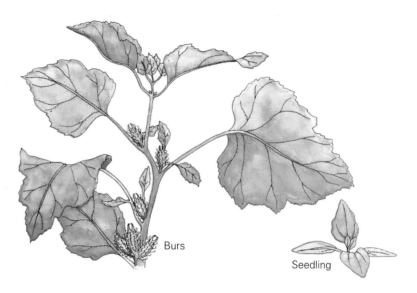

Burs

Seedling

Range: Throughout the United States and southern Canada (except in Quebec and northern New England).

Description: Plants grow 1 to 4 feet (30.5 to 122 cm) tall. Stems are erect, ridged, and hairy, some with reddish spots; stems are so branched that established plants look like a bush. Leaves are large, triangular to heart-shaped, and slightly lobed, with toothed edges. They're alternate on the stem and rough on both sides. Male flowers grow in short terminal spikes and drop soon after the pollen has been shed. The female flowers grow in clusters in leaf axils. Burs develop from the female flowers; they have two larger, sharp, incurved hooks at the top and are covered with hooked bristles, which attach to passing people or animals. Burs are light green, turning brown and woody as they mature. Blooms in August and September.

Life Cycle: Annual, reproducing by seeds.

Prevention and Control: Hoe or pull plants in the garden. Use dense mulches to smother seedlings. In fields, mow before the plants flower, repeating as needed during the season to prevent plants from flowering.

Notes: Cocklebur seedlings are poisonous to livestock. Cocklebur grows well in wet soils. Cocklebur can be confused with common burdock (page 230), but the former has elongated burs, whereas burdock has round burs.

Common Mallow
Malva neglecta   MALVACEAE

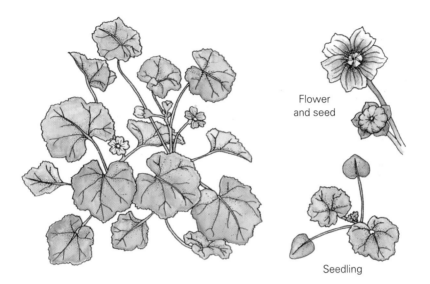

Flower
and seed

Seedling

Range: Throughout the United States and southern Canada.

Description: Stems grow 4 to 12 inches (10.2 to 30.5 cm) long. They branch at the base, appearing nearly erect or spreading close to the ground. Leaves are wide, rounded, slightly hairy, and sometimes slightly lobed, with softly toothed edges and long, slender petioles. Flowers are white to pale purple, have five petals, and are borne singly or in clusters from leaf axils. Seedpods are round and flattened and split into many pie-shaped segments. Blooms from April to October.

Life Cycle: Annual or biennial, reproducing by seeds.

Prevention and Control: Pull or hoe plants in the garden. Apply dense mulches to smother seedlings. Mow or cut larger plants in nearby areas to prevent them from setting seed.

Notes: Common mallow will grow in a wide range of soil conditions.

Common Ragweed
Ambrosia artemisiifolia

COMPOSITAE

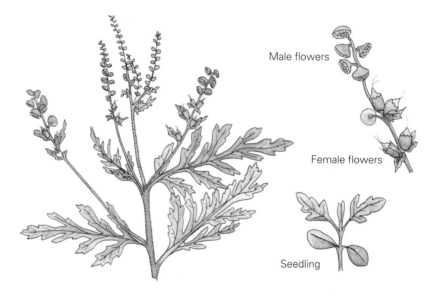

Male flowers

Female flowers

Seedling

Range: Eastern and north-central United States, and central and eastern Canada.

Description: Plants grow 1 to 3 feet (30.5 to 91.4 cm) tall. Stems are erect, unbranched or branched toward the top. Leaves are smooth, deeply lobed, and fernlike. They're sometimes opposite on the stem at the base of the plant, but they're more commonly alternate for the entire length of the stem. The flower heads are greenish spikes that grow at the tips of the branches and from the leaf axils. Seeds develop inside a brown woody husk with spines along the top. Blooms from July through September.

Life Cycle: Annual, reproducing by seeds.

Prevention and Control: Because ragweed is shallow-rooted and reproduces only by seed, hoeing and pulling are effective. Use dense mulches to smother seedlings. Mow nearby roadsides and other weedy spots before the plants bloom to prevent flower and seed formation.

Notes: Ragweed is a source of irritating pollen and is the most common cause of hay fever in fall. It some states and provinces, ragweed is considered a noxious weed and falls under weed-control ordinances. Ragweed grows in poor, dry soils but is adaptable to a wide range of conditions.

Corn Cockle
Agrostemma githago

CARYOPHYLLACEAE

Seedling

Range: Throughout the United States and southern Canada.

Description: Plants grow 1 to 3 feet (30.5 to 91.4 cm) tall. Stems are erect, are covered with soft hairs, and bulge slightly at the leaf joints. Leaves are lance-shaped, hairy, and opposite on the stem. Flowers are purplish pink and 1 to 2 inches (2.5 to 5.1 cm) wide, with five petals that have dark veins; they're borne one per stem and have long, narrow, green sepals. Seed capsules are puffy, with the sepals at the top; they hold many small, black, spiny seeds. The stems grow from a shallow taproot. Blooms from May to September.

Life Cycle: Winter annual, reproducing by seeds. Usually germinates in fall and sends up flowerstalks the next spring.

Prevention and Control: Pull or hoe plants before seeds set. Apply thick mulches to smother seedlings. Seed is rarely viable for more than a year if it's buried to a depth of 6 to 8 inches (15.2 to 20.3 cm).

Notes: Seeds are poisonous. Livestock and poultry must be kept off fields with corn cockle.

Corn Spurry
Spergularia arvensis

CARYOPHYLLACEAE

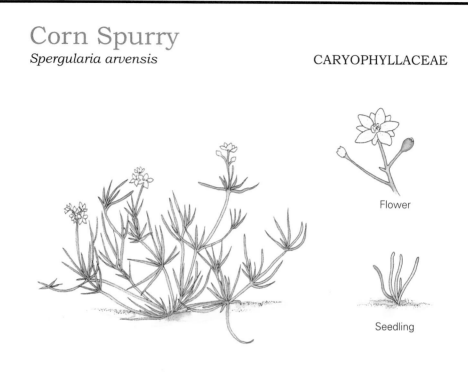

Flower

Seedling

Range: West coastal United States and Canada; most of eastern United States; also Colorado.

Description: Stems are 6 to 18 inches (15.2 to 45.7 cm) high and slender and branching. Leaves are threadlike, ½ to 1 inch (1.3 to 2.5 cm) long, with grooves on the underside; they're arranged in whorls on the stems. The small, white, five-petaled flowers are carried at the ends of stems, which bend down as the seedpods ripen. The seedpods are longer than the sepals and split into five sections. The seeds are dull black, circular, and flattened, with a pale narrow wing around the outer edge.

Life Cycle: Annual; flowers all summer; spreads by seeds.

Prevention and Control: Hoe or pull plants before seeds set. Use dense mulches to smother seedlings.

Notes: Corn spurry grows best in light, sandy soils or gravelly areas. The flowers are attractive to beneficial insects such as parasitic wasps (page 26), so a moderate number of corn spurry plants among tall or vigorous crop plants can be desirable.

Devil's Beggar-Ticks
Bidens frondosa   COMPOSITAE

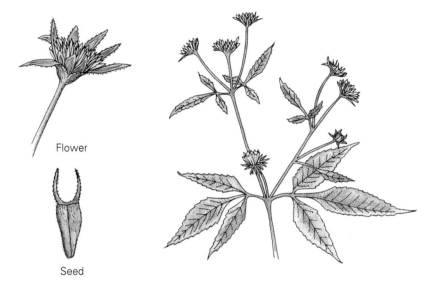

Flower

Seed

Range: Throughout the United States and southern Canada.

Description: Plants grow from 2 to 5 feet (61 to 152 cm) tall. Stems are usually smooth and are almost square; they grow in groups from a shallow, branched taproot. Leaves are opposite on the stem and are divided in three or five leaflets with pointed tips and toothed edges. They may have short hairs on the undersides but are always smooth on the upper surfaces. Flower heads are yellow-orange, with five petal-like outer flowers on each head. The seed is long and wedge-shaped, with two barbed spikes at the top. Blooms from July to October.

Life Cycle: Annual, reproducing by seeds.

Prevention and Control: Hoe or pull plants. Use dense mulches to smother seedlings. Mow or cut plants in nearby areas before they set seed.

Notes: Devil's beggar-ticks prefer rich, moist soil but will grow along roadsides, in waste places, and in damp areas. Animals may carry seeds into the garden. This weed can be an alternate host for Mexican bean beetle (page 43).

Field Dodders
Cuscuta spp.

CONVOLVULACEAE

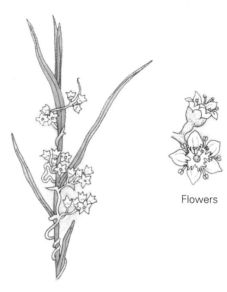

Flowers

Range: Throughout the United States south of Vermont and the Great Lakes, with the exception of much of the Pacific Coast states. Also found in prairie provinces in southern Canada.

Description: Stems may reach 7 feet (2.1 m) long, but because they grow in tangled masses on the host plant, the height is variable. Stringlike, yellowish, pinkish, or orange stems emerge from the ground. Dodders lack leaves because they don't produce chlorophyll. Instead, they have tiny suckers that attach to host plants. Once attached, the stem breaks from the root. The small, white, five-lobed flowers are produced in loose, rounded clusters. The calyx is large relative to the petals. Seeds are numerous, fairly small, and yellow to reddish brown. Blooms from July to September.

Life Cycle: Annual, reproducing by seeds.

Prevention and Control: Dodder seeds can be spread to gardens and fields mixed in small-seeded grains, with cover-crop seed or in hay used as mulch. If flowers haven't yet formed, immediately pull both the dodder and the host plant and compost them. If flowers have formed, pull both the dodder and the host plant and burn or dispose of them in the garbage. If necessary, solarize the soil for the summer months where dodder has been a serious problem. If you can't remove the host plant, continue to remove and destroy all visible dodder several times a season for up to 2 years. If dodder is mixed in with a cover crop, keep the area mowed for the season to make sure it doesn't set seed.

Notes: Field dodder is a parasite. It prefers open, dry sites.

Giant Ragweed
Ambrosia trifida

COMPOSITAE

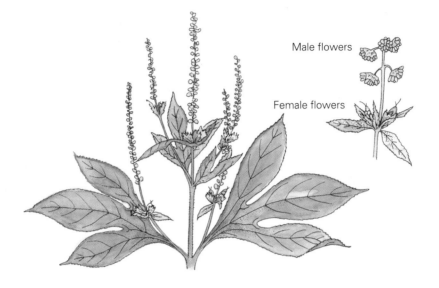

Male flowers

Female flowers

Range: Throughout the United States, with the exception of Pacific Coast areas, and into southern Canada from southwest Quebec to British Columbia.

Description: Plants can grow to 12 feet (3.7 m) tall, but are usually 2½ to 6 feet (76.2 to 183 cm) tall. Stems are erect, branched toward the top, covered with coarse hair, and rough. Leaves are hairy and divided into three or five deep lobes, with a border of leaf tissue along each side of the petiole. Flowers are greenish and grow on spikes at the tip of stems and in the leaf axils at the top of the plant. Blooms from July to September.

Life Cycle: Annual, reproducing by seeds.

Prevention and Control: Hoe or pull ragweed that appears in the garden. Apply dense mulches to smother seedlings. Frequently mow any ragweed that's growing in waste places to prevent the formation of flowers and seeds.

Notes: Ragweed is a source of irritating pollen and is the most common cause of hay fever in fall. In some states and provinces, ragweed must be controlled by law. Giant ragweed prefers moist soils but will grow in less ideal conditions. It's common in hedgerows and along the edges of fields and roadsides.

Jimsonweed
Datura stramonium

SOLANACEAE

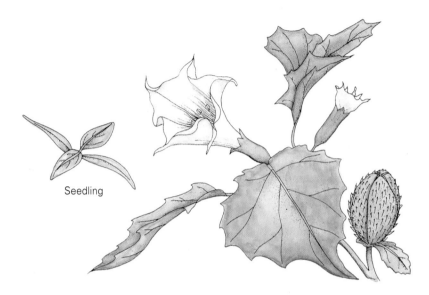

Seedling

Range: East, Midwest, Southwest, and along the Pacific Coast of the United States and southern Canada.

Description: Plants may grow to 5 feet (1.5 m) tall. They're bushy with spreading leaves, which are oval to triangular in shape with toothed edges. Stems are sometimes slightly purple. Flowers are white to pink and are a deep, funnel shape. Seed capsules are distinctly spiny and have four lobes. Seeds are kidney-shaped, flattened, and slightly pitted. Blooms from June to September.

Life Cycle: Annual, reproducing by seeds.

Prevention and Control: Pull and compost jimsonweed before seed capsules start to form; wear gloves when handling plants because they can cause skin irritation. Use dense mulches to smother seedlings.

Notes: Jimsonweed resembles eggplant and thrives in rich soil and full sun. It can harbor diseases and pests common to other tomato-family crops. The seeds are poisonous.

Lamb's-Quarters
Chenopodium album   CHENOPODIACEAE

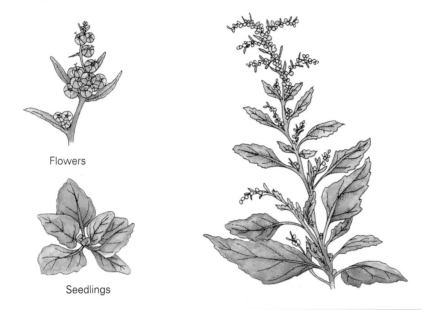

Flowers

Seedlings

Range: Throughout the United States and southern Canada.

Description: Plants grow 1 to 3 feet (30.5 to 91.4 cm) tall or more in rich soil. Stems are upright and branched, typically with grooves of lighter green or red running lengthwise. Leaves are egg-shaped or roughly triangular with toothed edges. They're alternate on the stems and generally wider on the bottom than the top of the plant. Green or reddish green, petal-less flowers grow in irregularly shaped spikes at the tops of branches. Blooms from early summer through fall.

Life Cycle: Annual, reproducing by seeds. In fall, very young plants can flower and set seed before frost.

Prevention and Control: Pull or hoe lamb's-quarters when they're young because they grow rapidly. In hot, dry weather, pulled seedlings can be left in the garden as mulch. Otherwise, compost them. Use dense mulches to smother seedlings.

Notes: Lamb's-quarters with a reddish purple sheen can indicate that the soil is nitrogen-deficient. Young leaves are edible, raw or cooked.

Marshpepper Smartweed
Polygonum hydropiper

POLYGONACEAE

Flowers

Range: Throughout southern Canada and the United States (except for southern Georgia and Florida).

Description: Plants are 6 inches to 2½ feet (15.2 to 76.2 cm) tall. Stems are prominently jointed, erect, smooth, and sometimes reddish. Leaves are alternate on the stem, narrow, lance-shaped, and pointed at the tips; they're smooth to slightly hairy. Petioles are small or absent. Flowers are small, four-lobed, and greenish white with pink edges; they grow in terminal spikes that droop in arches. The calyx, which sometimes has slightly reddish margins, protects the dull brown, lens-shaped or triangular fruit that contains a single seed. Blooms from June to November.

Life Cycle: Annual, reproducing by seeds.

Prevention and Control: Apply dense mulches to smother seedlings. Hoe or pull the plants. Remove pulled plants from the garden to prevent re-rooting from the stem nodes; dry in the sun before composting. Improving drainage helps to discourage the growth of smartweed.

Notes: Marshpepper smartweed prefers moist or boggy areas and is usually found in ditches, along shorelines, or in other low, poorly drained soils. Birds like the fruit and spread it to new ground. Stems and leaves are edible (they have a peppery flavor).

Mayweed
Anthemis cotula

COMPOSITAE

Seedling

Range: Throughout the United States and southern Canada.

Description: Plants can reach 12 to 18 inches (30.5 to 45.7 cm) tall. The multi-branched stem is erect and either smooth or covered with soft hairs. Leaves are alternate on the stem, light yellowish green, and finely divided into narrow segments. They have a distinctly bad odor when crushed. Small, white ray flowers surround a center of yellow disk flowers. Blooms from May to September.

Life Cycle: Annual, reproducing by seeds. In some climates, mayweed is a winter annual, germinating in late fall, overwintering, and sending up flower-stalks the following spring.

Prevention and Control: Hoe or pull plants in the garden. Use dense mulches to smother seedlings. Mow or cut plants in nearby areas to prevent formation of seeds.

Notes: Common names for this plant include stinkweed, fetid chamomile, dog fennel, and stinking daisy, all referring to the highly unpleasant odor that the leaves give off. Despite these names, it's attractive to beneficial insects and provides them with pollen and nectar. It's adapted to a wide range of soil conditions.

Mile-a-Minute
Polygonum perfoliatum

POLYGONACEAE

Flowers and fruits

Range: Southern New England, New York to Virginia, and west to Ohio; it's expected to spread over a wider eastern and southern range.

Description: Plants grow as a long, trailing vine, with a delicate, reddish stem bearing hooked barbs. Leaves are light green, alternate on the stems, and nearly perfectly triangular in shape, with hooks on the undersides. Distinctive cup-shaped, leafy structures circle the stems at intervals; this is where the small, white flowers (and later the fruit) emerge. Fruit are metallic blue and segmented; there's one shiny black seed in each segment. The vine grows very rapidly into a thick wave of vegetation that covers and smothers other plants, including trees. It produces many seeds continuously from June to October.

Life Cycle: Tender annual, killed by the first frost. Birds (and possibly other animals) feeding on the berries may spread seed over long distances. The seeds are also spread along streams because they can remain afloat in water for days.

Prevention and Control: Pull plants before flowers form. This task is easier before the barbs harden on the stems and leaves, but it can be done later (wear thick gloves and protective clothing because the tough barbs can seriously scratch skin). Check frequently for emergence of new seedlings. Repeatedly mowing or trimming plants to prevent them from flowering and setting seed will eventually control them as the vines die over the winter.

Notes: A native plant from Asia, it has been spreading from the original introduction site in Pennsylvania since the 1930s. It prefers extremely wet soils and full sun, but it can survive on drier sites and in part shade; it colonizes fields, stream banks, roadsides, and natural areas.

Morning Glories
Ipomoea spp.   CONVOLVULACEAE

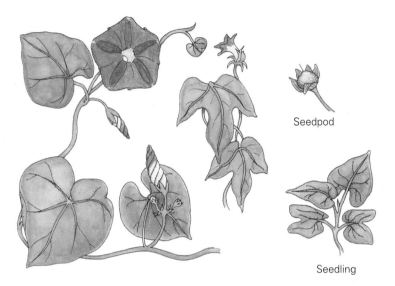

Seedpod

Seedling

Range: *I. purpurea* grows in the eastern half of the United States and Pacific Coast areas; *I. hederacea* grows in the eastern half of the United States (except in the most northern states).

Description: Stems grow from a few feet up to 10 feet (3 m) long, are slightly hairy, and twine around plants and objects in their path. Leaves are alternate on the stems with smooth edges and obvious veins arising from the midrib. Leaves of tall morning glory (*I. purpurea*) are heart-shaped, whereas leaves of ivy-leaved morning glory (*I. hederacea*) are three-lobed. Flowers are trumpet-shaped and pink, blue, purple, or white. They normally grow in groups of three to five from each flowerstalk. Blooms from July to September.

Life Cycle: Annual, reproducing by seeds.

Prevention and Control: Morning glories can become troublesome in warm regions. Pull every shoot in and around the garden, and allow the plant material to dry thoroughly to kill the vines before composting them. Use dense mulches to smother seedlings.

Notes: Watch for bird-sown morning glory vines growing in hedges and along fencerows. Don't let plants that spring up in nearby waste places flower or set seed.

Pennsylvania Smartweed
Polygonum pensylvanicum

Lady's Thumb
Polygonum persicaria

POLYGONACEAE

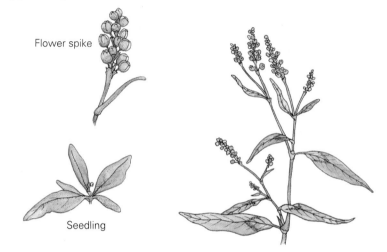

Flower spike

Seedling

Range: *P. pensylvanicum* is found in eastern and central United States as far west as Wyoming, and in southeastern Canada; *P. persicaria* has a similar range, including the northern half of the western United States into southern Canada.

Description: Plants grow up to 3 feet (91.4 cm) tall. Stems are erect, somewhat tough, and swollen at the stem joints. Leaves are alternate on the stem and long and pointed at both ends, and many of them have a darker splotch in the middle. The leaf has a short petiole extending from a sheath that encircles the stem. As the plant matures, lower sheaths dry and fall off; on *P. pensylvanicum* these papery sheaths have bristles. Flowers are pink or purplish, borne on short spikes, and are densely packed. Seeds are shiny and black. Blooms from late May to October.

Life Cycle: Annual, reproducing by seeds.

Prevention and Control: Pulling and hoeing are effective controls for these annual plants. Apply dense mulches to smother seedlings. Mow plants in ditches and roadsides to prevent them from setting seeds near your garden.

Notes: Pennsylvania smartweed can tolerate wet or compacted soils, shade, acidity, and low-nutrient levels. If it becomes a serious pest in the garden, it may indicate poor drainage or other problems with the soil. As the soil improves, smartweed populations will decrease.

Prickly Lettuce
Lactuca serriola   COMPOSITAE

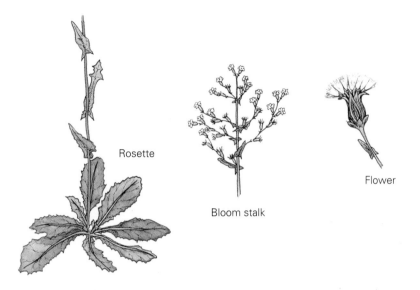

Rosette

Bloom stalk

Flower

Range: Throughout the United States and southern Canada.

Description: Plants may grow to 5 feet (1.5 m) tall. Stems are pale green and spiny, especially toward the bottom; they ooze a bitter, milky sap when cut. Leaves are alternate on the stem and sometimes blue-green, with short spines along the wavy or toothed margins. They clasp the stem tightly and have two lobes that project beyond the attachment point. The taproot is thick and deep. Flowers are numerous, small, and yellow. Seeds have a white tuft of hair at the end that enables them to be blown in the wind. Blooms from July to September.

Life Cycle: Annual, winter annual, or biennial, reproducing by seeds. The wind carries the seeds. Can sprout from the crown if only the foliage is removed.

Prevention and Control: Hoe or pull plants as you see them, cutting below the crown before they set seed. Apply dense mulches to smother seedlings. Prickly lettuce is rarely present in large numbers on cultivated land, but it can be a problem in old pastures or neglected fields. Mow or cut before flowering and again every 2 to 3 weeks thereafter to deplete the plant's reserves.

Notes: Most commonly found on light soils with good drainage. Prickly lettuce is an excellent plant for attracting beneficial insects; therefore, it could be left undisturbed in surrounding areas. However, because it can carry some of the same diseases as cultivated lettuce, it may help to remove it in surrounding areas if disease has been a continuing problem.

Prickly Sida

Sida spinosa

MALVACEAE

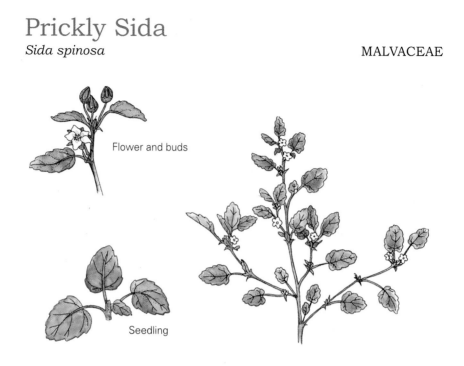

Flower and buds

Seedling

Range: Throughout the eastern two-thirds of the United States.

Description: Plants are 8 to 38 inches (20.3 to 96.5 cm) tall. Stems are erect, hairy, and many-branched. Leaves are alternate on the stem and lance-shaped with toothed margins. Two spiny projections grow from the base of each stem joint below the leaf petiole. The light yellow, five-petaled flowers also grow on short stalks from the stem joints. The calyx of the flower encloses the bottom of the seedpod. This also has five sections, each topped by two sharp beaks and containing a single seed. The plants grow from a long taproot. Blooms from June to October.

Life Cycle: Annual, reproducing by seeds.

Prevention and Control: Apply dense mulches to smother seedlings. Prickly sida is easy to pull when it's young and small (wear gloves to protect your skin from the spines). It grows a long, tenacious taproot early in the season, so the most effective control is cutting stems from the root with a very sharp hoe. Don't let plants flower and set seed in waste areas or along fencerows or roadsides.

Notes: Prickly sida thrives in the climate and soils of southern states.

Prostrate Knotweed
Polygonum aviculare   POLYGONACEAE

Flowers

Seedling

Range: Throughout the United States and southern Canada.

Description: Stems are 6 to 24 inches (15.2 to 61 cm) long and lie flat on the soil surface, forming wiry mats. Slender, ridged stems arise from thin taproots and branch in all directions; the joints of the stems have a papery covering. The stems may rise upward slightly at the flowering tips. Leaves are alternate on the stem, smooth-edged, and elongated, with somewhat pointed tips. Flowers are small and white or yellow and bloom where they join the stem. Seeds are dull brown and triangular. Blooms from midsummer to late fall.

Life Cycle: Annual, reproducing by seeds.

Prevention and Control: Pulling when the plant is young is the best control. Hoeing is effective on older plants, as long as the crown of the plant just at or slightly below the soil surface is severed from the roots. If knotweed is a serious problem, apply a dense mulch to smother weeds, and add organic matter or dig deeply, turning in compost or aged manure to aerate soil.

Notes: Prostrate knotweed grows where soils are hard and compacted. It's more likely to reside in permanent pathways than in the garden beds. Eliminate it from these areas by aerating with a spading fork and then covering with a deep mulch.

Prostrate Pigweed
Amaranthus blitoides

AMARANTHACEAE

Flowers

Range: Throughout southern Canada and the United States except the southernmost areas of Texas, Florida, and California.

Description: Stems are 8 to 24 inches (20.3 to 61 cm) long. Pigweed branches from the base and at nodes along each stem, spreading over the ground in a low mat. The reddish stems are smooth and commonly erect at the growing tips. Leaves are small and oval. Flowers are inconspicuous, lack petals, and are clustered in clumps that feel prickly to the touch. Seeds are lens-shaped and shiny black. Blooms from July to October.

Life Cycle: Annual, reproducing by seeds.

Prevention and Control: Smother seedlings with dense mulches. Hoe or pull plants. Because seeds are so plentiful and flowers so inconspicuous, be careful to remove plants early in the season. Don't leave pulled weeds in the walkways if the plants have flowers because the earliest seeds can mature on the pulled plants.

Notes: Prostrate pigweed prefers dry, sandy soils; however, it will grow in any garden soil that has good drainage.

Purslane

Portulaca oleracea

PORTULACACEAE

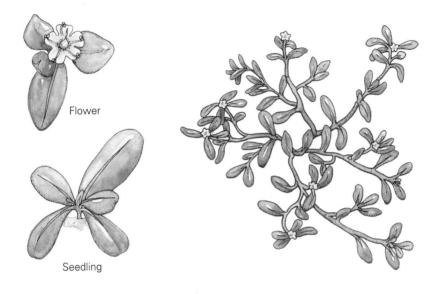

Flower

Seedling

Range: Throughout the United States and southern Canada.

Description: Stems grow to 1½ feet (45.7 cm) long, are smooth and succulent, and branch to form dense mats on the soil surface. The stems are usually tinged with red. Leaves are alternate or almost opposite on the stems and are rounded to oval in shape with smooth edges. Leaves may grow in a cluster at the tip of stems. Flowers are pale yellow and small and grow singly. The calyxes are green and enclose the petals, forming seed capsules that contain numerous tiny seeds. Blooms from July to September.

Life Cycle: Annual, reproducing by seeds.

Prevention and Control: Apply dense mulches to smother seedlings as they sprout. Purslane doesn't germinate until soils have warmed, so seedlings may germinate after the garden has been cultivated in spring. Pulling and hoeing are effective controls. Pulled plants shouldn't be left in the garden because little bits of stem can take root.

Notes: Stems and leaves of purslane are edible, raw or cooked.

Redroot Pigweed
Amaranthus retroflexus

AMARANTHACEAE

Flowers

Seedling

Range: Throughout the United States and southern Canada.

Description: Plants can grow to 6 feet (1.8 m) tall, but they're usually much shorter. Stems are slightly reddish, rough or hairy, upright, but sometimes branching at the top. Leaves are alternate on stems, dull green, and oval with pointed tips. Leaf edges are slightly wavy. Flower clusters look more like green bottle brushes than blooms; they grow in spikes. Seeds are shiny black or red-brown. The tough, deep taproot is distinctly red at the soil line. Blooms from July to October.

Life Cycle: Annual, reproducing by seeds. Plants germinating in spring grow 1 to 3 feet (30.5 to 91.4 cm) tall before blooming, but plants that germinate in late summer and early fall can produce seed when they've grown only a few inches. A single plant can produce thousands of seeds, which can remain viable in the soil for years.

Prevention and Control: Apply dense mulches to smother seedlings. Pull or hoe seedlings. Remove pulled plants from the garden and dry them in the sun before composting because they root easily. For severe infestations, cultivate the soil and leave it open for up to 2 weeks to allow seeds to germinate, then cultivate to kill the seedlings; repeat the cycle several times. Heavy infestations can also be choked out by growing cover crops.

Notes: Redroot pigweed grows in any garden soil.

Shepherd's Purse

Capsella bursa-pastoris   CRUCIFERAE

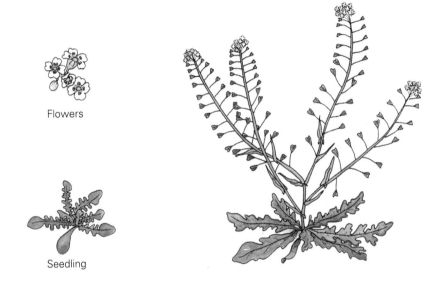

Flowers

Seedling

Range: Throughout the United States and southern Canada.

Description: Plants grow 8 to 18 inches (20.3 to 45.7 cm) tall. A basal rosette of lobed leaves commonly appears in late summer or fall, but it can also grow in spring or summer. After the rosette has overwintered or is well established in spring or summer, erect stems grow from the crown. Stems are branched and typically covered with tiny, grayish hairs. Leaves growing from the stems are smaller and narrower than those in the basal rosette. They clasp the stem and have slightly toothed edges with an overall arrow shape. Four-petaled white flowers grow in long stalks at the ends of branches. Seedpods develop at the ends of the long stalks and are triangular in shape. Blooms from March to November.

Life Cycle: Annual or winter annual, reproducing by seeds.

Prevention and Control: Use dense mulches to smother seedlings. Hoe or pull plants before they flower or set seed. Shepherd's purse roots easily, so remove pulled plants from the garden and compost them.

Notes: Shepherd's purse is present in almost all gardens, fields, and roadways. Its flowers are a rich source of nectar for beneficial insects; therefore, allow it to remain in waste areas and roadsides.

Spanish Needles
Bidens bipinnata

COMPOSITAE

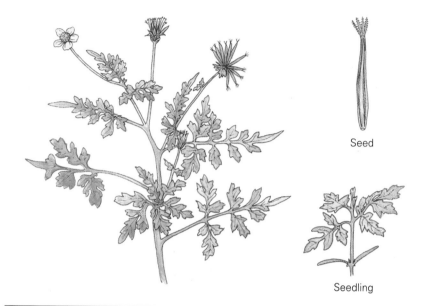

Seed

Seedling

Range: Throughout the eastern United States south of upper New York state, and west to Kansas.

Description: Plants grow 1 to 3 feet (30.5 to 91.4 cm) tall. Plants have a square stem that's sometimes hairy. Leaves are opposite on the stem and are fernlike leaflets with toothed edges. Flower heads are carried singly on long, leafless branches, toward the top of the plant. Pale yellow ray flowers surround darker yellow disk flowers in the center of each flower head. The long, slender seeds have three or four barbed spikes at the ends. Blooms from August to October.

Life Cycle: Annual, reproducing by seeds.

Prevention and Control: Apply dense mulches to smother seedlings. Hoe or pull plants. Watch waste places and areas along woods, walls, fences, and hedgerows for Spanish needles, and mow before flowers form.

Notes: Spanish needles grow in sandy or rocky soils, open fields, and slightly wooded areas. The barbed seeds stick to clothing and to the fur of passing animals, ensuring seed dispersal over a wide area.

Spotted Spurge
Euphorbia maculata

EUPHORBIACEAE

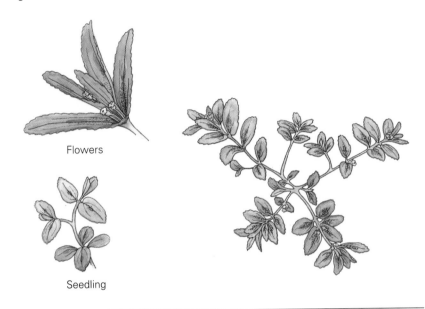

Flowers

Seedling

Range: Eastern two-thirds of the United States, and the Pacific Coast region north of central California; also areas in the eastern half of southern Canada.

Description: Plants are 1 to 2 feet (30.5 to 61 cm) long. The purplish, multi-branched stems form a mat that lies flat on the ground. Stems have milky sap. Leaves are hairy, opposite on the stem, and oval with serrated edges. There's a reddish area near the base of the leaf that gives the plant its name. Flowers are tiny and have petals fused together to form a cup; they're carried at the tops of branches on long stalks. The seed capsule is usually three-sided and contains small, pitted, triangular seeds. Blooms June to October.

Life Cycle: Annual, reproducing by seeds.

Prevention and Control: Apply dense mulches to smother seedlings. Hoe or pull plants. Spotted spurge germinates only in warm soils; look for seedlings in late spring and early summer.

Notes: Spotted spurge can grow well in slightly dry, gravelly, or sandy soils. It doesn't grow in shade; therefore, the dense canopy of an intensively planted garden bed helps inhibit growth of any spotted spurge that germinates later in the season.

Velvet Leaf
Abutilon theophrasti

MALVACEAE

Flower

Fruit

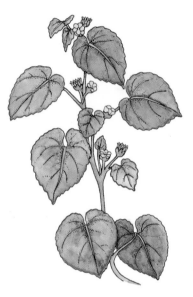

Seedling

Range: Throughout the United States except northern Maine, Michigan, Wisconsin, and the southeastern states.

Description: Plants grows 4 to 6 feet (1.2 to 1.8 m) tall. Stems are erect and covered with velvety hairs. Leaves are also covered with short, velvety hairs. They're alternate on the stem and heart-shaped with tapering, pointed tips. Flowers are borne on short stalks near the top of the plant. They're cream- to yellow-colored, about ¾ inch (19.1 mm) wide, with five yellow petals and many visible stamens around the taller pistils. Seedpods are 1 inch (2.5 cm) wide and cup-shaped, with stiff, prickly spikes around the edge; each pod contains as many as 15 prickly seeds. Blooms in midsummer, and seed sets in late summer to early fall.

Life Cycle: Annual, reproducing by seeds.

Prevention and Control: Apply dense mulches to smother seedlings. Pull or hoe plants. Mow plants in nearby waste places or along fencerows before seeds form.

Notes: Velvet leaf prefers rich, somewhat sandy soils in warm climates. Because the plant is so distinctive and grows only from seed, it's easy to eliminate from the garden.

Wild Mustards
Brassica spp.

CRUCIFERAE

Flower and seedpod

Seedling

Range: Throughout the United States and southern Canada.

Description: Plants grow up to 2 feet (61 cm) tall, depending on the species. Stems are erect and branched near the top. Leaves toward the bottom of the plant are lobed or deeply toothed; they become smaller toward the top. Small, bright yellow, four-petaled flowers are loosely clustered at the ends of branches. Seedpods are long and cylindrical and develop quickly. Seeds are dark brown or black. Blooms from early summer to late fall.

Life Cycle: Annual or winter annual, reproducing by seeds.

Prevention and Control: Use dense mulches to smother seedlings. Hoe or pull plants before seeds form. Seeds remain viable for many years in the soil. Mow plants along roadsides and field edges before seeds form.

Notes: Mustard flowers are an excellent source of nectar for beneficial insects, so allowing mustard to bloom in nearby areas can be useful. To avoid spreading seeds, pull plants immediately around the garden before the lower (earliest) flowers start to form seedpods; thoroughly dry the pulled plants before composting them. Leaves are edible.

Common Burdock
Arctium minus

COMPOSITAE

Seed

Range: Northern two-thirds of the United States; southern Canada.

Description: Plants grow from 1 to 5 feet (30.5 to 152 cm) tall. During the first year, the stems are short and hairy and grow from a crown, forming a dense rosette of large, somewhat fuzzy, heart-shaped leaves with noticeable veins. The second year, the stems are elongated, erect, and branched, and the leaves are alternate on the stem. The bottom leaves can be 1 foot (30.5 cm) or more long; leaves are smaller toward the tops of the stems. Flowers are small, reddish, surrounded by spiny bracts, and clustered. Seeds are round, spiny burs, about ½ inch (12.7 mm) wide. Blooms from July to October.

Life Cycle: Biennial, reproducing by seeds.

Prevention and Control: Pull or hoe seedlings and first-year plants. Dig up second-year plants, ensuring that as much of the large, deep taproot is removed as possible; burn any plants that have developing burs. Cut or mow down flowerstalks of burdock along roadsides and nearby areas before they set seed; repeated mowing will eventually kill established plants.

Notes: Burdock prefers fertile soil in undisturbed areas such as fencerows or unused farmland. Burs stick to anything, so seed is easily spread by animals and people.

Common Teasel
Dipsacus fullonum

DIPSACACEAE

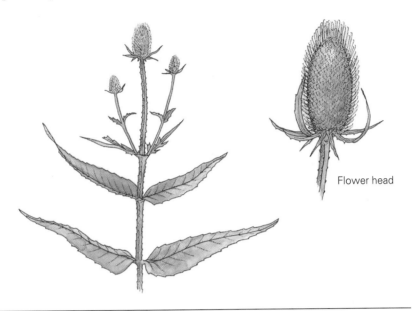

Flower head

Range: Eastern United States, from central Maine to North Carolina and westward in a narrow strip to Utah; northern Pacific coast south to central California.

Description: Plants may grow to 6 feet (1.8 m) tall. First-year plants grow in a rosette of narrow, scallop-margined, prominently veined, spiny leaves. Second-year plants grow tall, erect stems. Stems are sturdy, angled, and prickly and usually branch toward the top of the plant. The leaves are opposite along the stems and commonly form a bowl-like structure where their bases join around the stem. Leaves are narrow, toothed, and prickly at the edges and on the underside of the midrib. Flowers are white or purple with four petals and bloom in a large egg-shaped head that later becomes a prickly brown seedhead. Sharp, long bracts extend well beyond the central flower and become stiffly hooked at maturity. Blooms from July to October.

Life Cycle: Biennial, reproducing by seeds.

Prevention and Control: Apply dense mulches to smother seedlings. Pull or dig plants in the garden, taking out as much of the taproot as possible. If necessary to control plants in other areas, cut or mow before plants set seed, repeating until no more shoots appear.

Notes: Dried flower heads of teasel were once used to card wool. Today, the distinctive seedheads are used in dried flower arrangements.

Garlic Mustard
Alliaria petiolata

CRUCIFERAE

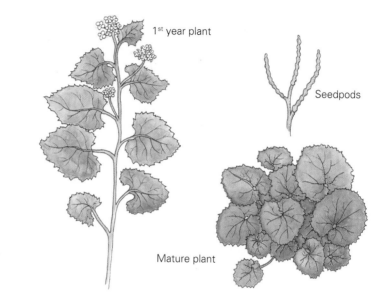

1ˢᵗ year plant

Seedpods

Mature plant

Range: From eastern Canada south to Virginia and west to Kansas and Nebraska.

Description: Mature plants reach 2 to 3⅓ feet (61 to 91.4 cm) tall. First-year plants form a low-growing rosette of leaves that remains green during winter. In the second year, erect, flowering stems form in early spring. Leaves are triangular to heart-shaped with toothed edges; they smell distinctly of garlic when crushed. Flowers are small, white, buttonlike, with four petals and are borne in clusters at the tops of stalks. Seedpods are short, narrow, and four-sided and stand erect from the plant; they contain shiny black seeds. Blooms in early spring, with seeds forming as early as mid-May; by late June most stems have dried up; however, the seedpods remain through summer. Seeds can remain viable for 5 years or more.

Life Cycle: Biennial, reproducing by seeds.

Prevention and Control: Apply dense mulches to smother seedlings (seedlings appear in fall). Hoe or pull plants anytime, making sure you remove the whole root because the plant can sprout from root pieces. Mow larger plants very early in the year before they set seed. Check for new shoots in a couple of weeks and mow again, repeating until no more shoots appear.

Notes: Garlic mustard tolerates poor, dry soil but thrives and is invasive in shaded and moist sites. It's commonly seen along roadsides and edges of woods. In some areas, this plant smothers native wildflowers—such as hepatica, trilliums, and wild ginger—that complete their life cycle in spring. The whole plant is edible, raw or cooked.

Henbit, Dead Nettle
Lamium amplexicaule

LABIATAE

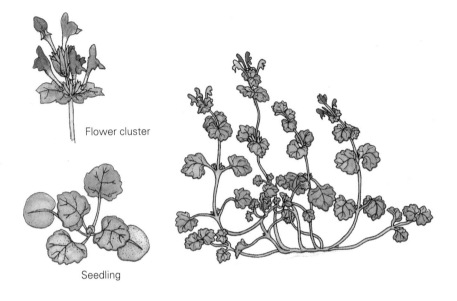

Flower cluster

Seedling

Range: Throughout the United States and southern Canada (except for the Dakotas, Montana, and part of Utah).

Description: Plants grow 4 to 16 inches (10.2 to 40.6 cm) tall. Stems are four-sided, branching, and upright. They tend to root where the lower joints of the stem come in contact with the soil. Leaves are opposite on the stem, hairy, and round, with deeply scalloped edges. Flowers are small and pink or purplish, with two lips and a long, tubular neck (corolla); they grow in whorls where upper leaves attach to stems. Blooms from April to June and again in September.

Life Cycle: Biennial or winter annual, reproducing by seeds and by rooting stems.

Prevention and Control: Apply dense mulches to smother seedlings. Hoe or pull plants, making sure that all pieces of roots are removed. Look for henbit early in the season, and control it before it drops seeds in the garden or adjacent areas. Remove pulled plants from the garden to prevent them from re-rooting; allow them to dry in the sun before composting.

Notes: Henbit prefers good soils and high-moisture levels. It prospers in cool, moist weather and is most troublesome in early spring and fall.

Poison Hemlock
Conium maculatum

UMBELLIFERAE

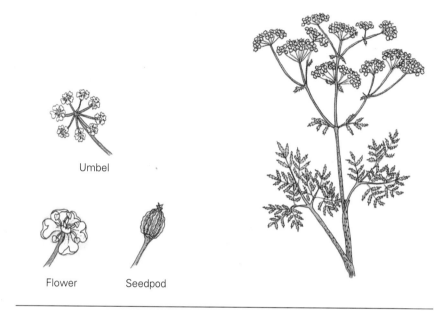

Umbel

Flower

Seedpod

Range: Throughout the United States and southern Canada (except for the north-central states and Canadian prairies).

Description: Plants grow to 2 to 7 feet (61 to 213 cm) tall. First-year plants form a low-growing rosette of leaves. Second-year stems grow tall, erect, and branched. The stems are ridged and typically spotted with small purple splotches. More leaves appear at the base than at the top of the stems. Leaves are compound and fernlike, with finely cut leaflets arranged along a central stalk; they're triangular in overall outline. The tiny white flowers appear in umbrella-shaped heads at the ends of branches. Fruit is small and round and divides down the center into two sections, each containing one seed. The plant has a long, white taproot. Blooms from June to September.

Life Cycle: Biennial, reproducing by seeds.

Prevention and Control: Wear gloves, long sleeves, and pants while handling this plant; all parts are poisonous and can cause skin irritation. Pull or dig the plants early in the season before seeds begin to form, taking as much of the deep taproot as possible. Dispose of the pulled plants by throwing them in the garbage or by burying them deeply. Infestations on cultivated ground are rare, although the plant sometimes migrates onto the edges of fields.

Notes: It's believed that Socrates was poisoned with a tea made from the poison hemlock plant. Whether the story is true or not, all parts of poison hemlock are fatally poisonous.

Queen-Anne's-Lace, Wild Carrot

Daucus carota   UMBELLIFERAE

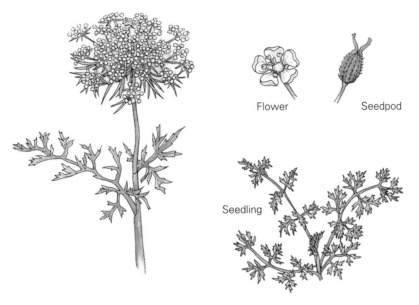

Flower   Seedpod

Seedling

Range: Throughout the United States and southern Canada (except for areas in the north-central states and Canadian prairies).

Description: Plants grow to 3 feet (91.4 cm) tall. First-year plants grow in a rosette of leaves from a white, fleshy taproot. Second-year plants grow tall, with erect, hollow stems that are ridged and hairy. Leaves are slightly hairy, compound, and fernlike. Leaves are alternate on the stems and attached to the stem by sheaths at their bases. Tiny white flowers form in flat, umbrella-shaped heads at the top of the plant. A single purplish flower commonly appears in the center of the flower head. As the flower heads mature, they cup inward. The light tan, seedlike fruits are ribbed and prickly. Blooms from June to September.

Life Cycle: Biennial, reproducing by seeds.

Prevention and Control: Apply dense mulches to smother seedlings. Pull or dig plants in the garden, making sure you remove as much of the taproot as possible. Mow or cut down plants in other areas before seeds set, repeating until no more new shoots form. If the disease aster yellows (page 181) has been a problem in garden plants, it may be helpful to control Queen-Anne's-lace in areas around the garden. Otherwise, it's such a valuable plant for attracting beneficial insects that it would be better to leave as much of it growing in nearby areas as possible.

Notes: Queen-Anne's-lace provides pollen and nectar for parasitic flies and wasps, minute pirate bugs, lady beetles, and many other beneficial insects that feed on pests of garden plants. The plant is common in dry soil, along roadsides and edges of fields.

Tansy Ragwort
Senecio jacobaea

COMPOSITAE

Flower

Seed

Range: Atlantic coast from Maine to Rhode Island; Maritime Provinces of Canada; Pacific coast from British Columbia to northern California.

Description: Plants grow to 4 feet (1.2 m) tall. First-year plants grow in a low rosette from a taproot. Second-year plants send up tall, erect stems. Stems are coarse and usually branch only at the top below the flowers. Leaves are deeply cut and lobed, with toothed edges. At the base of the plant the leaves may be hairy on the undersides. Upper leaves are alternate on the stem but clasp the stem. Flowers are round, bright yellow, and buttonlike and up to ½ inch (12.7 mm) across; they grow in wide clusters. Blooms from July to September.

Life Cycle: Biennial or winter annual, but can be a short-lived perennial. Reproduces by seeds and by root pieces.

Prevention and Control: Dig or pull plants in the garden, removing as much of the taproot as possible. In fields and waste places, mow early and often enough to prevent flowering and setting seed. In some western and eastern regions, watch for beneficial insects that have been released as a biological control for ragwort. These include the cinnabar moth, which has yellow-and-black-striped caterpillars that feed on the foliage, and a species of flea beetle and a large weevil, both of which have larvae that bore in the roots and kill the plants.

Notes: This plant prefers dry soil. It produces an alkaloid in the foliage that's toxic to horses and cattle.

White Campion, White Cockle
Silene alba   CARYOPHYLLACEAE

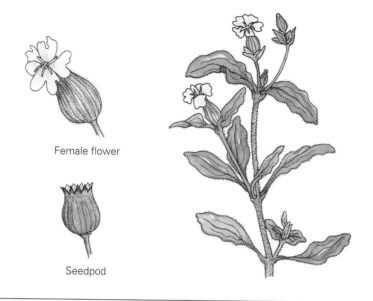

Female flower

Seedpod

Range: Eastern and north-central United States; Pacific Northwest United States, south to the middle of California; southern Canada from coast to coast.

Description: Plants grow 1 to 2½ feet (30.5 to 76.2 cm) tall. Stems are hairy, sticky, erect, and somewhat branching with an open habit. Leaves grow on stems in opposite pairs. They're hairy, light green, up to 4 inches (10.2 cm) long, and narrow with pointed tips. Flowers are held on long stems and are white to pink and fragrant, with five, deeply notched petals. They have a green-striped, bulbous tube below the petals. The seed capsule is toothed at the top and contains many flat, round, gray, bumpy seeds. Blooms from June to August.

Life Cycle: Biennial or short-lived perennial, reproducing by seeds and rootstock.

Prevention and Control: Apply dense mulches to smother seedlings. Hoe or pull plants, ensuring that the entire root is dug out. Mow or cut down plants before they set seed. Repeat the mowing until no shoots appear, or apply a dense mulch for one growing season.

Notes: This plant likes rich, well-drained soil and is commonly found along roadsides and bordering fields. It's an attractive plant for hoverflies and other beneficial insects, so it should be left to bloom in waste areas.

Broadleaf Plantain

Plantago major

PLANTAGINACEAE

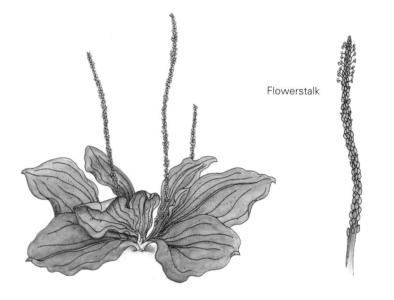

Flowerstalk

Range: Throughout the United States and southern Canada.

Description: Plants are 6 to 18 inches (15.2 to 45.7 cm) tall. Leaves grow in a flattened rosette of rounded, waxy, green leaves, 3 to 4 inches (7.6 to 10.2 cm) long. Leaves are thick and rough, with prominent parallel veins from the tip to the base. The leaf stems are stiff and wide and cup upward into a trough shape. Stems that carry flower and seed spikes are wiry and grow from the center of the rosette of leaves. Flowers are tiny and green, and seed capsules are brown or slightly purplish. They contain as many as 15 seeds each. Plantain can be much shorter and flatter in areas where it's mowed or trampled (such as in lawns). Blooms from May to September.

Life Cycle: Perennial, reproducing by seeds.

Prevention and Control: Dig or pull plants from gardens and lawns, ensuring that the entire root is removed. Where it is difficult to remove the root, repeatedly cut off the plant at the soil line until the root stops sprouting. Where plantain continues to invade lawns it is often a sign of compacted soil; therefore, aerate the lawn and spread a thin layer of compost to increase organic matter.

Notes: Plantain thrives in dense, compacted soils and shaded areas.

Buckhorn Plantain

Plantago lanceolata   PLANTAGINACEAE

Seedling

Range: Throughout the United States and southern Canada.

Description: Flowerstalks are 6 to 24 inches (15.2 to 61 cm) tall. Stems are wiry, erect, and leafless, bearing only the flowering spike. Leaves grow in a low rosette of narrow, lance-shaped, dull green leaves up to 1 foot (30.5 cm) long. Leaves narrow at the base and have three to five prominent veins that run lengthwise. The flower spikes are oval to elongate and are held considerably above the leaves. Flowers are tiny, greenish, and numerous and have distinctive long, yellowish or pale stamens that stick well out from the spike. Seed capsules grow in rows along the spike, and each contains two smooth seeds. Plants can be much shorter where they have been mowed or trampled. Blooms from May to October.

Life Cycle: Perennial, reproducing from seeds.

Prevention and Control: Dig or pull plants from gardens and lawns, ensuring that the entire root is removed. Where it's difficult to remove the root, repeatedly cut off the plant at the soil line until the root stops sprouting. If plantain continues to invade the lawn, the soil may be compacted, so aerate and increase organic matter.

Notes: Plantains prefer dense, compacted soil. Problems with plantain decrease as hardpan is broken up and aerated.

Canada Thistle
Cirsium arvense

COMPOSITAE

Seed

Seedling

Range: Northern United States and southern Canada from Quebec westward.

Description: Plants grow from 2 to 5 feet (61 to 152 cm) tall. The stem is thin and erect, with branches at the top. Leaves are 4 to 5 inches (10.2 to 12.7 cm) long, alternate on the stem, and deeply lobed with toothed, spiny edges. They're silvery and hairy on the underside. Flower heads are pink to purplish, are ¾ inch (19.1 mm) wide, and are borne in loose clusters at the top of the plant. Bracts beneath the flowers have weak bristles, but there are no spines on the stems bearing the flower heads. The seeds are flattened, ribbed, and oblong, with tufts of white hairs that allow them to be carried in the wind. Roots are deep, wide-spreading rhizomes. Blooms from July to October.

Life Cycle: Perennial, reproducing by creeping roots (rhizomes) and seeds. Seeds have a long period of viability, and roots sprout prolifically.

Prevention and Control: Wear thick gloves and pull or dig plants, removing every piece of root possible. Dry out root pieces in the sun before composting. After removing plants, sow a thickly planted cover crop to smother shoots and prevent seeds from germinating; apply a dense mulch to smother new shoots, or cut down new shoots monthly. Mow or cut nearby plants in field edges or waste areas before they flower; continue mowing monthly for several growing seasons to deplete roots. (This step may not kill plants but will prevent patches from spreading.) Apply dense mulches (cardboard, newspaper, plastic) for at least one and possibly up to three growing seasons to smother shoots. Corn gluten meal herbicides are effective at killing seeds before they emerge (but not shoots or roots). Sheep and goats will eat the thistles.

Notes: In some regions, biological control insects have been released to combat Canada thistle.

Chicory
Cichorium intybus

COMPOSITAE

Flowers

Range: Throughout the United States (except areas south of North Carolina and the Texas panhandle, as well as portions of north-central states); southern Canada from Nova Scotia to British Columbia.

Description: Plants grow from 1 to 6 feet (30.5 to 183 cm) tall. Stems are erect, branched, and hollow and ooze a milky juice when cut. Leaves at the base of the plant form a rosette of roughly lance-shaped leaves with deeply toothed to lobed edges. Leaves are alternate on the stem, smaller and less lobed than lower leaves; toward the top of the plant, they clasp the stem. Flowers are round and blue (occasionally white), with many petals and up to 1½ inches (38.1 mm) wide. Up to three flowers appear on each long stem arising from the uppermost leaves. Two rows of bristly bracts at the flower base are quite visible. Flowers close each evening. Plants have a deep taproot. Blooms from June to October.

Life Cycle: Perennial, reproducing from seeds and by spreading roots.

Prevention and Control: Pull or hoe plants, making sure to remove as much of the root as possible. Apply dense mulches to smother seedlings or shoots sprouting from roots. Repeatedly cut plants below the crown to eventually kill established roots. If it's necessary to control chicory in nearby areas, mow or cut plants before seeds form; otherwise, leave plants growing to attract beneficial insects.

Notes: Chicory prefers soil with a neutral to slightly alkaline pH and is most troublesome in limestone areas. It's most common along roadsides, fences, and unused land. It attracts beneficial insects. Roots are used as a coffee substitute or additive.

Coltsfoot
Tussilago farfara

ASTERACEAE

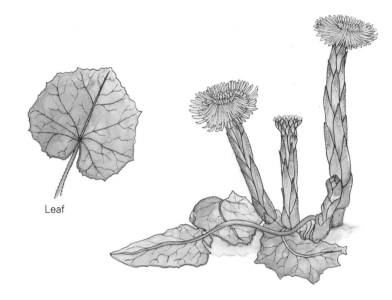

Leaf

Range: Northeastern United States as well as southeastern Canada; eastern areas west to Minnesota as well as eastern areas in Canadian prairies.

Description: Flowerstalks reach 6 inches (15.2 cm) tall and appear in early spring. They're erect, scaly, leafless, and somewhat woolly, with a purplish tinge. Leaves are heart-shaped, are 4 to 8 inches (10.2 to 20.3 cm) wide, and appear at the end of the flowering season. They have long petioles, and the undersides are covered with whitish hairs. Flowers are light yellow and up to 2 inches (5.1 cm) wide and resemble dandelions, with many narrow petals. Seeds have a tuft of hair that allows them to be spread by the wind. Blooms from April to May.

Life Cycle: Perennial, reproducing by seeds and roots.

Prevention and Control: Apply dense mulches to smother seedlings. Pull or dig plants, taking care to follow the spreading roots and dig them out entirely. Dry them in the sun before composting pulled plants. For serious infestations, apply dense mulches for a growing season to smother plants or mow plants every few weeks until roots stop sending up shoots.

Notes: Coltsfoot is adapted to a wide range of conditions and is commonly seen along roadsides and waste areas.

Common Milkweed
Asclepias syriaca   ASCLEPIADACEAE

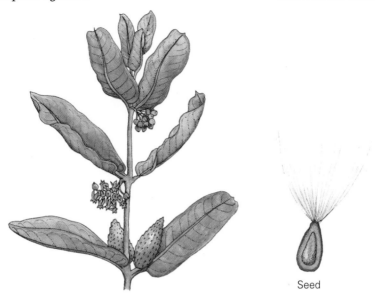

Seed

Range: Eastern half of United States (except for the Gulf Coast); southern Canada from New Brunswick to Saskatchewan.

Description: Plants grow 2 to 5 feet (61 to 153 cm) tall. Stems are upright, stout, fuzzy, and not branched. When cut, stems ooze a milky sap. Leaves are 4 to 8 inches (10.2 to 20.3 cm) long, opposite on the stem, broadly oblong and rounded, thick, and tough, with prominent veins; they're smooth on top, downy on the underside. Flowers are borne in large clusters from the upper leaves and stem tips. The star-shaped blooms are waxy, pinkish white to darkish pink and fragrant. Seedpods are large, teardrop-shaped, green, and spiny; they ripen into dry, grayish brown husks that split down one side to release seeds. Seeds are flat, brown, and oval and tipped with many feathery, silky white hairs. Plants have an extensive creeping root system (rhizomes). Blooms from June to August.

Life Cycle: Perennial, reproducing by seeds and by rhizomes.

Prevention and Control: It's usually sufficient to pull plants found in the garden, as long as underground rhizomes are also removed. Apply dense mulches to smother seedlings or shoots sprouting from roots. Don't let pods ripen on plants near your garden. Where the caterpillars of monarch butterflies are present, manage milkweed in nearby areas by cutting off flower heads before the pods start to ripen, and leave the leafy part of the plant for the caterpillars.

Notes: Common milkweed is found in old pastures, woods, roadsides, and gardens. Milkweed grows in many conditions but is most common in drier soils. It's the only food plant for the caterpillars of monarch butterflies.

Common Pokeweed
Phytolacca americana   PHYTOLACCACEAE

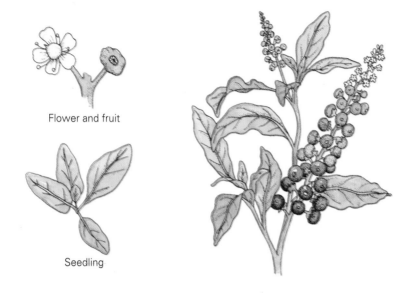

Flower and fruit

Seedling

Range: Throughout the United States from Maine to Minnesota, and southward, including the area between Florida and the eastern two-thirds of Texas.

Description: Plants grow 3 to 9 feet (91.4 to 274 cm) tall. Stems are thick, upright, and reddish. The stem is usually branched near the top. Leaves are alternate on the stem and oval, getting smaller toward the top of the plant. They're smooth, with alternate veins from the central midrib. The flowers grow in narrow, drooping, 4- to 6-inch (10.2 to 15.2 cm)-long strands, arising from stalks opposite upper leaves. The tiny, white flowers have five petals. They drop quickly and are followed by drooping clusters of dark purple berries, each containing 10 seeds. Plants grow from a large taproot. Blooms from June to September.

Life Cycle: Perennial, reproducing by seeds.

Prevention and Control: Use dense mulches to smother seedlings. Using gloves, pull or dig young plants before the large root develops. Large plants must be cut below the crown with a sharp spade, and as much of the root must be removed as possible. To clear ground of pokeweed, cut off and remove each group of stems, then continue to cut or mow the area every few weeks until they stop sprouting. Alternatively, after cutting down established plants, cover the entire area with a dense mulch (newspaper, cardboard, or plastic) for a growing season.

Notes: Pokeweed likes deep, rich, well-drained soils, but it doesn't survive long in a garden that's regularly cultivated. The entire plant is poisonous, except for young shoots.

Common Yarrow
Achillea millefolium

COMPOSITAE

Floret

Range: Throughout the United States (except areas in the Southwest) and southern Canada.

Description: Plants grow 1 to 2 feet (30.5 to 61 cm) tall. Stems are erect and usually simple but may branch toward the top. Stems may be smooth or slightly hairy. Leaves are delicate and feathery and give off an aromatic scent when crushed. They're covered with soft gray hairs and arise almost directly from the stem. Flowers are carried in flat, compound clusters and are usually white or yellow (rarely pinkish). Blooms from June to October.

Life Cycle: Perennial, reproducing by seeds and roots.

Prevention and Control: Pull plants in the garden before the they set seed, making sure that all roots are removed. Apply dense mulches to smother seedlings or shoots growing from roots. It usually isn't necessary or desirable to remove yarrow from nearby areas because the plants provide pollen and nectar for beneficial insects, particularly hoverflies, lady beetles, and parasitic wasps.

Notes: Yarrow grows in various conditions but is particularly common in thin, poor soils. Flowers dry well for winter arrangements.

Common Yellow Wood Sorrel

Oxalis stricta   OXALIDACEAE

Seedling

Range: Throughout the United States and southern Canada.

Description: Plants grow 4 to 18 inches (20.3 to 45.7 cm) tall. Young stems are generally erect but are thin and weak. As the plant grows, the stems branch in all directions and tend to spread low over the ground. Stems are light green and somewhat hairy. Leaves grow on long, thin petioles and are divided into three, heart-shaped leaflets with an obvious vein running down the center of each leaflet. Flowers are clear yellow with five petals. Seedpods are cylindrical and slightly hairy, with pointed tips. Seeds are tiny and are ejected quite a distance from the pod when it bursts. Blooms from May to October.

Life Cycle: Perennial, reproducing by seeds.

Prevention and Control: Hoe or pull plants before they set seed, removing all of the root. Plants can root readily from joints in the stem, so remove pulled plants from the garden and dry in the sun before composting. Use dense mulches to smother seedlings or shoots from pieces of root remaining in soil.

Notes: Wood sorrel is common with acid soil and in neglected areas, dry lawns, and bare soil. It grows quite well in shade.

Curly Dock
Rumex crispus

POLYGONACEAE

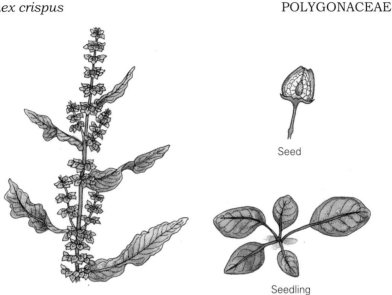

Seed

Seedling

Range: Throughout the United States and southern Canada.

Description: Plants grow from 1 to 4 feet (30.5 to 122 cm) tall. A dense rosette of thick, 6- to 12-inch (15.2 to 30.5 cm)-long leaves grows first from a thick, branching taproot. Later, flowering stalks grow from the rosette; stems are hairless and ridged, with enlarged joints; stems turn reddish brown in fall. Leaves are lance-shaped, with curly or wavy margins. Leaves growing on the stems are alternate, with short petioles growing from a papery sheath just above each leaf joint. The flower head has many branches with small, narrow leaves interspersed among the flowers. The small, greenish flowers become reddish brown as they age. The seeds are shiny, brown, and triangular, with a papery, winged covering. Blooms from June to September.

Life Cycle: Perennial, reproducing by seeds.

Prevention and Control: Pull or dig plants, making sure that the entire large, branched taproot is dug out of the soil. Removing dock is easiest when it's young, before the taproot has had a chance to grow deep. Apply dense mulches to smother seedlings or shoots arising from root pieces.

Notes: Curly dock is tolerant of poor conditions, but it's most common in moist soils. It commonly grows along roadsides and ditches, at the edges of fields, and in waste places.

Dandelion
Taraxacum officinale

COMPOSITAE

Seed

Seedling

Range: Throughout most of the United States and southern Canada.

Description: Flowerstalks grow to 1 to 12 inches (2.5 to 15.2 cm) high. Plants grow a basal rosette of lobed or toothed leaves arising from a deep, fleshy taproot. When leaves or stems are cut, they ooze a milky sap. Flower buds are nestled into the leaf rosettes at first, then grow above the leaves. Flower heads are bright yellow, 1 to 2 inches (2.5 to 5.1 cm) across; the flowerstalks are hollow, smooth, and pale on the outside. Seeds have tufts of hairs that allow them to drift in the wind. Plants can grow and flower as flat, low rosettes where they're repeatedly mowed or trampled. Blooms from March to December.

Life Cycle: Perennial, reproducing by seeds and from root crowns.

Prevention and Control: Where dandelions aren't desired, dig or pull plants before the seeds set, removing as much of the taproot as possible. For lawns, use a sharp, forked dandelion cutter to sever the taproot as deeply as possible, disturbing the soil as little as possible. (The larger the opening in the soil, the more likely it is that weed seeds will germinate in the opening.) Persistent plants may require digging several times to remove new shoots developing from roots. Dandelions provide a vital source of early pollen for bees and many other beneficial insects that feed on garden pests; therefore, it's neither necessary nor desirable to eradicate them from nearby areas.

Notes: Dandelion flowers can be used to make wine, the leaves can be cooked or eaten fresh, and the roots can be roasted for a coffee substitute.

Field Bindweed
Convolvulus arvensis   CONVOLVULACEAE

Seedpod

Seedling

Range: Throughout the United States (except for Florida and the extreme southern areas of Texas and the Southwest) and southern California.

Description: Stems are long, twining vines growing 2 to 7 feet (61 to 213 cm) long. They're smooth and thin, and they lie prostrate on the ground or climb up vegetation and objects. Leaves are alternate, simple, and smooth-edged, and many of them flare into two lobes at the base. Flowers are trumpet-shaped with a wide, round mouth; they're white or pink and 1 inch (2.5 cm) wide. The dark seeds have a rough, pebbly texture. Blooms from June to September.

Life Cycle: Perennial, reproducing by seeds and creeping roots.

Prevention and Control: Bindweed is difficult to eradicate because roots can extend for many feet in the soil. Dig or pull plants, making sure that the entire root is removed. Don't let it remain in the garden long enough to gain a foothold. For severe infestations, apply a dense mulch (newspaper, cardboard, or plastic that's well weighed down) to the area and to a wide area around the infestation to control spreading roots; leave in place for the entire season. Mow or cut plants in waste areas to prevent seeds from forming.

Notes: Bindweed likes rich soil, good drainage, and bright light conditions.

Field Horsetail
Equisetum arvense

EQUISETACEAE

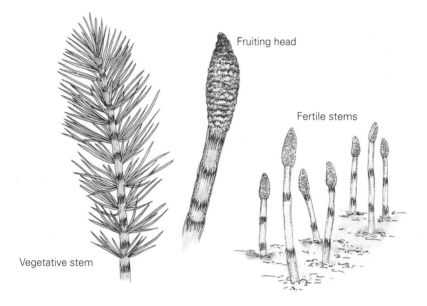

Fruiting head

Fertile stems

Vegetative stem

Range: Throughout the United States (except in the Southeast) and southern Canada.

Description: Plants grow up to 18 inches tall (45.7 cm). Stems are stiff, erect, hollow, jointed, and very tough. They're either vegetative (which means they don't produce flowers) or fertile (which means they produce flowers). Fertile stems appear first in spring. They aren't branched; they have prominent, swollen joints and what looks like small oval pinecones (the fruiting heads) at the tips. The stem dies back after the fruiting heads shed their spores. Later the vegetative stems appear; these have whorls of long, thin branches arising from each leaf joint. The roots are strong rhizomes that can grow many feet deep in moist soils.

Life Cycle: Perennial, reproducing by spores and by creeping roots.

Prevention and Control: Pull or dig plants, removing as much of the root as possible; this is a temporary measure because shoots eventually grow back from the pieces of root left in the soil. Repeated removal, combined with keeping the soil cultivated and open, discourages horsetail sufficiently for the season to allow garden crops to grow. Smothering plants with dense mulches (cardboard, newspaper, or plastic) can provide temporary control; however, shoots can eventually penetrate even asphalt surfaces. Where possible, for long-term prevention of horsetail invasions, dry out the site by improving drainage, and enrich the soil with compost and organic matter; make sure that the soil is well drained over winter.

Notes: Horsetail thrives in moist, sandy, or gravelly soil, especially along edges of woods and fields and in ditches.

Goldenrods
Solidago spp.

COMPOSITAE

Florets

Range: Many species throughout the United States and southern Canada.

Description: Plants grow from 2 to 5 feet (61 to 152 cm) tall. Stems are generally solitary, but they may be clustered. Leaves are numerous and crowded, especially toward the middle to the top of the plant. They're narrow and lance-shaped and have prominent, parallel veins and sharply toothed margins. Leaf undersides may be slightly hairy. Basal leaves usually die and drop as the season progresses. The many-branched flower heads are carried at the top of stems. Flowers are yellow to yellow-green and bloom on long spikes that droop in graceful arcs. Blooms from July to October.

Life Cycle: Perennial, reproducing by seeds and creeping rhizomes.

Prevention and Control: To remove plants from the garden, hoe or dig plants, removing as much of the root as possible. It may be necessary to dig established roots several times throughout the season whenever new sprouts appear. Apply a dense mulch to smother seedlings or shoots. It usually isn't necessary or desirable to control goldenrod in nearby areas and roadsides because it's an important source of pollen and nectar for bees and many beneficial insects.

Notes: Goldenrod can grow in any type of soil, but it does require good light. It's an important source of pollen and nectar for honeybees and other beneficial insects, such as minute pirate bugs and hoverflies. Contrary to popular belief, goldenrod doesn't cause hay fever; that's because it isn't pollinated by spreading pollen in the wind.

Ground Ivy
Glechoma hederacea

LABIATAE

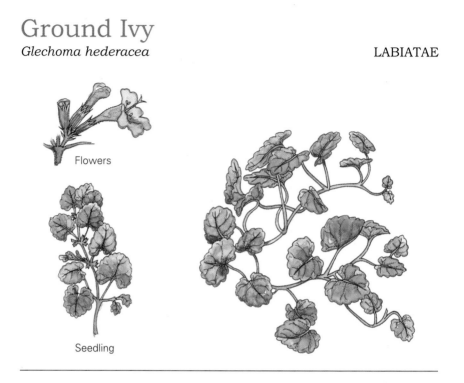

Flowers

Seedling

Range: Throughout the eastern half of both the United States and southern Canada, except for Florida and southern Georgia.

Description: Stems grow 15 to 30 inches (38.1 to 76.2 cm) long, usually spreading along the ground. Stems are four-sided and branching and commonly root at the stem joints. Leaves are round or kidney-shaped, bright green, and opposite on the stem, and they have scalloped margins. Flowers are blue or purplish and grow from the point where the leaf meets the stem on upright branches. They're small and trumpet-shaped, with two lips. Blooms from April to July.

Life Cycle: Perennial, reproducing by seeds and creeping stems.

Prevention and Control: Hoe or pull plants, making sure to take all roots and connecting stems. Remove pulled plants from the garden and dry them in the sun to prevent stems from sprouting roots when they're composted. Apply dense mulches to smother seedlings and shoots developing from fragments of stems left in the garden or to smother dense patches on lawns.

Notes: Ground ivy, a mint relative, prefers rich soils that are somewhat moist. It grows well in shade and typically tries to form a groundcover under trees.

Heal-All
Prunella vulgaris   LABIATAE

Flowers

Range: Throughout the United States (except for regions in the north-central states) and southern Canada.

Description: Stems are up to 24 inches (61 cm) long; they're four-sided and can be erect or prostrate on the soil. Leaves are opposite on the stems, hairy when young, and smooth as they mature; they have smooth or slightly toothed margins and are spaced widely along the stems. Flower spikes are thick, grow at the tips of branches, and have a pair of visible bracts below them. The small, tube-shaped flowers have two lips and are blue, purple, or pink (rarely white) with green or purplish calyxes. Where plants are mowed or trampled, they grow into dense, prostrate mats. Blooms from May to October.

Life Cycle: Perennial, reproducing by seeds and runners (stolons) that root at the joints.

Prevention and Control: Apply dense mulches to smother seedlings and young plants. Dig or pull plants, removing all of the connected above-ground runners and roots. Remove pulled plants from the garden and allow them to dry in the sun to prevent stems from sprouting roots before composting them.

Notes: Heal-all thrives in moist areas and is common in lawns and along roadsides.

Hedge Bindweed
Convolvulus sepium

CONVOLVULACEAE

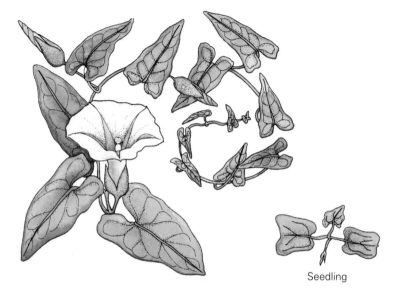

Seedling

Range: Eastern and northwestern United States and southern Canada.

Description: Stems grow 3 to 10 feet (91.4 to 305 cm) long and trail on the ground or twine up plants and over objects. Stems are usually smooth, but they may be covered with small hairs. Leaves are alternate on the stem and arrow- or heart-shaped, with pointed tips and squared-off lobes at the base. Flowers are trumpet-shaped, white or pinkish, and 1 to 2 inches (2.5 to 5.1 cm) wide. Roots are very long and shallow. Blooms from June to August.

Life Cycle: Perennial, reproducing by seeds and creeping underground stems (rhizomes).

Prevention and Control: Removing this invasive plant from gardens requires persistence in pulling it every time a shoot appears. Pull out roots and shoots, remove the pulled plants from the garden, and dry them in the sun before composting them. To remove a large patch of bindweed, apply a dense mulch (cardboard, newspaper, or plastic that's well weighed down) to the affected area and to a wide border around it; leave the mulch for the entire growing season and watch for roots spreading from under the mulched area. Limiting the area of moist soil in the garden by using a drip irrigation system helps prevent bindweed roots from re-colonizing garden beds because dry soil deters them. To control bindweed in hedges, cut the stems near the ground to kill tops and prevent seeds from forming.

Notes: Hedge bindweed can climb nearby plants or fences, but without a support it will trail along the ground. It's quite invasive, and it will quickly cover the edges of roadways or fields, choking out less-vigorous plants. Bindweed likes rich, moist soils and good light. It grows quickly in the cool conditions of spring and fall, and in coastal areas it may continue to grow all winter.

Hoary Vervain
Verbena stricta

VERBENACEAE

Flowers

Seed

Range: Midwest, the Great Plains, Texas, and along the Pacific coast in the United States.

Description: Plants grow 1 to 4 feet (30.5 to 122 cm) tall. Stems are erect and simple or branched toward the top, and they're covered with soft, white hairs. Leaves are opposite on the stem and oval, with toothed edges. They have a coating of soft, white hairs that makes them look almost downy. Flowers grow in slender, upright spikes of small purple, pink, or white blooms; flowers open in succession from the bottom to the top of the spike. Seeds are dark brown. Blooms from June to September.

Life Cycle: Perennial, reproducing by seeds and by creeping underground roots (rhizomes).

Prevention and Control: Apply a dense mulch to smother seedlings. Pull or dig plants in the garden, removing the whole root system. Remove pulled plants from the garden to prevent them from rooting again, and dry them in the sun before composting. Cut or mow plants in nearby areas before they flower.

Notes: Hoary vervain likes dry, gravelly soils and grows well where fertility is low. It's unlikely to infest garden areas that are well tended and have high levels of organic matter.

Horse Nettle
Solanum carolinense

SOLANACEAE

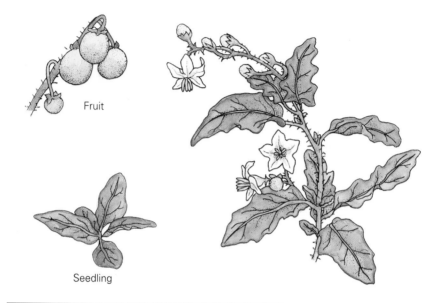

Fruit

Seedling

Range: In the eastern half of the United States, in the West from Idaho and Arizona to California (except the state of Washington), and in southern Canada.

Description: Plants grow 1 to 3 feet (30.5 to 91.4 cm) tall. Stems are stout, erect, and branched or unbranched, with yellowish spines. Leaves are up to 5 inches (12.7 cm) long, alternate on the stem, and oblong or oval, with wavy or lobed edges. The leaves also have prickly, yellow spines along the veins and the leaf stem. The flowers are star-shaped, 1 inch (2.5 cm) wide, and white, pale blue, or violet. They bloom in small clusters, and each flower has a green calyx with five sepals at its base. Numerous seeds develop within a round, yellow-orange berry, which is ½ inch (12.7 mm) wide; the berries wrinkle as they mature. Blooms from June to September.

Life Cycle: Perennial, reproducing by seeds and creeping underground roots (rhizomes).

Prevention and Control: Wearing gloves, pull or dig plants before they flower and dig up the entire root system; remove the plants from the garden and dry them in the sun before composting. Cut or mow nearby plants in fields and along roadsides before they flower; repeat mowing as new shoots appear. To clear a heavily infested area, dig plants and then apply a dense mulch (newspaper, cardboard, or plastic) to smother new shoots for the growing season.

Notes: Horse nettle grows best in sandy soil in full sun. It's poisonous.

Purple Loosestrife
Lythrum salicaria   LYTHRACEAE

Seedstalk

Range: Northeastern United States to Virginia and Missouri and western Washington state; eastern Canada and southern British Columbia.

Description: Plants grow 2 to 4 feet (61 to 122 cm) tall. Stems are stout and erect. Like the leaves, they may be smooth or have small, downy hairs. Leaves are opposite each other on the stem or arise in three-leaved whorls that clasp the stem. They're smaller and more lance-shaped toward the top of the plant; leaves at the base are more heart-shaped. Flowers are a clear purple color and very showy. They have six petals, grow in slender, upright, tapering spikes that are wider at the base, and are interspersed with leafy bracts. Blooms from June to September.

Life Cycle: Perennial, reproducing by seeds.

Prevention and Control: Loosestrife— along with its entire root system (which isn't extensive)—must be dug out to be eliminated, preferably before plants flower. Apply a dense mulch to smother seedlings. Cut or mow established plants and continue to mow every few weeks until plants stop sending up shoots, or mulch with newspaper, cardboard, or plastic for a growing season. Where loosestrife continues to be a problem, improve the drainage of the site if possible.

Notes: Loosestrife can grow in a range of conditions, but it thrives in moist, swampy conditions. It's an invasive weed that has become a serious pest in wetlands, where it chokes out native plants needed to sustain wildlife. The seeds float and are readily carried by flowing water to new sites. Although once considered an ornamental, it's now recognized as a serious problem and shouldn't be planted.

St.-John's-Wort

Hypericum perforatum

GUTTIFERAE

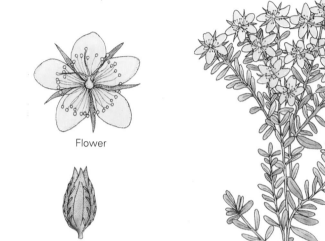

Flower

Seedpod

Range: Throughout the eastern half of both the United States and southern Canada; also southern British Columbia and Pacific Northwest states.

Description: Plants grow 1 to 2 feet (30.5 to 61 cm) tall. Stems are smooth, erect, and multibranched with a woody base. The numerous leaves are each 1 inch (2.5 cm) long, oblong, and dotted with tiny pinhole spots that let light through. They're opposite on the stem and attached directly to the stem. The stems carrying the blooms are quite leafy. Flowers have five yellow-orange petals with dark dots at the edges of the petals. The flowers are 1 inch (2.5 cm) wide and have noticeable, long stamens growing in three distinct groups. The seedpods are round with pointed tips and contain three chambers with numerous seeds. Blooms from June to September.

Life Cycle: Perennial, reproducing by seeds and creeping roots.

Prevention and Control: Apply a dense mulch to smother seedlings. Using gloves, pull or dig plants, removing the entire root. To clean a heavily infested area, cut or mow the plants and continue to mow every few weeks until the roots stop sprouting, or apply a dense mulch (cardboard, newspaper, or plastic).

Notes: St.-John's-wort prefers dry, gravelly, or sandy soils; it won't grow in damp areas. It contains a compound that irritates the mouths of livestock that graze on it. It can also cause an allergic reaction and severe burns on skin with exposure to sunlight. In some regions, insects that eat St.-John's-wort are being released as a biological control.

Sheep Sorrel
Rumex acetosella

POLYGONACEAE

Seedling

Range: Throughout the United States and southern Canada.

Description: Plants grow up to 6 to 18 inches (15.2 to 45.7 cm) tall. Young plants form a rosette of leaves, which are 1 to 3 inches long (2.5 to 7.6 cm) and arrow-shaped. Thin, erect, flowering stems grow from the center of the rosette; they branch toward the top of the stem. Leaves growing from stems are narrower than those in the rosette and have two distinct basal lobes. Stems and flowerstalks are reddish. Small, red or yellowish flowers grow on branching, upright spikes. The fruit is shiny, triangular, and yellow or reddish brown. Plants have widely spreading root systems. Blooms from May to October.

Life Cycle: Perennial, reproducing by seeds and extensive creeping roots (rhizomes).

Prevention and Control: Apply a dense mulch to smother seedlings. Pull or dig plants, along with the roots. Remove plants from the garden to prevent them from rooting, and dry them in the sun before composting. Improve soil fertility and add lime to raise the soil pH, which inhibits the growth of sorrel.

Notes: Sorrel typically indicates poor fertility. It grows on acidic, shallow, dry, or gravelly ground.

Stinging Nettle
Urtica dioica

URTICACEAE

Flowers

Range: Eastern half of the United States (except Florida), eastern Washington state, Idaho, Colorado, northern Texas, and southern Canada.

Description: Plants grow 2 to 6 feet (61 to 183 cm) tall. Stems are erect and ridged and covered with hairs that sting bare skin, leaving red welts. Leaves are also covered with stinging hairs; they're opposite on the stem, rough, dark green, oval to heart-shaped with coarsely toothed margins. Tiny green flowers bloom in clusters on drooping spikes originating from points where leaves meet the stem and at the tips of stems. Fruits are tiny, grayish brown, and lens-shaped. Blooms from June to September.

Life Cycle: Perennial, reproducing by seeds and creeping roots (rhizomes).

Prevention and Control: Wear boots, thick pants, and tough gloves, and use a sharp spade to dig stinging nettles. Follow the spreading roots through the soil and lift them. Let the plant dry in the sun before composting (continue to wear gloves when handling the wilted plant material). Cut or mow plants and continue to mow every few weeks when shoots reappear, or apply a dense mulch (cardboard, newspaper, or plastic) for a growing season.

Notes: The leaves are edible as steamed greens.

Tall Ironweed
Vernonia altissima   COMPOSITAE

Flowers

Seed

Range: Eastern half of the United States south of Vermont and New Hampshire.

Description: Plants may reach 10 feet (3.1 m) tall. Stems are smooth and branch widely toward the top. Leaves are alternate on the stem, lance-shaped with pointed tips, and up to 10 inches (25.4 cm) long, with small, pointed teeth at the margins. They usually point upward, rather than horizontally from the stem. Flowers are reddish purple and ½ inch (12.7 mm) wide; they grow in loose, open clusters. Green, sharply toothed, leaf-like structures enclose the base of the flower heads. Blooms from August to October.

Life Cycle: Perennial, reproducing by seeds and creeping roots (rhizomes).

Prevention and Control: Dig or pull plants, along with the roots. Mow or cut plants in the late summer before they set seeds. Apply dense mulch (cardboard, newspaper, or plastic) to smother seedlings or shoots developing from roots of plants that have been mowed down. Improve the drainage of garden soils to discourage tall ironweed.

Notes: Tall ironweed prefers very moist, rich soils. It's an attractive food plant for bumblebees, so you may not want to eradicate plants in areas near the garden.

Wild Garlic
Allium vineale

LILIACEAE

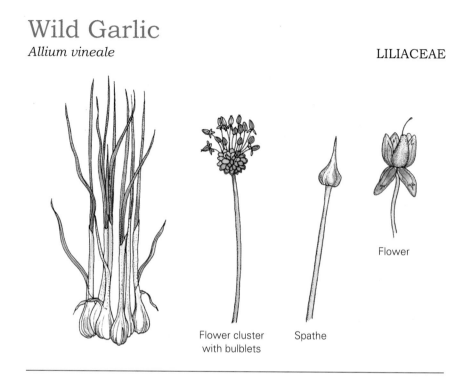

Flower cluster
with bulblets

Spathe

Flower

Range: Throughout the United States.

Description: Plants grow 1 to 3 feet (30.5 to 61 cm) tall. Stems are stiff and erect, with leaves growing only from the lower half. Leaves are hollow with a basal sheath that encircles the stem. In some areas, wild garlic will flower and set seed. The flower head is umbrella-shaped and made up of whitish green, pink, or purplish red flowers on a short stock; plants set seeds in early spring. The plant produces small, grain-sized, aerial bulblets on the top of the stem and larger bulblets underground toward the end of summer. Blooms from May to June.

Life Cycle: Perennial, reproducing from seeds, aerial bulblets, and bulbs.

Prevention and Control: Dig up every plant, removing as many underground bulbs as you can find. Cultivate regularly to control developing shoots; this is most effective in dry soil. If wild garlic is a serious problem, apply a dense mulch (newspaper, cardboard, or plastic) to heavily infested areas for an entire season. Improving the soil drainage helps discourage the growth of the weed.

Notes: Wild garlic tolerates almost any environment, but it grows best in heavy, fertile soil. Leaves smell like garlic.

Yellow Rocket, Winter Cress
Barbarea vulgaris   CRUCIFERAE

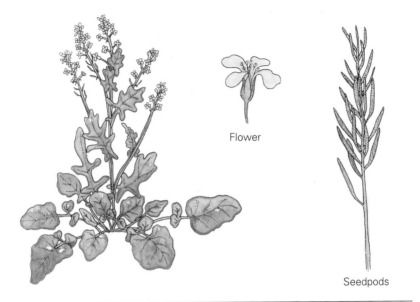

Flower

Seedpods

Range: Northeastern United States south to Arkansas, areas in the north-central states, and Pacific Northwest; southeastern Canada.

Description: Plants grow 1 to 2 feet (30.5 to 61 cm) tall. During the first year, a rosette of leaves forms close to the ground. Leaves are glossy and lobed; the rounded terminal lobe is so large that lower lobes look more like smaller individual leaves than portions of the same leaf. In spring of the second season, stems grow from the crown. The stems are hairless and may be ridged. Leaves are alternate on the stems and lobed at the base; they become less lobed and shorter toward the top of the stem. Flowers are bright yellow, have four petals, and grow in loose clusters at the end of each branch. They're followed by 1-inch (2.5 cm)-long seedpods with tiny yellow seeds. Plants have a deep taproot. Blooms from April to August.

Life Cycle: Short-lived perennial, reproducing by seeds; in some areas it grows like a winter annual.

Prevention and Control: Hoe or pull plants, removing the deep taproot. Cut or mow heavily infested areas before plants set seed, repeating mowing every few weeks until they stop sending up shoots, or apply a dense mulch (newspaper, cardboard, or plastic) for the growing season. It may not be necessary or desirable to control rocket in nearby waste or weedy areas because it's an excellent source of food for bees and beneficial insects.

Notes: Rocket likes rich soils with good moisture levels and quickly colonizes newly cultivated areas. It provides some of the earliest pollen and nectar in spring for beneficial insects and bees. It's edible.

Japanese Honeysuckle

Lonicera japonica   CAPRIFOLIACEAE

Flower

Berries

Range: Eastern half of the United States north to Michigan.

Description: Plants grow up to 30 feet (9.1 m) long. Stems are woody and trail or climb over vegetation and objects. Stems lying on the soil surface sprout roots at the leaf joints. Leaves are opposite on the stem, slightly hairy, and oval. Paired, highly fragrant, and white, pink, or yellow flowers arise from each side of the leaf joints just above the leaf. The five petals form a long tube with two uneven lips. Berries are purplish black and shiny. Two or three seeds are enclosed in each berry. Blooms from June and July.

Life Cycle: Perennial, reproducing from seeds, trailing stems, and underground rhizomes.

Prevention and Control: Pull seedlings as soon as they appear. Dig deeply to remove established rhizomes and rooting stems; continue to watch for new shoots, and remove them as they appear. This job takes several seasons; honeysuckle is vigorous and spreads rapidly. To slow the spread of plants, cut or mow plants in uncultivated areas before they set fruit (which is spread by birds), and continue to mow periodically for several seasons, or pasture goats in the area.

Notes: Honeysuckle twines up fences or nearby trees, or if it doesn't have support, it trails along the ground. Berries are a favorite food of many seed-spreading birds. In the southern states, leaves remain on the plant all winter.

Kudzu

Pueraria lobata

LEGUMINOSAE

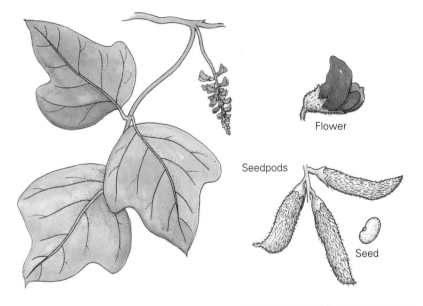

Flower

Seedpods

Seed

Range: Southeastern half of the United States and mid-Atlantic states.

Description: Plants reach to up 60 feet (18.3 m) long in one season, smothering vegetation and growing over objects. When young, the stems of the vine are slightly hairy, but as they age, they become woody and smooth. Leaves are divided into three leaflets; they're usually lobed and alternate along the stem. Flowers are small, reddish purple, and grape-scented and resemble pea flowers; they're borne in clusters. The large, upright petal is bright yellow at the base. Seedpods grow up to 4 inches (10.2 cm) long and look like hairy pea pods. Kudzu grows from a large, deep, starchy, tuberous root. Blooms from late August to September.

Life Cycle: Perennial, reproducing mainly by runners and stems that root at the leaf joints; also may sometimes spread by seeds.

Prevention and Control: Cut vines and dig out as much of the deep roots as possible. Because each piece of root can sprout, continue to watch for shoots, cutting or digging them as they appear or mowing closely every month for two growing seasons. Apply a dense mulch (newspaper, cardboard, or plastic) for one or more growing seasons to smother shoots—it may take 2 to 3 years to eliminate established vines.

Notes: The branching stems of kudzu twine around upright supports or trail long distances across the ground.

Multiflora Rose

Rosa multiflora

ROSACEAE

Rose hips

Range: Throughout most of the United States except the Rocky Mountain, desert, and southeastern coastal plain areas; parts of eastern Canada.

Description: Plants grow to 10 feet (3.1 m) tall. Stiff thorns protect the stems. The deciduous leaves are compound, divided into seven to nine oval leaflets, with sharp-toothed edges; they're arranged along a central stalk with a single middle leaflet at the tip. Leaves are fuzzy on the undersides. The flowers are white or light pink, fragrant, and about ¾ inch (19.1 mm) wide; they grow in clusters. Flowers are followed by bright red, pea-sized hips that can persist on the canes until spring. Blooms from May to June.

Life Cycle: Perennial, reproducing by seeds and from cane tips that root where they touch the soil.

Prevention and Control: Dig out plants invading gardens, removing as much of the roots as possible (wear heavy gloves to handle the canes). To clear thickets of rose, cut stems at the soil line, then continue to mow at monthly intervals, or apply a dense mulch (newspaper, cardboard, or plastic) for at least one growing season. Eliminating this rose may take several seasons.

Notes: A full-grown multiflora rose is a huge shrub, with long stems that stand erect for 4 to 5 feet (1.2 to 1.5 m), then arch back to the ground. The hips are an excellent source of vitamin C and are relished by birds, which help spread the seeds.

Poison Ivy

Toxicodendron radicans (Rhus radicans)   ANACARDIACEAE

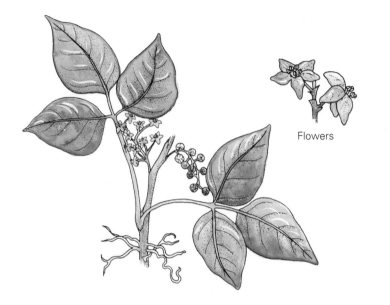

Flowers

Range: Throughout the United States (except for Alaska and California) and southern Canada.

Description: Poison ivy grows either as a shrub or as a climbing vine. All parts of the plant contain an oil that causes painful and itchy skin blisters. Each leaf is made up of three leaflets, 2 to 4 inches (5.1 to 10.2 cm) long, with pointed tips borne on long petioles. Leaves may be hairy or shiny, with smooth or slightly toothed edges. Shape and characteristics of the leaves vary; however, the leaves do turn red in fall. Flowers grow in clusters and are tiny and yellow-green, with five petals. Flowers are followed by small, hard, dry, white or grayish white fruit. Blooms from late May to July.

Life Cycle: Perennial, reproducing by seeds and creeping roots that grow from joints in the lower stems.

Prevention and Control: Wear protective clothing (gloves, long-sleeved shirt,

pants, and boots) when working around this plant. Dig out roots as soon as you notice the characteristic three leaflets. In fall, about a week after the first hard frost, look for the leaves turning reddish orange, and dig out the plants. Put pulled plants and roots into heavy plastic bags, then discard them in the garbage, or allow pulled plants and roots to dry in the sun, then bury them. Don't compost poison ivy, and don't burn it because it produces toxic smoke. Note that some people are extremely sensitive to poison ivy and shouldn't attempt to control it until winter when leaves have fallen from the stems. Cut stems off at ground level, then apply a dense mulch (newspaper, cardboard, or plastic) for at least one growing season.

Notes: The toxic oil can remain for years on tools that come in contact with this weed. If you come in contact with poison ivy, immediately wash your skin thoroughly with soap and lots of water for 15 minutes; wash clothing with strong detergent.

Poison Oak

Toxicodendron toxicarium (Rhus toxicodendron) ANACARDIACEAE

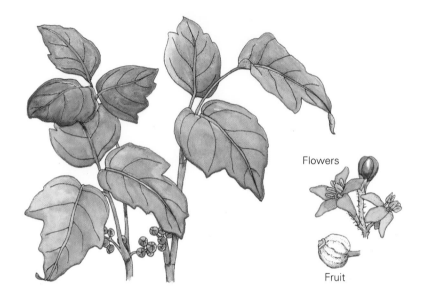

Flowers

Fruit

Range: Southeastern United States from New Jersey to Florida, west to Missouri, Oklahoma, and Texas; related species in California.

Description: Plants grow to 4 to 6 feet (1.2 to 1.8 m) tall. All parts of the plant contain an oil that causes painful and itchy skin blisters. Stems are slender and woody. Unlike poison ivy, poison oak doesn't grow roots from stem joints, nor is it a climber. Leaves have soft hairs and are divided into three leaflets. Leaflets are also hairy and are variously shaped. Many have deep teeth or lobes and are shaped like maple or oak leaves. Flowers grow in clusters and are small and whitish with five petals. Green to light tan berries form in fall. Blooms from May to June.

Life Cycle: Perennial, reproducing by seeds and underground roots.

Prevention and Control: Wear protective clothing (gloves, long-sleeved shirt, pants, and boots) when working around this plant. Dig out roots as soon as you notice them. Put pulled plants and roots into heavy plastic bags, then discard in the garbage, or allow pulled plants and roots to dry in the sun, then bury them. Don't compost poison oak, and don't burn it because it produces toxic smoke. Cut stems off at ground level, then apply a dense mulch (newspaper, cardboard, or plastic) for at least one growing season.

Notes: The toxic oil can remain for years on tools that come in contact with this weed. If you come in contact with poison oak, immediately wash your skin thoroughly with soap and lots of water for 15 minutes (contrary to myth, this won't cause the rash to spread); wash clothing with strong detergent.

Bermudagrass
Cynodon dactylon   GRAMINEAE

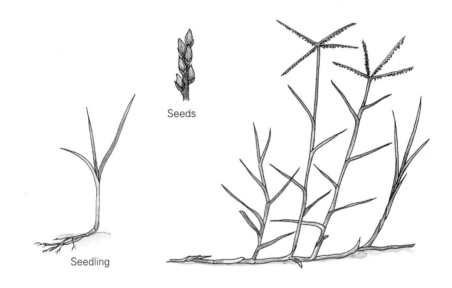

Seeds

Seedling

Range: Southern two-thirds of the United States; hardy only south of Pennsylvania.

Description: Stalks grow up to 1⅓ feet (40.6 cm) tall, but the rest of the plant is prostrate and creeping, forming dense sod. Rooting stems (stolons) lie along the soil surface, branching, rooting, and carrying the wiry stems. Leaves are fine, narrow, short, and gray-green, with a fringe of hairs just above the sheath where they attach to the stem. The flower head is divided into three to seven 1- to 2-inch (2.5 to 5.1 cm)-long spikes that radiate from the ends of erect stalks. Two rows of deep orange, prickly seeds develop along each spike. Roots are thin, scaly rhizomes. Blooms from June to August.

Life Cycle: Perennial, reproducing by rhizomes, stolons, and seeds.

Prevention and Control: Pull or dig plants, removing all roots and stolons. Allow pulled plants to dry in the sun before composting. In gardens with heavy infestations, apply a dense mulch (newspaper, cardboard, or plastic) for a growing season. In southern areas, solarizing the soil for the hottest part of the season can kill the roots. On the northern edge of its range, fall plowing to expose roots to heavy frosts can kill the plant.

Notes: Bermudagrass can be used as a lawn or pasture grass in dry, sandy soils. If lawn plants are creeping into gardens, establish a mowed strip between the lawn and the garden or install an edging strip as a barrier to keep bermudagrass in bounds.

Crabgrasses

Digitaria spp.

GRAMINEAE

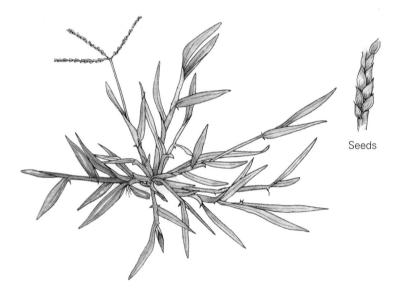

Seeds

Range: Throughout the United States and southern Canada. Large crabgrass (*D. sanguinalis*) isn't found in North Dakota; smooth crabgrass (*D. ischaemum*) isn't found in southern Florida, west Texas, or parts of the Southwest.

Description: Plants grow 15 inches (38.1 cm) (smooth crabgrass) to 3 feet (91.4 cm) (large crabgrass) tall. Stems can be erect or spread on the ground. They can root from joints of the stem lying on the soil, so crabgrass commonly forms a dense mat. Leaves of large crabgrass are hairy, narrow (¼ inch [6.4 mm] wide), and elongated. Leaves of smooth crabgrass are smaller and smooth, with a blue to purplish cast. Crabgrass flower heads grow in terminal spikes on upright stems. Tiny hairs grow both from the areas where leaves arise from their sheaths and on the bracts below the florets. Blooms from July to September.

Life Cycle: Annual, reproducing by seeds or from roots growing from stem joints.

Prevention and Control: Pull or dig plants before they set seed, removing all stems and roots. In lawns, fertilize in early spring to promote the growth of desired grasses and decrease the openings in the turf that allow crabgrass seed to germinate. Corn gluten meal herbicides can be used on lawns to stop crabgrass seeds from germinating (this has no effect on growing grasses). Repeated mowing only encourages crabgrass to grow in a spreading mat; because they can continue to flower and set seed, mowing isn't a control method.

Notes: Crabgrass is most common in dry and sandy soils, but it will grow in other conditions.

Foxtails
Setaria spp.

GRAMINEAE

Seed

Seedling

Range: Throughout United States and southern Canada.

Description: Green foxtail (*S. viridis*) grows 1 to 3 feet (30.5 to 91.4 cm) tall. It has erect or ascending stems that branch close to the base. Leaves are hairless but rough, and there's a fringe of hairs around the base of the leaf where it meets the stem. Flower heads are long, bristly, green spikes, 1 to 3 inches (2.5 to 7.6 cm) long with tips curving downward. Seeds are green and ¹⁄₁₆ inch (1.6 mm) long. Yellow foxtail (*S. glauca*) is shorter, growing 1 to 2 feet (30.5 to 61 cm) tall, and usually grows in clumps. The leaves have a few long hairs at the base where they attach to the stem. Its seeds are larger than green foxtail's and are yellowish. Foxtails may be shorter and more spreading in habit where they have been mowed or trampled. Blooms from June to September.

Life Cycle: Annual, reproducing by seeds.

Prevention and Control: Apply dense mulches to smother seedlings. Pull or dig plants in the garden as early as possible to ensure that no seeds have set. If renovating a field, mow before seeds form, and repeat if necessary; the following spring, cultivate several times before planting a cultivated crop. Several years of cultivating to control foxtail before it can set seed is usually enough to deplete the supply of viable seeds in the soil.

Notes: Foxtails tolerate a wide range of conditions and are commonly found along roadsides and in waste areas. They don't reproduce by underground stolons or rhizomes as many grasses do, so digging up scattered clumps is relatively easy.

Johnsongrass
Sorghum halepense

GRAMINEAE

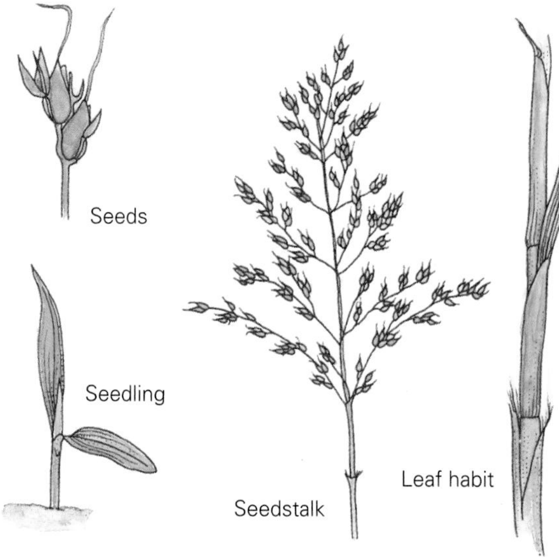

Seeds

Seedling

Seedstalk

Leaf habit

Range: Southern two-thirds of the United States and areas in Washington State and Oregon.

Description: Plants grow 1½ to 6 feet (45.7 to 183 cm) tall and have strong, erect stems. They look somewhat like slender corn plants. Leaves are 6 to 20 inches (15.2 to 50.8 cm) long and smooth, with a white vein down the center. Flowers are loose, upright, hairy, and purplish. The seeds are red-brown. Roots are fleshy, scaly rhizomes that may grow quite deep from established plants. Blooms from June to October.

Life Cycle: Perennial, reproducing by seeds and roots.

Prevention and Control: Dig Johnsongrass out of the garden, removing all roots. Apply a dense mulch (newspaper, cardboard, or plastic) for at least one growing season. The mulch may have to stay in place for two seasons. For serious infestations in fields, frequent mowing or close grazing is necessary to deplete the deepest growing roots.

Notes: Because established Johnsongrass clumps are very difficult to kill, remove small plants as soon as they're seen throughout the season.

Quackgrass, Couchgrass

Agropyron repens   GRAMINEAE

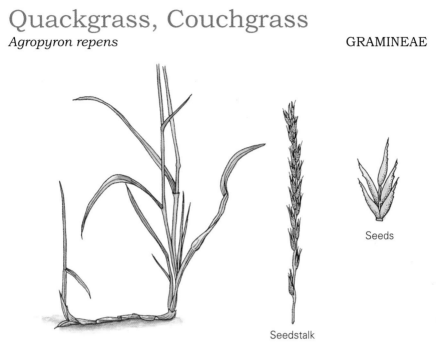

Seeds

Seedstalk

Range: Throughout southern Canada and the United States except the southernmost states.

Description: Plants grow to 2 to 3 feet (61 to 91.4 cm) tall. Stems are smooth, with three to six joints. Leaves are narrow, with pointed tips; they're ribbed and rough to the touch on the upper surface, smooth on the undersides. A distinguishing characteristic of quackgrass is the pair of clawlike appendages clasping the stem at the base of each leaf. Flowers are 2- to 6-inch (5.1 to 15.2 cm)-long spikes, with two opposite rows of tiny flowers arising from sharp and tiny bracts. The seeds are tiny, yellow-brown, and grain-shaped. Roots are tough, fibrous rhizomes, with many scaly joints. Blooms from late May to September.

Life Cycle: Cool-season perennial, reproducing by seeds and rhizomes.

Prevention and Control: Pull or dig plants from gardens, following along the lengths of roots to remove as much as possible. Dry pulled roots in the sun before composting. Continue to hoe or pull plants as shoots reappear. To clear infested areas, mow closely, then apply a dense mulch (newspaper, cardboard, or plastic) to smother shoots; or seed a smother crop (such as successive crops of buckwheat, followed by winter wheat or rye). Mulch heavily for several feet around all garden areas to prevent quackgrass from invading from nearby areas. Quackgrass roots are easiest to remove from deep, friable garden soils, so lighten heavy soils by digging in compost and green-manure crops.

Notes: Quackgrass is adapted to many soil conditions but prefers full sun; it's commonly seen in gardens, lawns, pastures, and neglected areas.

Glossaries

The following definitions help to explain many of the technical terms found throughout the book. They also elaborate on concepts, processes, and structures of organisms mentioned in the text. Terms are organized according to the section of this book they correspond to: Insects, Diseases, and Weeds.

Insects

Abdomen The last section of an insect's body, following the head and thorax. Digestive and reproductive organs are found in the abdomen.

Antenna Paired, segmented structures, also called feelers; one on each side of the head. Aids sensory perception. Plural is *antennae*.

Beak Long, stylus-like mouthpart used by sucking insects to pierce the surface of a plant or animal; hollow and jointed. One or more tiny needles in the beak pierce the tissue.

Brood All the insects that hatch from eggs laid by a given mother, or those that hatch and mature at the same time. Commonly used to refer to bees.

Caterpillar Larval stage of a butterfly or moth. Segmented or wormlike, with a distinct head, 12 simple eyes, a pair of very short antennae, and usually six well-developed legs, as well as two to five pairs of prolegs.

Chitin A hornlike substance that forms a layer of the exoskeleton.

Chrysalis The tubular, hard pupal shell of a butterfly.

Class The largest subgroup of a phylum. Insects belong to the class Insecta or Hexapoda (meaning "six-legged").

Cocoon The silken pupal case of a butterfly or moth.

Compound eye The eye of an insect, composed of many separate hexagonal lenses fitted closely together; sensitive to movement and color. Larvae lack compound eyes.

Crawler The first active instar of a scale.

Cuticle The outer layer of the exoskeleton.

Dormant Inactive; in suspended animation; hibernating. Dormancy occurs in winter.

Elytra The hard, opaque wing covers of beetles, which meet in a straight line down the insect's back and cover most of the thorax and abdomen, giving an armored appearance.

Exoskeleton The hard outer covering or skeleton that protects an insect's body like armor. Forms a jointed frame.

Family The largest subdivision of an order. Each family contains a group of related genera (*see* Genus). Family names end in "-idae."

Frass The sawdust-like excrement of borers such as the peachtree borer and the squash vine borer.

Genus The largest subdivision of a family. Each genus is made up of a small group of closely related members. Plural is *genera*.

Gregarious Living in groups, as in ants, aphids, and honeybees.

Grub The larva of a beetle. Grubs are plump, flat, or wormlike, with well-developed heads and three pairs of legs. They pupate in the soil or other protected sites.

Hibernation A winter period of suspended animation passed by many insects that live more than one season. Usually spent in soil or garden debris.

Honeydew A sweet substance secreted by aphids, which is relished by ants. Also produced by mealybugs, scales, and whiteflies.

Host plant The plant on which an insect feeds, lives, or lays eggs.

Instar The form of an insect between each molt. Most insects pass through three to six instars.

Larva Immature form of an insect that is more or less wormlike; may be legged or legless; may be smooth or covered with spines or tufts of hair. They have chewing mouthparts. Plural is *larvae*.

Maggot The larva of a fly, usually a small, white, legless worm without an obvious head. Mouthparts are hooked. Maggots tend to feed inside the host plant or animal.

Mandibles The strong chewing jaws of arthropods.

Maxillae Second pair of jaws just behind the mandibles.

Metamorphosis A form change during which an insect molts and passes through nymph to adult stages (incomplete metamorphosis) or through larval to pupal and adult stages (complete metamorphosis).

Molt A shedding of the exoskeleton so that an insect can grow. The old skin splits after a new one has formed beneath it.

Nymph An immature adult with undeveloped wings and, in some cases, different markings from the adult.

Ocellus The simple, single-lensed eye of an insect. It perceives light but produces no image. Insects usually have them as well as compound eyes. Found at the base of the antennae or on top of the head. Larvae rely on them entirely. Plural is *ocelli*.

Order The largest subgroup of a class. Insects are divided into 26 orders. Each order contains a large group of insects that share similar wing structures.

Oviparous Egg-laying.

Ovipositor The egg-laying organ in female insects.

Parasite An insect that lives and feeds in or on another insect or animal for at least part of its life cycle.

Pheromone A chemical substance, such as a sexual attractant, secreted by an insect to create a response in others of its species.

Phylum A major division of the animal kingdom. Insects belong to the phylum Arthropoda (meaning "joint-legged").

Predator An insect that feeds on another live insect or animal.

Proboscis Long, retractable sucking tube through which nectar is syphoned by insects such as butterflies and moths.

Proleg A plump, fleshy, false leg that enables larvae to move more easily. Caterpillars may have up to five pairs, which are sometimes hooked to enable them to hang from a host plant.

Pubescent Downy; covered with short, fine hairs.

Pupa An inactive stage between larva and adult in which adult features develop. The pupa may be encased in a chrysalis or cocoon, or it may roll itself in a leaf. Plural is *pupae*.

Pupate To turn into a pupa.

Scavenger An insect that feeds on dead plants, dead animals, or decaying matter.

Sessile Incapable of movement; immobile. Some female scales are sessile.

Species The fundamental unit in classification. The species refers to a single insect that may be distinguished from others in its genus by a particular feature or habit. Plural is *species*.

Spiracle One of many tiny holes in the thorax and abdomen of an insect that serve as breathing pores.

Thorax The center section of an insect's body, between the head and the abdomen. Wings and legs are attached to the thorax.

Vector A disease carrier.

Viviparous Bearing live young. Aphids can be viviparous.

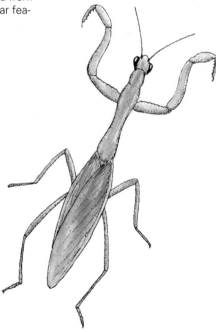

Diseases

Acervulus A shallow, saucer-shaped mass of hyphae with a depression in the center that bears conidiophores—stalk-like filaments that have conidia (asexual spores) at the tips. Spores are released when the acervulus grows and ruptures cells of the host plant. Plural is *acervuli.*

Alternate host One of two plants upon which a parasitic fungus must live.

Anthracnose A disease characterized by lesions that show on the epidermis. Caused by fungi that produce asexual spores in acervuli.

Ascomycetes A fungal group characterized by a membranous sac, or ascus, in which the cells divide to form ascospores. Yeasts, molds, and mildews are ascomycetes. Ascospores are sexual.

Bacteria One-celled microorganisms that reproduce by division. Bacteria are dependent on either dead or living organic matter for food.

Bacteriophage A virus-like organism that destroys bacteria.

Basidiomycetes A group of fungi characterized by mycelium with cross walls and the production of sexual spores on club-shaped filaments called basidia. Rusts, smuts, and mushrooms are basidiomycetes.

Blasting Failure to produce fruit or seeds.

Blight General description of diseases that cause sudden leaf, flower, or stem death.

Blotch A superficial spot or necrotic area.

Canker A diseased or dying area on a stem. Most commonly applied to woody plants.

Carrier A plant or animal bearing an infectious disease agent without showing symptoms. Carriers can transmit the disease to other organisms. Most bear the disease agent internally, although the term can be used when the agent is carried externally.

Causal organism The organism responsible for causing a disease.

Certified seed Seed monitored to ensure varietal purity and freedom from disease organisms.

Chlamydospore An asexual spore formed by a mycelial cell. Thick-walled, chlamydospores are resting spores that can remain dormant until conditions are correct for development.

Chlorosis Yellowing caused by partial failure of chlorophyll development. Symptomatic of many diseases.

Coalesce To grow together to form one spot or splotch.

Conidia Asexual spores formed at the tips of conidiophores. Produced most numerously during the height of the growing season, conidia are wind- or rain-borne.

Conidiophore Hyphae on which conidia are produced.

Damping-off Used to describe the death of seedlings, emerged or not, caused by a number of organisms.

Defoliate To cause most leaves on a plant to die and drop.

Dieback Progressive death of branches or stems from the tip backwards toward the main stem or trunk.

Enzyme A chemical produced by cells which brings about changes in processes such as ripening or digestion. Some pathogenic bacteria produce enzymes that damage host plants.

Epidermis The outermost layer of cells of a plant part.

Epinasty An abnormal growth pattern of leaves caused by rapid growth of cells on the upper surface, resulting in a downward cupping of the leaf.

Escape Applied to plants that are not resistant to a particular pathogen but do not acquire it.

Exudate Any substance produced within a plant that is then released or discharged through natural openings or injuries.

Facultative parasite An organism that can grow on either living or dead organic matter.

Fasciation Plant distortion caused by injury or infection resulting in flattened or curved shoots. Stems may look fused.

Flagellum A whiplike filament of a cell enabling it to swim through liquids.

Fruiting body The fungal structure containing or bearing spores.

Fungus A plant that lacks chlorophyll and is dependent upon either dead or living organic matter for food supplies. Fungi reproduce by both sexual and asexual spores and are composed of a body of filaments called hyphae that form branched systems called mycelia.

Gall A localized swelling composed of unorganized cells. Caused by bacteria, fungi, or insects.

Gamete A mature sex cell.

Girdle A lesion that encircles the stem or root, causing death.

Haustorium A specialized fungal hypha that penetrates the cells of a host plant and absorbs food from them.

Host A plant infected or parasitized by a pathogen.

Hyperplasia Abnormal increase in cells, resulting in formation of galls and tumors.

Hyphae Threads or filaments of a fungal mycelium or body.

Lesion A spot or area of diseased tissue.

Mildew A fungus that grows on the surface of plant parts.

Mold A fungus that produces a woolly growth on the surface of plant parts.

Mosaic A disease caused by a virus, characterized by mottled patterns of yellow and green on the leaves.

Mycelium The vegetative body of a fungus, composed of many hyphae.

Necrotic Dead. (Necrosis is death.)

Nematode Nonsegmented, microscopic roundworms that live in soil, water, plants, animals, and dead organic matter. Some nematodes are plant parasites.

Nodule A lump or knot.

Obligate parasite A parasite that can live only on living matter.

Parasite An organism that obtains its nutrients from a secondary organism.

Pathogen An organism capable of causing disease in other organisms.

Penetration peg A strong hypha anchored to the host surface with a sticky substance. Produced in order to bore into a host.

Perfect stage The period of a fungal life cycle when spores are produced sexually.

Phloem The vessels in the plant that carry dissolved sugars from leaves to the rest of the plant. One of the two vessels in the vascular bundle.

Phycomycetes One group of fungi. Characterized by sexual reproduction and few cross walls in the hyphae.

Primary infection The first infection by a fungus after a resting period.

Pustule A blisterlike structure.

Pycnidium A flask-shaped, fruiting body of a fungus that contains asexual spores. Usually located near the surface of the host.

Pycnium The flask-shaped, fruiting body of a rust fungus that contains pycniospores. These spores are unisexual and are usually fertilized by insects feeding on the nectar produced in the pycnium.

Resistance Ability of a plant to remain relatively healthy despite infection by a pathogen. Resistance is an inborn quality and is not caused by environmental factors.

Resting spore A spore that can remain dormant for long periods of time before germinating. Most resting spores are very thick-walled.

Ring spot Symptomatic of some diseases. Ring spots are brownish yellow on the margin and green in the center.

Rogue To remove a plant. Plants infected with some diseases are normally rogued to prevent the spread of the disease.

Rosette Formation of short-stalked leaves that radiate from a central stem. Some diseases produce an unnatural rosette in their hosts.

Russet A corky, roughened area on the skin surface. Russeting can be caused by pathogens, insects, or cultural techniques.

Rust The disease caused by a rust fungus, or the fungus itself. Rusts may have one or more hosts through their life cycles and, in some cases, have as many as five types of spores.

Saprophyte An organism that feeds on dead organic matter.

Scab A disease that is characterized by rough, scaly tissue on the skin surface.

Sclerotium A resting mass of fungal hyphae that does not contain spores but that is capable of becoming dormant and remaining so for many years before resuming growth.

Scorch A burning of tissue caused by a pathogen or by environmental conditions.

Secondary infection A disease caused by infectious material following a primary infection or produced by reproductive material that has not undergone a resting period.

Shothole A disease symptom in which small round holes die and drop out of leaves.

Sign Any visible portion of a pathogen. Signs can include mycelia, spores, fruiting bodies, or even a mass of bacteria.

Smut A disease caused by a smut fungus, or the fungus itself. Smuts are characterized by the formation of dark masses of resting spores.

Sporangium A fungal fruiting body that produces asexual spores.

Spore A single cell or multicelled reproductive unit. Fungi produce sexual and asexual spores. The resting structures of some bacteria are also called spores.

Strain Synonym for *race* when describing plant pathogens. A strain, or race, is a subgroup within a species that differs in host range or effect from other members of the species.

Summer spore A spore that proliferates during the best growing conditions and that does not rest between release and germination.

Susceptible Without inherent resistance to a pathogen.

Systemic Applied to a pathogen or chemical that travels throughout the plant body. Many systemics travel through the vascular system.

Thallus The vegetative body of a thallophyte, a simple plant, including fungi, algae, bacteria, slime molds, and lichens.

Tolerant Capable of sustaining an infection by a pathogen, or of enduring environmental stress or injury without much damage.

Toxin A poison.

Vascular Applied to the vessels in the plant that carry water or nutrients. Respectively, these are the xylem and phloem vessels.

Vector An organism or agent that transmits diseases. Many insects are vectors of plant diseases.

Vein-banding A symptom of some viral diseases in which regions along the veins are a darker green color than regions between veins.

Virulent Strongly capable of producing disease.

Virus An obligate parasite composed of genetic materials and protein that is capable of reproducing within living materials.

Wilt Drooping plant tissue as a consequence of insufficient water supply. Some diseases cause wilt by plugging the vascular system.

Xylem The vessels that carry water in the plant.

Yellows Disease that causes abnormal yellowing of leaves and stems.

Zoospore A spore that swims.

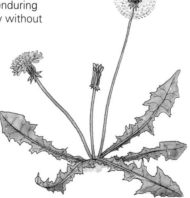

Weeds

Achene A dry, one-seeded fruit that does not open readily. The seed is distinct from the fruit. Common among members of the composite family.

Acute Sharply pointed.

Alternate An arrangement of leaves, branches, or flowers in which each is placed singly at different heights along the stem.

Annuals Plants that live from seed to maturity, reproduction, and death in only one growing season.

Anther The part of the stamen that bears pollen.

Apex The uppermost point; tip.

Awn A bristlelike appendage. Found most commonly on grass flowers.

Axil Upper angle where a leaf or branch joins the stem.

Axillary Situated in an axil.

Barb A rigid bristle or point, usually reflexed.

Beak A long, prominent point.

Berry A fleshy fruit containing two or more seeds, such as a tomato and a grape.

Biennial Living two growing seasons, usually flowering during the second.

Bipinnate Twice-pinnately compound.

Blade The flat, expanded part of the leaf.

Bract A small, rudimentary or under-developed leaf. Often found in flower clusters.

Bristle A stiff, hairlike growth.

Bulb An underground bud with fleshy scales or bracts.

Bulblet A small bulb borne on the inflorescence or stem.

Calyx All the sepals of a flower cluster considered collectively; the outer perianth whorl.

Capsule The dry, dehiscent fruit of two or more carpels.

Carpel One of the ovarian portions of a compound pistil.

Chlorophyll The green pigment necessary for photosynthesis, developed in the chloroplasts of plant cells.

Clasping Applied to leaves that partly or completely surround a stem, as seen in grasses.

Compound leaf Leaf in which the blade is divided into two or more sections, or leaflets.

Cordate Heart-shaped, with the point away from the base.

Corolla The inner set of floral leaves, or petals. Sometimes fused, as in morning glories.

Corymb A raceme with the lower flowerstalks longer than those at the tip, so that the head gives a flattened appearance. Outer flowers open first.

Culm The stem of a grass. Usually hollow except at the nodes.

Decumbent Lying flat, with the tip pointing upward.

Decurrent Extending along the sides of another, as in leaves where the blades extend as wings along the petiole or stem.

Dehiscent Opening by valves or slits, as in a seed capsule. Poppy capsules are dehiscent.

Dentate Toothed, with outward-pointing teeth.

Dioecious A plant bearing only one sex on a plant; male and female flowers are on separate plants.

Disk flower The tubular flowers in the center of the head of many composites. The yellow center of the daisy is composed of disk flowers.

Divided Separated to the base.

Drupe A single-seeded fruit with a fleshy outer part. Stone fruits such as peaches and cherries are drupes.

Elliptic Oval in shape.

Entire Describes a smooth leaf margin. Not toothed, lobed, or serrated.

Fibrous Fine adventitious roots, usually in a mass.

Floret An individual flower of a cluster, head, or spike.

Fruit The ripened ovary or ovaries with attached parts.

Grain Fruit of grasses particularly; seed coat and ovary walls fused into one body.

Habit The general growth pattern of a plant or its mode of growth, such as shrubby, trailing, or erect.

Habitat The environmental conditions of a specific place in which a plant grows.

Head A short, compact flower cluster of sessile or nearly sessile florets.

Herbaceous Not woody.

Imperfect Describing flower lacking either stamens or carpels. It is "imperfect" because it has only one sex.

Indehiscent Applied to a seedpod or capsule that does not readily open at maturity.

Internode The part of a stem between two nodes.

Involucre A whorl of small leaves or bracts just under a flower or flower cluster. Generally protects reproductive structures.

Lanceolate Lance-shaped, several times longer than wide, and tapering to a pointed apex.

Leaflet One part of a compound leaf.

Legume A member of the family Leguminosae. Characterized by a fruit that splits readily along two sides at maturity, such as a pea pod.

Lobed Divided to about mid-point.

Mericarp One of the two carpels of a fruit of the parsley family.

Midrib The central rib or vein of a leaf or other organ.

Monoecious Having both male and female flowers on the same plant, such as many kinds of squashes.

Netted Applied to veins, meaning they form a network pattern.

Node The part of a stem where leaves or branches emerge.

Nut A hard, indehiscent, one-seeded fruit.

Obovate Ovate, but with the narrower end at the bottom.

Opposite Two leaves or buds at a node.

Ovary The part of the pistil bearing the ovules.

Ovate Egg-shaped, with the broader end at the bottom.

Ovule An undeveloped or immature seed.

Palmate Radiating from a central point like a fan or the fingers on a hand.

Palmately compound Leaflets radiating from a central point.

Panicle An inflorescence. A branched raceme with each branch bearing a cluster of flowers. Overall, a panicle is shaped like a pyramid.

Pappus A ring of fine hairs developed from the calyx. A pappus often acts as a dispersal mechanism, as in dandelion seeds.

Peduncle Stem of a solitary flower or flower cluster.

Perennial Growing three or more seasons.

Perfect Applied to flowers having both stamens and carpels.

Perianth The floral envelope, the calyx and corolla together. Most often used to describe flowers without clear divisions between calyx and corolla, such as lilies.

Petal One of the leaves of the corolla, usually colorful.

Petiole The stalk of a leaf.

Phloem The vessels in the plant that carry dissolved sugars from leaves to the rest of the plant. One of the two vessels in the vascular bundle.

Pinnate Similar in appearance to a feather, having leaflets along each side of a common axis.

Pinnately compound Leaflets arranged on each side of a common axis.

Pinnatifid Leaflets cleft to the middle or beyond.

Pistil The seed-bearing organ with a style (a tube bearing the stigma at its apex), stigma (the part of the pistil that receives the pollen grains), and ovule.

Pistillate Having pistils and no stamens. Female.

Pod Usually describes a dry, dehiscent fruit.

Pollen The spores or grains borne by the anther, which contains the male element.

Prickle A stiff, pointed outgrowth from the epidermis or bark.

Procumbent Trailing on the ground without rooting.

Prostrate Lying flat on the ground. Some prostrate stems can root.

Pubescent Covered with short, soft hairs.

Raceme An inflorescence composed of pedicled florets growing from a common axis. Flowers open from the base upward.

Ray flower A flower growing on the margin of the disk flowers, strap-shaped. The white petals of the daisy are ray flowers.

Rhizome Underground or barely superficial reproductive stem.

Rhombic Shaped like an equilateral parallelogram, usually having oblique angles.

Rib A primary vein in a leaf or flower.

Rootstock Roots that can develop adventitious buds. Often used to mean underground reproductive stems as well.

Rosette A cluster of leaves, usually basal and shaped like a rose, or radiating from a center.

Runner A slender, trailing stem that takes root at the nodes.

Sepal One of the divisions of a calyx.

Serrate Having sharp teeth that point forward.

Sessile Without a petiole or stalk.

Sheath A long structure surrounding an organ or part.

Simple leaves Leaves in which the blade is in one piece, not divided.

Spike A flower spike with sessile or nearly sessile flowers.

Stamen The pollen-bearing, or male organ, of a flower.

Staminate Having stamens and no pistils. Male.

Stipule A basal appendage of a petiole.

Stolon A stem that bends to the ground and takes root at the tip or nodes.

Succulent Fleshy tissues storing much water.

Taproot A central, tapering, main root with smaller lateral roots. A carrot is a taproot.

Tendril A slender organ, leaf, or stem with which a plant clings to a support.

Terminal At the end of a stem or branch.

Thorn A stiff, sharply pointed, and somewhat degenerate branch.

Toothed Dentate. Having pointed edges along the margins.

Trifoliate A compound leaf with three leaflets, such as poison ivy.

Tuber A modified underground stem that usually stores food. Reproductive. A potato is a tuber.

Umbel A flower cluster that is shaped like an umbrella, such as dill flower heads.

Utricle A small, one-seeded fruit.

Valve The separate parts of a pod or capsule.

Vascular bundle The term applied to describe phloem and xylem vessels, or veins, in plants. Nutrients and water travel through these vessels to each part of the plant.

Veins The vascular bundles of leaves, containing phloem and xylem vessels.

Whorled An arrangement of three or more structures at a node.

Xylem Vessels in which water is carried from roots to the rest of the plant. One of the two vessels in vascular bundles.

Resources

Many organic gardening products are becoming available at local garden centers. If you cannot find what you need locally, there are many fine mail-order suppliers on the list that follows. Inclusion in this list does not imply endorsement of these companies by Rodale. Rather, these companies are listed because they offer a range of helpful organic products.

A-1 Unique Insect Control
5504 Sperry Drive
Citrus Heights, CA 95621
Phone: (916) 961-7945
Fax: (916) 967-7082
Web site: www.A-1Unique.com

Applied Bio Pest
Unit 129
587 West Channel Islands Boulevard
Port Hueneme, CA 93033
Phone: (805) 984-9224
Fax: (805) 984-1517
Web site: www.biopest.com

Arbico
18701 North Lago Del Oro Parkway
Tucson, AZ 85739
Phone: (520) 825-9785
Fax: (520) 825-2038
Web site: www.arbico.com

Beneficial Insectary
9664 Tanqueray Court
Redding, CA 96003
Phone: (800) 477-3715
Fax: (888) 472-0708
Web site: www.insectary.net

Bountiful Gardens
18001 Shafer Ranch Road
Willits, CA 95490
Phone: (707) 459-6410
Fax: (707) 459-1925
Web site: www.bountifulgardens.org

Buena Biosystems
P.O. Box 4008
Ventura, CA 93007
Phone: (805) 525-2525
Fax: (805) 525-6058
Web site: www.buenabiosystems.com/
homepage.htm

Burpee
W. Atlee Burpee & Co.
Warminster, PA 18974
Phone: (800) 333-5808
Fax: (800) 487-5530
Web site: www.burpee.com

Cook's Garden
P.O. Box 5010
Hodges, SC 29653-5010
Phone: (800) 457-9703
Fax: (800) 457-9705
Web site: www.cooksgarden.com

Fedco Seeds
P.O. Box 520
Waterville, ME 04903-0520
Phone: (207) 873-7333
Fax: (207) 872-8317
Web site: www.fedcoseeds.com

Gardens Alive!
5100 Schenley Place
Lawrenceburg, IN 47025
Phone: (812) 537-8650
Fax: (812) 537-5108
Web site: www.gardensalive.com

Gardener's Supply Co.
128 Intervale Road
Burlington, VT 05404
Phone: (888) 833-1412
Fax: (800) 551-6712
Web site: www.gardeners.com

The Green Spot, Ltd
93 Priest Road
Nottingham, NH 03290-6204
Phone: (603) 942-8925
Fax: (603) 942-8932

Harmony Farm Supply
P.O. Box 460
Graton, CA 95444
Phone: (707) 823-9125
Fax: (707) 823-1734
Web site: www.harmonyfarm.com

Hydro-Gardens
P.O. Box 25845
Colorado Springs, CO 80936
Phone: (888) 693-0578
Fax: (888) 693-0578
Web site: www.hydro-gardens.com

Irish Eyes & Garden City Seeds
P.O. Box 307
Thorp, WA 98946
Phone: (509) 964-7000
Fax: (800) 964-9210
Web site: www.irish-eyes.com

Johnny's Selected Seeds
Foss Hill Road
Albion, ME 04910
Phone: (207) 437-4301
Fax: (800) 437-4290
[Fax outsite continental U.S.:
(207) 437-2165]
Web site: www.johnnyseeds.com

The Natural Gardening Company
P.O. Box 750776
Petaluma, CA 94975
Phone: (707) 766-9303
Fax: (707) 766-9747
Web site: www.naturalgardening.com

Natural Insect Control
R.R. #2
Stevensville, Ontario,
Canada L0S 1S0
Phone: (905) 382-2904
Fax: (905) 382-4418
Web site: www.natural-insect-control.com

Nature's Control
P.O. Box 35
Medford, OR 97501
Phone: (541) 245-6033
Fax: (800) 698-6250
Web site: www.naturescontrol.com

Peaceful Valley Farm Supply
P.O. Box 2209
Grass Valley, CA 95945
Phone: (888) 784-1722; (530) 272-4769
Fax: (530) 272-4794
Web site: www.groworganic.com

Planet Natural
1612 Gold Avenue
Bozeman, MT 59715
Phone: (800) 289-6656; (406) 587-5891
Fax: (406) 587-0223
Web site: www.planetnatural.com

Rincon-Vitova Insectaries
P.O. Box 1555
Ventura, CA 93002
Phone: (800) 248-2847
Fax: (805) 643-6267
Web site: www.rinconvitova.com

Snow Pond Farm Supply
53 Mason Street
Suite 104
Salem, MA 01970
Phone: (978) 745-0716
Fax: (978) 745-0905
Web site: www.snow-pond.com

Territorial Seed Co.
P.O. Box 157
Cottage Grove, OR 97424
Phone: (541) 942-9547
Fax: (888) 657-3131
Web site: www.territorial-seed.com

Worm's Way
7850 North Highway 37
Bloomington, IN 47404
Phone: (800) 274-9676
Fax: (800) 316-1264
Web site: www.wormsway.com

Suggested Reading

Bradley, Fern Marshall, and Barbara W. Ellis, eds. *Rodale's All-New Encyclopedia of Organic Gardening*. Emmaus, PA: Rodale, 1992.

Ellis, Barbara W., and Fern Marshall Bradley. *The Organic Gardener's Handbook of Natural Insect and Disease Control*. Emmaus, PA: Rodale, 1996.

Flint, Mary Louise. *Pests of the Garden and Small Farm: A Grower's Guide to Using Less Pesticide*. Oakland, CA: University of California, 1998.

Flint, Mary Louise, and Steve H. Dreistadt. *Natural Enemies Handbook: The Illustrated Guide to Biological Pest Control*. Oakland, CA: University of California, 1998.

Hynes, Erin. *Rodale's Successful Organic Gardening: Controlling Weeds*. Emmaus, PA: Rodale, 1995.

Michalak, Patricia. *Rodale's Successful Organic Gardening: Controlling Pests and Diseases*. Emmaus, PA: Rodale, 1994.

Olkowski, William, et al. *The Gardener's Guide to Common-Sense Pest Control*. Newtown, CT: The Taunton Press, 1995.

Smith, Miranda, and Anna Carr. *Rodale's Garden Insect, Disease & Weed Identification Guide*. Emmaus, PA: Rodale, 1988.

Uva, Richard H., et al. *Weeds of the Northeast*. Ithaca, NY: Cornell University Press, 1997.

Whitson, Tom D. *Weeds of the West*. Newark, CA: The Western Society of Weed Science, 1992.

Web Sites

Biological Control: A Guide to Natural Enemies in North America
www.nysaes.cornell.edu/ent/biocontrol

Biological Control Virtual Information Center
www.ncsu.edu/biocontrol/biocontrol.html

Integrated Pest Management Project, University of California Statewide
www.ipm.ucdavis.edu/

Photo Credits

AG Stock USA/Jack K. Clark 160 (*left*)

AG Stock USA/Debra Ferguson 177

AG Stock USA/Harold Kaufman 164, 180

AG Stock USA/Howard Schwartz 166 (*right*), 167 (*right*), 176 (*right*)

E. R. Degginger/Color Pic, Inc. 143

Phil Degginger/Color Pic, Inc. 150

Alan and Linda Detrick 159, 169, 174, 178

James F. Dill 145, 147, 148 (*left and right*), 149, 156, 158, 160 (*right*), 163, 166 (*left*), 167 (*left*), 173, 179, 184

Philip B. Hamm, Extension Plant Pathologist, Oregon State University 181

Holt Studio International/Photo Researchers 157 (*left*)

Holt Studios/Nigel Cattlin/Photo Researchers 157 (*right*)

Bill Johnson 172

Margaret McGrath 162

Kathy Merrifield/Photo Researchers 151 (*left*)

Robert Mulrooney/University of Delaware 146, 154 (*left and right*)

Cynthia Ocamb 151 (*right*), 168

Rich Pomerantz 175 (*right*)

Positive Images/Karen Bussolini 170

Joseph Postman, U.S. Department of Agriculture, Agricultural Research Service, National Clonal Germ Plasm Repository, Corvallis, Oregon 185 (*right*)

Rob and Ann Simpson 176 (*left*)

Ron West 142, 152, 153, 155, 161, 165, 171, 175 (*left*), 182, 183 (*left and right*)

Rick Wetherbee 144

Index

Note: Page references in **boldface** indicate illustrations.